Prisoners of Hope

Prisoners
of
Hope

Exploiting the
POW / MIA
Myth in America

SUSAN KATZ
KEATING

Random House / New York

Library of Congress Cataloging-in-Publication Data

Keating, Susan Katz.

    Prisoners of hope : exploiting the POW/MIA myth in America / Susan
Katz Keating.

        p.   cm.

    Includes bibliographical references and index.

    ISBN 0-679-43016-4

    1. Vietnamese Conflict, 1961–1975—Prisoners and prisons.

  2. Vietnamese Conflict, 1961–1975—Missing in action—United States.

  3. Prisoners of war—United States. 4. Prisoners of war—Vietnam.

I. Title.

DS559.4.K43 1994

959.704'37—dc20   94-20322

Manufactured in the United States of America on acid-free paper

24689753

First Edition

To my husband, Michael, for whom I, too,
would spend a lifetime searching.

A Note to the Reader

I was the editor of a small-town newspaper in California when I was hired as a reporter for *The Washington Times*. I arrived in D.C. in June 1985, hoping to find that one big story we journalists all dream of writing. Within a few months, I thought I had found it; I was certain that live American POWs remained against their will in Vietnam. I became obsessed with finding the POWs, and in the process managed to annoy my editors, my friends, and my boyfriend (who married me anyway). As the years went on, though, and no POWs surfaced, I began to realize a curious phenomenon about this story. It is deceptive, in that once you scratch the surface, you are convinced that POWs exist; but after you really dig, you discover the truth as put forth in this book.

Acknowledgments

The writing of this book was, among other things, an exercise in time management. While completing the various stages, I gave birth to two babies, oversaw my oldest daughter entering kindergarten, lost some original chapters in the course of a software disaster, and wrote while recovering from injuries received in a car accident. As such, I could not have finished this project without the support of a small army, whose members assisted in many significant ways.

The most important help came from my family, to whom I give my first and most effusive thanks.

At the top of the list is my husband, Michael, who never questioned that I should quit work to gamble on this uncertain venture, and who believed that nothing could interfere with its completion.

I am also enormously grateful to my children. Erin, with her constant sunny enthusiasm for the book, made me remember that writing is, in fact, fun. Kelly and Courtney, who spent their first months of life sleeping long hours on my lap while I worked, were amazingly adaptable and accommodating companions.

My mother, Eithne Scott, was a great cheerleader and dispenser of moral support. Every writer should have such a fan club.

I am indebted to the many people who helped with the voluminous research that took over nine years. Steve Boras merits special thanks for his time and expertise. He was indispensable. B. G. Burkett selflessly contributed key information and advice. Paul Olenski provided a rare window to one of the most intriguing episodes of the Vietnam War, the defection of Pvt. Bobby Garwood. I was touched by Paul's loyalty when he agreed to speak on condition I mention a fallen comrade, Curtis Brown; I am pleased to keep my end of the bargain. Bill Schulz of *Reader's Digest* generously passed on research material.

I am also grateful to Nathan Adams, Broadus Bailey, Robert K. Brown, Brig Cabe, Nicholas Cain, Joe Canole, Scott Celley, Dr. Michael Charney, Jim Coyne, Dan Cragg, Representative Bob Dornan, Jerry Gilbert, Mary Hotze, Ken Majeski, Hank Newkirk, Mark Salter, Keith Schneider, Steve Solarz, Jay Sullivan, Judge Norman Turner, Jimmy Walker, and Richard Woodley.

I am indebted to my contacts within the Department of Defense; the National Archives and Records Administration; the U.S. Army; the U.S. intelligence community; and a certain foreign embassy. I wish I could thank them all by name, but appreciate their need for anonymity. They know who they are.

I also appreciate the ongoing help from *Washington Times* librarians David Dickson, Clark Eberly, and John Haydon, who patiently fielded my many requests and saved me hours of time and aggravation.

I owe much to former POWs who, over the years, have shared their stories with me. They include, but are not limited to, Everett Alvarez, Jack Bomar, Dieter Dengler, Jeremiah Denton, Doug Hegdahl, Howard Hill, Rodney Knutson, Representative Pete Peterson, Robinson Risner, Admiral James Stockdale, Richard Stratton, Orson G. Swindle III, Leo Thorsness, and Jim Warner. I am especially thankful for insights from the heroic Col. James "Nick" Rowe, may he rest in peace.

Special mention goes to another POW hero, Senator John McCain, who graciously returned every phone call and answered every question.

This book would have taken a completely different form if not for the many MIA families who kindly took me into their confidence. They include, but also are not limited to, Dolores Alfond, Marie Barzen, Dan Borah, Kay Bosiljevac, George Brooks, Carol Collins, Donald Carr, Jr., Matthew Carr, Kenneth Carr, Bob Dumas, Kathryn Fanning, Mary Lou Hall, Anne Hart, Ann Holland, Earl Hopper, Albro Lundy III, Barbara Robertson, Shelby Robertson Quast, Robin Owen Sampley, and the late Marian Shelton.

I learned much from MIA cousin Karen Kirkpatrick, who did not always agree with my conclusions, but who nevertheless eloquently explained the bureaucratic and emotional complexities of searching for a loved one. She has my admiration.

I also wish to thank my father-in-law, John Keating, who gave me the benefit of wisdom gained during two tours as a fighter pilot in Vietnam.

This book was brought to fruition with the assistance of beneficent enablers. My editors at *The Washington Times* allowed me to stake out a beat that was never really mine. Joe Finder helped me find my superbly talented agent, Henry Morrison, who was instrumental in designing the proposal sent to Random House. My editor, Bob Loomis, made me the envy of my writer friends, and for good reason. Bob is a teacher and true guardian of the written language. I shall miss working with him.

Last, but far from least, I thank Marge Herring of Riverside Poly High School, who contributed in more ways than she knows.

Contents

Part Two

The True Conspiracy 123

Prologue

On October 12, 1990, a horse-drawn caisson carried the body of Marian Shelton through the grounds of Arlington National Cemetery. A large procession followed, proud in its grief, immersed in tragedy. Professional watchers—film crews, reporters, and photographers—silently blessed the crisp light of autumn for so vividly accenting this beautiful drama. For this was more than just a funeral, more than just another hero's burial. This was an event, marking the death of MIA wife Marian Shelton, the last casualty of the Vietnam War.

The funeral party halted in self-conscious solemnity beside a freshly prepared grave. The military honor guardsmen loaded their weapons. They lifted their rifles in unison, preparing for the hero's send-off. They fired: once, twice, and again until they finished the requisite number of volleys.

All those present, mourners and journalists alike, could not escape knowing that this was more than just gunfire. This was an echo of the last sound ever heard by Marian Shelton.

It was this very echo that opened Marian's death to exploitation, that made it useful to people who traffic in such matters. Her death by gunshot wound was parlayed into an opportunity. It was milked for meaning by activists, charlatans, politicians, and journalists who profit from the Vietnam War's sad legacy of men still missing in action.

This MIA industry has nurtured an American myth, that the missing men are still alive, are being held captive against their will, and—if we act quickly—will one day return home.

The myth has infiltrated mainstream culture. POW "never forget" flags are waved over U.S. military installations and some state capitols. The flags have appeared on national television, flying over the Super Bowl; on stickers adorning every type of motor vehicle from pickup trucks to Mercedes-Benzes; and next to Old Glory herself on flagpoles outside American Legion posts and similar organizations all across the country.

The myth is so powerful it has spawned round after round of government investigations, all leading to the conclusion that there is no solid evidence of live Americans held in Southeast Asia. The best known of these panels is the Senate Select Committee on POW/MIA Affairs, known as the Kerry Committee, formed in 1991 after a spate of phony photographs revitalized the POW issue. The committee spent hundreds of thousands of dollars and generated reams of paperwork in a volatile, year-long investigation that only confirmed the conclusions of previous committees.

Despite the consensus of the various committees, the U.S. government still operates on the assumption that men remain alive in captivity. The Pentagon remains obligated to continue the search for MIAs or their remains and frequently dispatches intelligence agents, excavation teams, and expert negotiators to Southeast Asia. These and other MIA-related efforts cost the U.S. government $100 million per year. The POW myth is such that it even turned Marian Shelton's grievous death by her own hand into a symbol of heroism.

Yet Marian's death must not go unheeded. It must be remembered, examined, and mourned; for it is testament to a much broader tragedy. The tragedy is rooted in Marian's life story, which itself has something of a mythic quality.

Marian grew up in the small town of Owensboro, Kentucky. Even as a child, she knew what it meant to miss a loved one; her brother had vanished without a trace while fighting in World War II. When Marian was thirteen, she fell in love with one of her schoolmates, Charles Shelton. It was, she once told me, the first time her pain over the loss of her brother had been eased.

Charles and Marian dated throughout their teens, even after Charles, who was slightly older, left for college. As everyone expected, the two married right after Marian's high school graduation. Charles later joined the Air Force and became a pilot. Marian bore five children. It was an exciting life that took the family to stations around the world.

The Sheltons were living on Okinawa in 1965 when Charles was transferred to Udorn Royal Thai Air Base. This time, the family could not move with him. Charles would be flying missions over Vietnam. The family celebrated their final Easter together, then saw Charles off to war.

Nine days later, there was bad news. On April 29, his thirty-third birthday, Captain Shelton was shot down over Laos. Like Marian's older brother, Charles was now missing in action.

Marian returned to the United States to raise the couple's five children. The youngest was just over a year old. Marian established a household routine, all the while fully expecting each phone call, each knock on the door, to bring news that Charles was coming home.

Years passed, and that news never came. Eventually, the government shifted Charles from the list of men missing to that of men killed in action.

Marian refused to accept the verdict. "I always felt Charles was alive," she once told me. "We were so close. I can't explain it, but I would have known if he were dead."

She pressed hard for information on Charles. She phoned the Air Force constantly, wanting to know what had been done to find her husband. Officials who dealt with Marian found her irritating but admired her perseverance. They dubbed her "the Kentucky Colonel."

Marian's efforts brought a certain measure of success. She learned from government reports that Charles had ejected safely from his crippled aircraft and had radioed that he was in good condition on the ground in Laos. A villager who saw the entire episode told U.S. authorities the airman had been captured alive by Pathet Lao troops. A band of Montagnard tribesmen also said they had seen Shelton captured alive.

The government had reports indicating that Charles had been taken to a cave near Sam Neua, Laos, and was probably held with another American pilot, David Hrdlicka. For several years after their capture, Shelton and Hrdlicka were the subject of many live sighting reports. None could be verified, but they created the impression that Charles was alive. One unsubstantiated report said that in 1968 Charles was moved to a special camp for incorrigibles in either Hanoi or China. He was also said to have been rescued by Montagnards in 1976, and then recaptured by enemy forces.

Bolstered by this information that she had forced out of the government, Marian vowed she would spend as much time as it took to find her husband. "If it takes ten years, twenty years, whatever. I will hold on."

She held on for twenty-five years. In that time, she watched her children grow up and set out on their own. She hooked into a network of informants who passed on enticing clues about Charles. At one point, the sources told Marian about a secret CIA mission code-named Duck Soup, in which Charles had supposedly been rescued and then returned to his captors. The sources were only half right; there had been a secret "Duck Soup" program, but it had not pertained to POWs.

The informants also said that Charles, while chained to a desk and in the company of armed guards, had attacked and killed three of his captors with his bare hands. They said that Charles had been rescued once, then deliberately returned to captivity to protect the identity of his rescuers.

Marian believed the stories. In 1973 she went to Indochina in search of Charles and bribed a boatman to smuggle her into Laos. After seven weeks overseas, she returned home with no new information.

Marian grew to symbolize the fledgling MIA movement. She was a perfect spokesperson: articulate, personable, and steeped in tragedy. In 1987 Hollywood producers sought to revive the old *Queen for a Day* television show and chose Marian as a pilot episode contestant. Her wish was for the producers to find Charles. Failing that, she asked that she and her five children be taken to the Vietnam Veterans Memorial for Mother's Day. The television show was canceled before it was even taped, but the producers— members of a group not normally known for compassion—were so touched by Marian's plight that they granted her wish, anyway.

Marian supported the efforts of other MIA hunters. She mortgaged her house to pay the legal bills of one activist who persuaded her he was the victim of government subterfuge. She joined in the lawsuit of two others who sought to force the White House to do more in the search for POWs.

Eventually, the search for Charles took its toll. In late 1990 Marian started to show signs of strain. Friends noticed she was different. She stopped returning phone calls. She gave away her travel hot pot and portable iron, saying she no longer needed them.

The night of October 4, Marian was alone in the California home she had purchased in Charles's name. She sat down at the kitchen table. She wrote a letter to her children, explaining she had done the best she could to find their father. She placed the note on the table alongside a rosary. And then, for the first time in twenty-five years, she removed the POW bracelet with Charles's name on it. She placed it on the table with the other items.

Shortly after 11 P.M., Marian walked outside. In her hand was a .22-caliber pistol. She held the barrel to her head and pulled the trigger. She died from a single shot. The search for Charles had ended.

The story is monumentally sad. But the Sheltons represent only one of many MIA families still caught in the debilitating aftermath of Vietnam. Convinced that their loved ones are still alive, thousands of mothers, fathers, sisters, brothers, children, and wives continue to this day to wait up nights, listening for the sound of a long-vanished step.

Their stories are both poignant and heart-rending. A young woman from Washington State was not yet born when her uncle, an enlisted marine, disappeared while on a night patrol in Vietnam. The marine's niece was raised to believe she would one day be part of a family gathering to welcome home the long-lost uncle. She became so enveloped by the fantasy that in 1992, at the age of eighteen, this beautiful young girl completely devoted herself to finding POWs. She moved in with a group of POW activists, mostly unemployed middle-aged men sharing a house near Washington, D.C. She was on call around the clock to work on the MIA issue. She received no pay for her work and was expected to supply her own food and clothing besides.

A Massachusetts woman remarried after her pilot husband was presumed killed in Vietnam. In 1990, seventeen years after the airman disappeared, the woman was contacted by a Vietnamese group that claimed the missing pilot was alive. As proof, the Vietnamese sent a dog-tag rubbing. The woman did not realize that Vietnam is home to a thriving cottage industry producing fake dog tags and other phony evidence. She took the clumsy rubbing to mean her first husband might still be alive. The single sheet of paper, sent from abroad by unscrupulous con artists, caused the woman to doubt the past seventeen years of her life. "I truly thought he had not survived," she said. "I never would have remarried if I had thought there was the slightest glimmer of hope."

In some cases, hope has driven family members to remarkable lengths. In 1972, with the war still raging, the mother of a missing serviceman managed to get into Laos in search of her son, whom she believed had phoned her from a prison in Phnom Penh. She did not find him. In 1993 an MIA daughter took time off from her job as a college professor to hike through remote mountain territory in Vietnam. She was looking for a tribal chieftain whom she believed had information on her father. She learned nothing.

One MIA father talks each night to his son's green beret, hoping the missing soldier will somehow hear his assurances of love. An MIA wife who remarried in the mid-1970s still cries spontaneously during flashbacks of the husband who disappeared over Laos in 1969. Another wife bakes chocolate chip cookies and always has them on hand for her missing husband.

The dedication and love of these families are both inspirational and enviable. Who among us would not like to be as cherished by our families as these men are by theirs? And who does not feel awed by the MIA wives, whose steadfast devotion stands in stark contrast to the disposable loyalties of modern marriage?

David Hrdlicka's wife, Carol, has described her dedication in straightforward terms: "My family will not rest until we find the fate of David."

Carol Collins, the former wife of a missing Army captain, Donald Carr, has described what it is like to endure such a quest: "You become obsessed. You cannot eat, sleep, work, because you would waltz with the devil to bring one man home."

In 1990, though, Marian Shelton had an even better reason than most for obsessing on the search for Charles. Even though the Pentagon knew Charles was dead, it had continued to promote him through the years, so that the man who disappeared as a captain is now known as Colonel Shelton. More significantly, as a result of Marian's relentless lobbying, the Pentagon had changed her husband's listing from MIA back to POW. Charles Shelton remains the only American so classified from the Vietnam War. The government did this as a symbolic gesture, but Marian took it as further proof that Charles was still a prisoner. Tragically, she went to her grave trying to secure his release.

But the sad truth is, no matter how long she might have tried, Marian never could have brought Charles home. Nor can any other MIA family expect to welcome their own missing men. Neither Charles Shelton, David Hrdlicka, nor any other involuntary MIA will ever return alive, for the simple reason that no POWs remain in Southeast Asia.

PART ONE

The Setup

How the U.S. government mismanaged the POW issue in such a way as to undermine its own credibility

1

Perspective

I once tried to gauge Marian Shelton's sense of her own objectivity on POWs. "I know you believe men are being held in Southeast Asia," I said. "How much of that belief is colored by what happened to Charles?"

It was an unfair question. Her husband's disappearance was the framework of Marian's view on POWs. It was unreasonable to ask her to step outside that experience.

Marian was gracious enough to answer me anyway. "I learned about this issue because I wanted to find my husband," she said. "That's what got me involved. But his case is not the only source of evidence on POWs. Even without Charles, even if he had never been shot down, there is plenty of good, strong evidence."

What evidence was most convincing? I asked.

"Look at what happened with the French. Vietnam held back French prisoners for years after the war with France was over. If Vietnam did it to them, they would do it to us."

Others have pointed to this precedent, as well. Professional activists such as Ted Sampley, Jack Bailey, and Mike Van Atta have cited the French experience as proof the Vietnamese like to keep POWs for long periods of time. They say it means Americans were held after March 1973, when all prisoners were supposedly returned during Operation Homecoming. MIA family members have drawn the same conclusion. Karen Kirkpatrick, who is a cousin of the missing Donald Carr, has told me of the French connection. So has Ann Holland, wife of MIA Melvin Holland.

It would be a compelling argument, if true. The basic premise, that French and American POWs received similar wartime treatment from their Vietnamese captors, is correct. But the concurrent assumption, that Hanoi held back French prisoners, is false. It is based on a misconception of what happened to the French POWs who did not return home.

To understand how the fate of the nonrepatriated French prisoners differs from that of American MIAs, it is important to know something about the French involvement in Vietnam. Unlike the United States, which sent its regular troops to war, France fought in Indochina with a special category of troops called the French Union Forces. This group included some French nationals but was made up mostly of outsiders from colonial units and the Foreign Legion. The colonial troops included men from Algeria, Senegal, and Morocco. The legionnaires came from all over, including Communist Czechoslovakia, Hungary, Poland, Romania, and the Soviet Union.

When France withdrew from Vietnam in 1954, the two nations set up an exchange of prisoners. More than twenty-five thousand French forces did not return from captivity. When France pressed for an accounting, Vietnam answered that it had no French POWs.

A number had already been returned—not to France, but to their original homelands. It was a particularly cruel fate for the more than one thousand legionnaires sent back to the Communist countries they had escaped years earlier. In most cases, the returnees were met by vindictive officials who had them arrested, tortured, or killed.

Some French prisoners remained in Vietnam voluntarily. They came from a special class of POW. Some were mainland French legionnaires who had been loyal to the Vichy regime, but most were colonial troops with only peripheral ties to France. They had arrived in Indochina directly from Africa, with perhaps a short stint in France for military training. The Viet Minh correctly judged that the colonial troops would be susceptible to propaganda. The Communists enticed large numbers to remain in Vietnam, where a good many had already married local women and started families.

To their great dismay, the deserters found that reality was nothing like the paradise they had been promised. The colonials and their families were forced to live in isolated ghettos, where they could not interact with mainstream society. They enjoyed even fewer privileges than the meager ones allotted to ethnic Vietnamese. Eventually, the deserters realized that whatever France had in store for them would be better than life in Communist Vietnam. They then asked to be returned to French control.

The French government agreed to accept them, but in a manner designed to save face. The deserters were found guilty of treason, sentenced to ten years in prison, then granted an immediate amnesty. About one thousand of that class left Vietnam under the amnesty program, with the last few trickling out around 1972. Today the only Frenchmen living in Indochina are there by choice.

American POW activists have misconstrued these circumstances to fit their own agenda, interpreting them to mean that Vietnam held French prisoners for nearly fifty years after the war. But what is most enlightening, in terms of the French experience, is what happened to the POWs. Their fate was so terrible that it had a profound impact on French military memory, something I glimpsed in 1990s Washington at a British embassy reception.

A French military attaché was one of the guests, and I asked him about POWs in Vietnam. The very mention of that topic caused him to brim with emotion. "It was inhuman, what they did to our men," he said. "They were masters of brutality."

This came starkly to light in 1954, in the wake of the catastrophic battle of Dien Bien Phu. After France suffered this pivotal defeat, which would prompt its withdrawal from Vietnam, more than ten thousand troops from the French Union garrison were captured by the Viet Minh. Battle-weary and injured, the POWs were in no condition to undertake a trek through the mountains in monsoon season. Yet that is what they were forced to do, as the Viet Minh took them to prison camps located as far as 530 miles away.

The men were made to march quickly. One group covered 310 agonizing miles in only twenty-four days, a rate of 13 miles per day. The rapid pace was enforced by a constant supply of fresh guards, who rotated in at regular intervals.

Food was grossly inadequate. The prisoners were given cold rice once a day, in portions geared toward the body weight of the comparatively small Vietnamese. The captives suffered from chronic dysentery. They lost additional fluid through heavy perspiration. Most of the men quickly shed life-sustaining body weight.

No special care was given the wounded. Men who should have been airlifted to the nearest hospital immediately were instead dragged across the mountains by weary compatriots who refused to leave them. It was the best course of action, given the circumstance. Unlike the Japanese on Bataan, the Viet Minh did not bother to kill the thousands of prisoners who fell by the roadside. Those unfortunates were simply abandoned where they lay, to die quickly or linger on for days.

It was a march on which health and strength were relative terms. An artilleryman with a pierced diaphragm carried forty-four-pound rice bags so his fellows could eat. Men ravaged by dysentery pooled their meager strength to carry a legionnaire with a shattered thighbone. Others pitched in to transport a paratrooper who had artillery fragments imbedded in his eyes.

Once in the camps, prisoners had to survive as best they could on their own resources. They were left without treatment; French military doctors were held in a special camp reserved for officers, and the sites for enlisted men did not have medical cadres.

A few hospital camps were set up shortly before the cease-fire in 1954, but the French doctors who served in them reported that the conditions were appalling. Viet Minh cadres who were barely qualified to give injections took it upon themselves to perform major surgery on men who needed expert medical treatment.

A legionnaire arrived at one hospital camp in desperate condition. His arm had been shattered by machine-gun fire and left to fester for the duration of a twenty-five-day forced march. The Viet Minh medics operated on him without anesthetics or antibiotics.

Numerous soldiers developed bone infections after their fractures were left untended for months. They suffered excruciating pain when the infections were finally scraped out, again without anesthetics.

In the regular camps, where enlisted personnel were held, the biggest threat was the drinking water, which came directly from streams and rivers and was teeming with deadly bacteria.

Camp 5-E, located in the jungle surrounding Ngoc Lac in the north, was particularly hard hit. From March through September 1952, 201 out of a total 272 inmates died of drinking contaminated water. During a one-month period in 1954, 120 out of 250 men died under similar conditions less than fifty miles away, at Camp 70.

Some of the prisoners' illnesses could have been helped; as a matter of course, France sent in planes to air-drop medicine, food, and clothing into the camps. The supplies were never put to the use for which they were intended. Prison guards intercepted the packages and kept the goods for themselves.

After the war ended, 10,754 French troops—far fewer than the 26,225 who were missing—returned from captivity. The French Union High Command was shocked to note that returned POWs typically weighed 100 pounds or less. They had reached this appalling condition after less than six months in captivity.

What was even more shocking was that these skeletal survivors were the lucky ones. They were fortunate to be only sick and starving, and not sick, starving, and seriously wounded. Not one prisoner with a wound to the abdomen, chest, or skull managed to survive the camps.

Of those returned, 6,132 were so ill they required immediate hospitalization. It was too late for some; despite the best efforts of French medical experts, sixty-one repatriated POWs died within a few months.

The French scholar Bernard B. Fall wrote of these horrors in 1958, advising U.S. military leaders to note the Vietnamese attitudes toward POWs and military medicine: "This needs to be known in the West, since future complications in the area may compel friendly forces to face the same foe once more under similar conditions."

Despite this warning, the United States entered its own phase of the war expecting a certain measure of civil conduct by the enemy. The United States assumed Hanoi would abide by the sections of the 1949 Geneva Convention that addressed the protection of POWs.

But Hanoi circumvented the convention, claiming the American captives were not prisoners of war but criminals. As such, they were kept in subhuman conditions.

The survivors' stories are the stuff of nightmares. One who came back with horrifying tales was Dr. F. Harold Kushner, an

Army flight surgeon. Kushner was captured in 1967 and held four years in Quang Nam in South Vietnam. In February 1971 he was marched for fifty-seven days to Hanoi, where he was relieved to be held in the relative luxury of a prison. He was released a short time later, during Operation Homecoming.

Kushner estimated that the mortality rate among Americans held in the south was 45 percent. He was not officially allowed to treat his fellow prisoners but did what he could surreptitiously. In extreme cases, the Viet Cong let him help obviously dying men. The Viet Cong's medicine—caffeine, aspirin, and epinephrine—was useless. Ten POWs died in Kushner's arms at Quang Nam.

In Kushner's camp, the diet consisted of about three cups of rotten, feces-laden rice per day. The men had no shoes and minimal clothing. It was cold in the mountains, and the prisoners had no blankets. They improvised, wrapping themselves in old burlap rice sacks. In mosquito season, there were no nets to protect them from the bloodthirsty swarms.

Disease was rampant. Kushner said that after six months in captivity, the typical American POW had lost about half his weight and had developed a distended belly and muscle atrophy; he suffered from chronic malaria plus an enlarged liver and spleen; his feet and ankles were swollen from fluid retention, complicated by the lack of protein. In addition, his body was covered with open sores. He defecated about forty times a day.

The prisoners had a formula for diagnosing their most debilitating illness. A man with ten to twenty bowel movements a day was suffering from common diarrhea. Anything more than that was dysentery.

The campgrounds were littered with feces. The men, most of whom had open sores on the soles of their feet, developed severe infections from stepping in the human waste. There was no medicine to fight the infections. Nearly all the POWs were afflicted with worms. The men would literally pluck the parasites from their mouths and noses. Weak as they were, the prisoners were made to perform slave labor in the fields or mountains, carrying trees or hundred-pound baskets of manioc root.

Colonel James "Nick" Rowe, a courageous POW later assassinated in the Philippines, told me that while he was held in the South, he contracted several life-threatening tropical diseases, including amoebic dysentery, malaria, beri-beri, and jaundice. Rowe said his captors allotted him two cans of rice a day. He tried to supplement the diet by hunting for snakes and rats when he could, but the chance rarely presented itself. "I was kept in a cage made of slender saplings measuring three by four by six feet. I couldn't stand up or stretch out to my full length. Plus they had me in leg and arm irons."

These conditions were trying enough on their own, without the added stress of repeated torture. The Viet Cong used both physical and psychological methods on Rowe and his fellow inmates.

"We had guys who died after torture sessions," Rowe said. But those same sessions had little physical impact on the torturers. "They used methods where they didn't have to exert themselves. Instead of beating you with an ax handle, like they did in Korea, the Viet Cong would truss you up and let the ropes do the work."

They were just as creative psychologically. "If you can't take being alone, for example, that's an effective way to break you," Rowe said. "Or, they would find individuals who had personality conflicts and put them together."

Other methods included being set up for what turned out to be a fake execution or being forced to watch the real executions of fellow inmates.

The psychological abuse had a direct impact on the men's physical health. It caused some to fall prey to "give-up-itis," in which they grew so depressed they refused to eat or otherwise care for themselves.

Prisoners held in the North supposedly had better conditions, because they were kept in prisons instead of cages and received better rations. Former POWs, however, tell stories of such savagery that it is hard to imagine the northern prisons being looked on as a better alternative to anything.

Orson G. Swindle III was held in downtown Hanoi at the infamous Hoa Lo prison, dubbed the Hanoi Hilton by inmates. At one point, Swindle was put through nearly three weeks of continuous torture.

"I spent twenty days chained to a stool without sleep," Swindle told me. "One day I went berserk, and they let me sleep for a day, then kept me up for another ten days. They had me in a bright room and whacked me with a thick pole if they caught me sleeping. It was fairly effective. I did a lot of hallucinating."

John McCain was captured in 1967 after bailing out of a crippled Navy fighter jet. He broke both arms and a leg during ejection and was further roughed up on the ground by an angry mob. Someone smashed his shoulder with a well-placed blow of a rifle butt. Someone else drove a bayonet deep into his foot.

McCain was taken to prison, where his wounds were left untreated for four days. He developed an infection so severe that on the fourth day he believed he was dying. He asked to see a doctor. His captors told him he was beyond medical help.

His life was saved by accident, when the North Vietnamese learned that his father was Admiral John S. McCain, Jr., commander in chief of U.S. forces in the Pacific. Young McCain was promptly treated.

The following year, the Communists offered McCain an early release. He refused on the grounds that other men should be set free first. The POWs had their own code of conduct governing when a man could accept release. The procedure was that sick and wounded would be released first, followed by enlisted men by date of capture, then officers by date of capture. McCain would not violate the code. In retaliation, his captors rebroke his leg, broke an arm, smashed his teeth, and meted out other tortures.

In 1970 McCain again incurred wrath when he refused to meet with members of the American antiwar movement. As punishment he spent the entire summer confined to a tiny cell.

Retired Air Force Colonel Jack Bomar was tricked into meeting an American war protestor at the Hanoi Hilton shortly after being captured in 1967. Bomar was still recovering from wounds related to his shoot-down but was able to walk with crutches. Thinking he was going to meet with a friend of his family, Bomar was disappointed to find a radical professor from Berkeley, California, waiting to see him. Bomar told the professor his low opinion of the antiwar movement.

"I was hurt pretty badly after that, and I never saw another bandage, I never saw another anything," Bomar said. "In fact, I spent a lot of time in solitary confinement, and I got selected to get worked over by Fidel, this Cuban. He cost me years of agony."

Bomar had daily sessions with "Fidel" for more than a year. In one incident alone, Bomar sustained a broken cheekbone, a burst eardrum, and four broken teeth (incredibly, a group of POW activists went to Cuba to find Fidel in 1993, not to exact retribution, but to request his cooperation in the ongoing hunt for MIAs).

Each POW story, it seems, is more horrifying than the last. George McKnight's throat was plugged with a towel while a guard repeatedly jumped up and down on his stomach. Robinson Risner was hung by ropes for hours at a time, with sixty-pound bars attached to his ankles. Jim Bell spent thirty days handcuffed in a narrow pit beneath his cell, with no way to fend off disease-infested rats and mosquitoes.

All these hardships—torture, starvation, disease, physical trauma, and depression—wreaked havoc on the POWs' health. Military doctors who studied the men when they returned found that the average man released during Operation Homecoming had fourteen medical diagnoses. This was after going through the Vietnamese equivalent of a restoration program, designed to get the men into good condition for release. But a few extra rations and the cessation of torture could not cure the men's multitude of illnesses. The ailments spanned a wide range, but the most common included malaria, systemic infestation by worms, severe hearing and vision problems, nerve damage, and the effects of extreme malnutrition. Other common diagnoses included acute upper respiratory infections, bronchitis, pneumonia, dysentery, and bacterial skin infections.

Certain types of injuries were more or less common depending on where a man was interred. Prisoners held in the North had a higher instance of peripheral nerve injury resulting from rope torture. Those held in the South suffered more from malaria, malnutrition, skin disease, and psychiatric problems.

The men who did survive, however marginally, owed much to the company of their fellow prisoners. Navy doctors cited prisoner-to-prisoner communication as possibly the most important factor for survival. Communication prevented many from falling victim to the "give-up-itis" that had been so prevalent among POWs in the Korean War. More importantly, communication kept the internal "911" system in operation, summoning help for the needy.

Many a prisoner survived his ordeal only because his compatriots literally would not let him die. Tales abound of POWs giving up their own scant rations for the sake of another or forcing a man to eat, drink, and cleanse himself.

The system didn't always work. In his 1976 book *P.O.W.*, John G. Hubbell tells the heartbreaking story of a prisoner known only as "the Faker," who had been singled out for unspeakable torture by Fidel. The other prisoners watched helplessly as, over time, the Faker gradually lost his mind from the constant beatings.

The man refused to feed himself, would not make eye contact, and never spoke. When he finally broke silence, it was in response to a special gift, a banana, that had been smuggled in to him. The Faker said there was a microphone inside the banana, and he would not eat it. The prisoners worked hard to bring the Faker back from the brink, but he was suspicious of their intent, thinking they meant to hurt him. He continued to refuse help and was so withdrawn he did not even recognize pictures of his own family. He never came back from Vietnam.

Those who did return existed within a window of survivability. Their healthy American bodies held out, desperately, for up to eight years at a stretch. Those with dysentery and other progressively life-draining illnesses could not have existed much longer under the inhospitable conditions.

In fact, the returnees' bodies were so stressed by captivity, they took years to recover. Follow-up studies conducted by the Navy showed that even with the best medical treatment, repatriated Navy prisoners suffered from poor health for two to three years after their return. It wasn't until five years after Operation Homecoming that the men established a pattern of good health. It should be noted that these were the optimal POWs. They were aviators, which means they were well educated, older and presumably more mature, in good physical condition, and held in the North. Army and Marine POWs, primarily held in the South, fared on the whole less well.

Nevertheless, the POW activists claim that Americans have survived in Vietnam for an additional twenty years after Operation Homecoming, in the harsher settings of southern-style camps. In making this assertion, the activists have a ready supply of explanations for how this could be so.

When asked about the long-term effects of torture, the activists behave as if torture is dangerous only while it is being applied and that complications of the injuries inflicted—a crushed kidney, for example—are not a factor. The activists sound almost heartened when they say that the worst of the torture was meted out during the war and that the POWs would no longer be subject to the life-threatening abuse reserved for enemies.

But the Vietnamese have such cultural disregard for human life, it is unlikely they would have eased up on their maltreatment of men they had been conditioned to hate. I have heard testimony to this effect from a longtime enemy of Vietnam, the Montagnard tribesmen.

Montagnards now living in the United States have told me the Vietnamese treated the tribesmen with great cruelty, even when the two groups were not directly engaged in warfare. One member of the Koho tribe told of the time Vietnamese soldiers burst into his village while on their way to fight some other enemy. The soldiers demanded food, but the villagers had none; they had just consumed the last of their rice stores. The soldiers then slit open the villagers' bellies and ate directly from the stomachs of the live Montagnards.

The activists also have a simple explanation for how the POWs could withstand prolonged bouts of illness. They say the men developed immunity—a medical impossibility, since you cannot become immune to a chronic disease you have already contracted. In this way, the activists sidestep the matter of how a man can survive twenty years of chronic dysentery, malaria, or beri-beri.

The activists similarly evade another key question. When asked how the POWs could endure the debilitating depression and other problems of prolonged solitary confinement in primitive compounds or secret caves—where the POWs are almost always portrayed as being held—the activists have no answer. They instead point to their misconception of the French experience, saying that if French POWs survived long past 1954, Americans could endure past Operation Homecoming.

If only it were true. But the only real parallel between the French and American POWs is that both suffered horribly at the hands of their Communist captors. Indeed, the French experience only underscores how unlikely it is that any Americans remained in captivity for more than a short time after Operation Homecoming. The Vietnamese did not keep long-term hidden caches of men. They killed off and tortured whom they could and returned whomever they had to. In terms of the Americans, that obligation meant giving back the men they were known to hold: the men on the POW list.

2

The List

Navy Seaman Doug Hegdahl was barely twenty-one years old in 1969, when he was released after a comparatively short stay in Hanoi's Hoa Lo prison. As he marched through the gates on his way to freedom, Hegdahl seemed overjoyed, repeatedly whistling the same few bars of a jaunty children's song. His former captors did not react to the annoying sameness of the tune. They ignored the broad grin and friendly nods Hegdahl gave them, as if he were saying good-bye to party hosts instead of prison guards. The Vietnamese were used to Hegdahl's irritating, odd behavior. They were glad finally to be rid of him.

It is difficult to fault the Vietnamese for their simmering dislike of Hegdahl. He had literally fallen into their hands under unbelievable circumstances and had continued to confound them ever since. The Vietnamese would have liked him even less had they known that beneath his grinning, whistling exterior, Hegdahl had transformed himself into a vital intelligence link, a lifeline for more than 250 prisoners trapped inside the Hanoi Hilton.

Hegdahl's role began in 1967, when he was an exuberant nineteen-year-old stationed on board the guided-missile cruiser USS *Canberra*. In the early morning hours of April 6, Hegdahl was sleeping below decks as the *Canberra* cruised the Gulf of Tonkin.

He was awakened by the whistles and thuds of a night bombardment. He couldn't believe his luck: here was a chance to see a real live fireworks display! Hegdahl bounded up topside. As he stood by the rail, the concussion of the ship's giant guns blew him overboard. The ship disappeared into the darkness, oblivious to the flailing sailor.

Hegdahl spent ten hours without a life jacket, struggling to keep afloat. He was a powerful swimmer, but his strength was nearly gone when a group of Vietnamese fishermen finally pulled him from the water.

"I didn't think of myself as being captured," Hegdahl told me. "I thought of myself as rescued."

The fishermen turned him over to North Vietnamese troops. Hegdahl's captors did not believe he had been so foolish as to fall off a ship in enemy waters; they thought he must be some kind of superfrogman dispatched to swim ashore and spy on the North. But Hegdahl persisted with his story, and his captors eventually concluded they had a complete idiot on their hands.

For his part, Hegdahl knew it was better to be thought a fool than a "criminal aggressor." He played to his audience, passing himself off as a simpleton who could barely operate a mop. After two and a half years, his captors were convinced Hegdahl had been thrown overboard by shipmates who were just as sick of him as they were. They offered him an early release.

The offer was not as unusual as it may seem. Two years earlier, Hanoi had instituted an early-release program to reward POWs who admitted to being "war criminals" and who demonstrated sufficient repentance. The system was designed to prompt competition among the POWs and turn them against one another. A small number of prisoners did fall victim to the scheme and worked to ingratiate themselves with their guards. In general, though, the POWs resisted the program, and adhered to their code governing acceptance of early release.

When the Vietnamese offered early release to Doug Hegdahl, he at first refused, saying it was not his turn to go. But the Vietnamese insisted, as did Richard A. Stratton, a Navy pilot who was Hegdahl's commanding officer in prison.

"I ordered him to accept," Stratton told me. "He was far too valuable to be kept inside the compound."

That was because Hegdahl, who disarmed his captors with his foolish behavior, had spent his internment memorizing the names and ranks of about 250 fellow inmates, set to the tune of "Old MacDonald Had a Farm."

Stratton and other inmates believed it was vital for Hegdahl to sing his song in Washington. The men realized that to the outside world, many of them had simply vanished; without Hegdahl, they feared, their fate might never be learned.

They were right. In 1969, when Hegdahl was released, Hanoi admitted holding only fifty-nine American POWs. All other MIAs were mystery cases. Both North Vietnam and the Defense Department knew that any man who was unaccounted for was as good as dead. The Pentagon wanted to locate as many men as possible, to force an accounting from Hanoi. American officials knew that fifty-nine was a suspiciously low number, but the United States had no way to determine the truth. Hegdahl's version of "Old MacDonald" provided the breakthrough the Pentagon was looking for. Retired Air Force Colonel Howard Hill, a former Pentagon spokesman who was himself held in the Hanoi Hilton, told me just how much impact Hegdahl's mission had: "Up until that time, we had no accounting for those men, whether they were alive or dead. In one move, this increased our knowledge four hundred percent."

Such was the wartime process of accounting for missing men. Information came out at its own pace and was applied piecemeal to the MIA puzzle.

There are now 2,231 names on the government's official

Vietnam MIA list. It continues to be a valued document, central to virtually everyone's view of the POW issue. The Pentagon, the State Department, Congress, and other government agencies refer to it when dealing with the Vietnamese or speaking to the press. Activists use it in their publicity and fund-raising drives, and MIA families turn to it as a source of hope.

But the list is no longer the lifeline it was in Doug Hegdahl's day. If anything, it is a piece of propaganda, the hodgepodge product of special interests, misguided intentions, and political pressures. It vastly overstates the number of missing Americans and gives the false impression that more than two thousand men were thought to be alive after Operation Homecoming. It has been used by activists to bolster their claims that the men are still out there, huddled in their cages, living off the hope that their names will somehow make it to the outside world.

The sad truth is, at least half the men on the list are known to be dead. Of those not known dead, about 80 percent are thought to be dead, with possibly a handful remaining at the end of Operation Homecoming.

The government has known from the outset that it would never learn the fate of every man who disappeared in Vietnam. That is the nature of warfare. Nearly 80,000 American soldiers remain unaccounted for from World War II; more than 8,000 are missing from Korea. On the Communist side, a staggering 300,000 troops are still missing from the Vietnam War alone. When compiling its statistics from Indochina, the Pentagon realized it could not expect absolute answers but could only find a point from which to begin to solve the question of the missing men.

During the Vietnam War, accounting for MIAs was not a matter of the highest national priority—the Pentagon had other, more pressing concerns—but still it was pursued from many angles and with great diligence. By war's end, it seemed as if the task had been taken up by offices within all five concentric rings of the Pentagon and then some. The agencies' names present a mind-numbing mix of acronym soup: DOD, DIA, CIA, MACVSOG, DIOR, DCSINT, JPRC, JCS; plus the individual services, the State Department, and the Pentagon's Office of the Comptroller.

Each had its own special interest and varied its methods accordingly. Some counted only the dead. Others counted both the dead and the wounded. Still others kept a tally of missing civilians. One group included deserters and men who were Absent Without Leave (AWOL) and excluded those who were listed as Killed in Action/Body Not Recovered (KIA/BNR). One organization confined its tallies to pure numbers and did not keep records of names until after the war. Another was interested in whether men vanished under hostile or nonhostile circumstances.

Information came from a variety of sources, including eyewitness reports, investigative review boards, and human memory banks like Doug Hegdahl. Despite all the microtracking, accounting errors crept in.

The memory banks were particularly vulnerable to error. Some, like Hegdahl, gave firsthand information of men he knew to be alive, but many other lists had a much broader scope. In an effort to help as many men as possible, some of the human memory banks included on their rolls the names of all men who were thought to have been POWs. If a man's name was found scratched in a cell, he was included. If a man was rumored to have been seen in prison, his name was memorized. In this way, many men who were already dead were reported as live POWs.

The top secret MACVSOG (Military Assistance Command, Vietnam Studies and Observation Group) also provided erroneous information. During the war, one of MACVSOG's assignments was to search for and rescue prisoners. Part of that effort, codenamed "Brightlight," included forays into Laos and Cambodia. Because U.S. involvement in those areas was secret at the time,

MACVSOG deliberately misreported the results of its cross-border investigations. Men known to be dead under precise circumstances were vaguely described as missing from obscure situations in Vietnam.

Other accounting errors were deliberately created by pilots who witnessed aircraft crashes. In a practice that dates back to previous wars, pilots sometimes thought they were helping widows and orphans by claiming to have seen evidence of another man's survival, when in fact they had seen just the opposite.

Sharon Walsh, an MIA wife who advertised overseas for her missing husband, learned that for twenty years she had been the victim of such a deliberate false report.

John Walsh's squadron commander, who was flying in the airplane next to Walsh when he was shot down, finally admitted in 1991 that he had "flat-out lied" about the airman's survival. He had lied to protect Mrs. Walsh from the shock of learning she was a widow and to keep her on the military payroll, which was more lucrative than the lump-sum distribution of death benefits.

The families learned of the deliberate misreporting soon after Operation Homecoming. Lieutenant Commander George Coker, a Navy pilot who flew in Vietnam, explained the process in October 1973, when he spoke before a meeting of the National League of Families: "A guy is flying, he does see his wingman shot down. Two guys go in, and they're deader than a doornail. He's thinking to himself, 'If I report that they're dead, the wife's going to be brokenhearted, she'll get death gratuities, and that's it. If I report him MIA, his pay keeps going, and it will cushion the blow for a little while.' "

Lieutenant Commander Coker said that another widespread practice, protecting the families' pride, inadvertently created hope that certain men had survived when in fact they had not:

"I just saw your son fly into the ground. Do you think I'm going to tell you that? Hell, no. . . . If I tell you your son got target fixation and flew into the ground, to my way of thinking, what I would be saying to you is, 'You know, what you had for a son is a real idiot.' That's not true, so what am I going to say? 'Well, he flew down, and he probably lost control, he was probably hit by a [rocket] or something and lost control of the aircraft and went in.' But now I've given you a shred of hope. . . . So now he has the option of ejecting.''

Admiral James Stockdale and General John W. Vessey, Jr., the presidential envoy on POW/MIAs, also spoke of the phenomenon in 1992 testimony before the Kerry Committee. Admiral Stockdale said he had once seen an aircraft crash that certainly left the pilot dead, but he had been uncertain how to report the incident.

"I went up to see [the captain] and I said, 'I'm just getting started in this thing.' And I sent the message, whether I should have called [the missing pilot] KIA or MIA. . . . He said, 'I did this in World War II, and, of course . . . there's a great temptation to do the wife a favor. But in the long run I think you do her an injustice, because you're giving her the wrong message. If you think he's dead, say he's dead.' ''

Stockdale said he did report the man as dead, but he subsequently heard many stories of deaths being misreported. "I've been told that people who were seen to spin in the traffic pattern and crash in their plane were listed as MIA for that same darned reason," Stockdale said. "We ought to think of a better way to compensate families besides lying to them."

General Vessey testified that he, too, knew the practice to be widespread: "It's something that drives our making inaccurate reports, the very fact that you deprive your comrade's family of their livelihood by declaring him dead. So the inclination has been, if there's any doubt at all, move toward the [classification of] missing rather than face facts."

Not all misreporting, however, sprang from good intentions.

The MIA list was also skewed by men who vanished via the underground European and Japanese "railroads."

The railroads were unique in that they masked a man's disappearance in a way that ordinary desertion did not. Normally, when a soldier left his unit with no intention of coming back, he left enough of a trail to show that he had, in fact, deserted. The railroads helped effect a clean getaway and left only questions in their wake.

Their methods came to light after a well-publicized case exposed the most active railroad, a Japanese-based group called "Beheiren," also known as "Peace to Vietnam."

Agents from Beheiren were trolling for prospects in a Tokyo bar one evening in 1967 when they overheard four young sailors grousing about life in the Navy. The youngsters, all aged nineteen or twenty, were mostly frightened. They were stationed aboard the aircraft carrier *Intrepid,* which was headed for the Gulf of Tonkin. A friendly Japanese, really a Beheiren operative, injected himself into the conversation. He was sympathetic and said he would help the four if they decided not to go back to the ship. The "*Intrepid* Four," as the sailors came to be known, accepted the offer. They eventually wound up in Sweden. One of the sailors, Craig Anderson, returned to the United States in 1970 and spun a remarkable tale.

As Anderson told it, the sailors had had no political motives when they decided to jump ship; they had made the decision on impulse, with no money and no idea what they would do or where they would go. But Beheiren already had that angle covered. The "peace committee" hid the men, then used them during a press conference denouncing the war in Vietnam.

"We really got picked up in this current," Anderson told reporters. "They were political scientists, authors, intellectuals. We were in completely over our heads."

The sailors were then horrified to find themselves on board a Soviet ship, headed for Moscow.

"We thought, 'What are we doing?' " Anderson said. "We had an identity crisis. Here we were U.S. Navy men aboard a Russian ship."

Unknown to Anderson and company, that had been the plan all along, that the four should go to the Soviet Union. It was only natural, given the circumstances. According to secret Soviet documents I obtained in the course of writing this book, the entire episode was orchestrated by the Soviet KGB spy agency.

A top secret report dated November 25, 1967—one month after the men deserted—outlined an ambitious program centered around the four puzzled sailors: "We have received foreign reports which attest to the great influence of the courageous action of four American sailors on public opinion in many countries," began the report, signed by former KGB chief Yuri Andropov. "To advance the goals of development of the widest possible campaign against American aggression in Vietnam, we recommend implementing the following measures."

The report then outlined plans to use the sailors in various propaganda stunts. The *Intrepid* Four would sign leaflets asking their fellow servicemen to lay down arms, among other protests. Andropov also wanted the four deserters to lead a worldwide youth movement aimed at ending U.S. involvement in Vietnam. The KGB envisioned a multimedia campaign to include radio, press, TV ads, and yet more leaflets, to coincide with an antiwar mobilization week set to begin that December.

The worldwide youth movement never got under way, but the sailors did appear in a second antiwar press conference aired on Soviet television.

As an indication of their naïveté, Anderson said the four had expected they would at some point return to the United States as free men. When they learned they could not, they decided to settle in Sweden, where they were left to their own devices.

In retrospect, Anderson said, he and his mates had been used. "We were exploited, pure and simple. First by this group in Japan who were promoting their left-wing ideology, and then by the Russians."

The KGB and Beheiren continued their cooperative effort. I obtained a second top secret KGB report, dated February 24, 1968, in which the Soviet spy agency summarized Beheiren's most recent work with deserters. The document also told of plans that were under way: "At the present time, [Beheiren] is preparing to illegally transport from Japan three American servicemen who abandoned their units . . . preparing to send them to Europe through the Soviet Union."

Through these reports and other secret intercepts, the United States was able to identify some of the men who had disappeared via the Japanese railroad. Others vanished more successfully and were placed on the MIA list. Their names are deleted from the list from time to time when a missing man surfaces and solves his own case. One former MIA turned up in 1989 in Sydney, Australia; he identified himself as a deserter and was taken off the list. Others will likely never turn up. One loyal American from an elite unit chose to remain in Laos, his former commander told me, "because he didn't want to go back to his mama in San Diego."

Others on the MIA list included some who returned to the United States undetected after having gone AWOL in Vietnam. The men were able to escape Vietnam in the final days of the war, when anyone who looked American was allowed to scramble aboard an evacuation jet without showing identification. Some of these men were discovered years later by accident, in the course of getting a traffic ticket or applying for a marriage license. By the time they were caught, some had already been transferred to the list of deserters.

Richard Dienst walked away from his unit in Vietnam in 1967. He returned to the United States in 1971 and never tried to hide his identity. In 1982 a police officer stopped him for having an outdated license plate sticker. A computer check showed he was wanted for desertion. Two Marine Corps deserters, Bernard E. Kiel and Albert E. Clark III, were found in 1992. They were returned to Marine control, to be processed for discharge.

The addition and subtraction of deserters helped keep the MIA list in a state of flux. The Pentagon estimates that as many as two hundred AWOL servicemen may have been on the list at one time or another.

These factors all helped make the list subject to interpretation, so that when the war ended, there was a certain amount of governmental confusion over how many men were genuinely missing. There was even more ambiguity after Operation Homecoming, when returned POWs gave sometimes contradictory reports on men who remained unaccounted for. The DIA and the secretary of defense at first could not agree on the exact number of MIAs; but by May 1973, two months after Operation Homecoming was completed, the Pentagon's official MIA tally reflected the DIA's listing of 1,303 MIAs. That number declined gradually over the years, as various cases were solved.

Then, in 1977, the administration ordered hundreds of men reclassified from MIA to Killed in Action/Body Not Recovered; the Pentagon was obliged to remove those men's names from the list. By the end of 1978, there were only 224 official MIAs. In 1979, though, MIA families enlisted Congress and the courts to force the Pentagon to include on the list all men who had ever been designated KIA/BNR. As a result, names that had only recently been taken off the list were reinstated, and the names of

1,200 men who had never even been on the list, because they were known to have died, were added. By the end of 1980, the MIA count stood at 2,500, higher than it had at any other time, either during or after the war.

Government agents assigned to solve MIA cases were upset by the forced adjustments. They were especially disturbed by the inclusion of the 1,200 men who were known to have died. "It literally caused ulcers at DOD," one official told me. "These additional names were not vague discrepancy cases. We knew they were dead. Now we had to pretend we didn't know what became of them. And of course the families latched onto this one shred of hope, and no one dared tell them, 'Look, your son died years ago.' "

The Pentagon tried to compensate for its misleading official list by compiling internal lists of genuine unresolved cases. One of the internal lists was of men who were known to have survived the incident that had led to their disappearance; this was called the "Last Known Alive" list. In 1987 the tally was 269.

"We did not expect these guys to turn up in captivity," the official told me. "We expected the Vietnamese to tell us what happened to them."

As of May 1994, 179 cases from the Pentagon's internal Last Known Alive list were resolved. It now contains 90 names.

Another list was compiled in 1987 at the behest of General Vessey. The "Vessey Discrepancy Cases," as they came to be known, were 380 cases of priority interest. As of May 1994 there were 73 names on the discrepancy list.

Unfortunately, the Vessey list has only confused matters further. It contains legitimate unsolved cases that are also on the Last Known Alive list, but it also includes KIA/BNR cases that are conclusive but for the physical evidence of a body.

Army Sergeant James McLean is one such case. Sergeant

McLean disappeared in South Vietnam on February 9, 1965, while working with an advisory team assigned to the South Vietnamese Army. He was captured by the Viet Cong. Another POW who escaped captivity later reported he had been held with Sergeant McLean, who was alive but was suffering from severe malaria. After Operation Homecoming, other former POWs said they knew nothing of Sergeant McLean. In March 1992 U.S. investigators interviewed a nurse who said that Sergeant McLean had been a patient at a hospital she worked at in Vietnam. She said that McLean had arrived at the hospital in April 1965, extremely ill with malaria, and had died after ten days.

Vessey's list also includes two civilian missionaries captured around the time of the 1968 Tet offensive. Henry Blood and Elizabeth Olsen both died in captivity, according to a returned prisoner who was held along with them. The repatriated POW, Michael Benge, reported that he personally had buried Olsen and witnessed the burial of Blood. The missionaries' remains have not been located.

Before it was disbanded at the end of 1992, the Kerry Committee sought to rectify some of the many discrepancies in accounting for MIAs. Committee investigators tried to restructure the original lists from source documents belonging to the various services and commands. The search lead investigators on a far-flung scavenger hunt, from the National Archives' Suitland Reference Branch in Maryland to the headquarters of the Pacific Command in Hawaii. Committee staffers gathered volumes of documents but were also surprised to find that many records were no longer available.

The Army's deputy chief of staff for intelligence could not find any of his agency's extensive POW/MIA records from the Vietnam era. Similarly, intelligence files from MACVSOG were also missing.

The Army and other agencies with missing files did not know when their records had disappeared or whether they had been lost, destroyed, or somehow misfiled.

Some, it turns out, had been misappropriated by a well-known military historian who had long been considered above reproach. The historian, Shelby L. Stanton, is a former Green Beret executive officer, the equivalent of an office manager, who has written several densely detailed books about U.S. involvement in Vietnam. Part of his credibility as a historian was based on his claim to being a highly decorated Special Forces adventurer. In 1992 I wrote an exposé on Stanton for *The Washington Times,* describing how the famed historian had fabricated his military background and had manufactured some of the material in his writings, as well.

Stanton's connection to the pirated POW records first surfaced long before I reported it as part of the 1992 exposé. Stanton himself revealed his involvement in May 1985, when he phoned a Pentagon official to say he possessed original case reports on close to one thousand MIAs. Stanton wanted the Pentagon official to help him sell the files to Time-Life Books.

The official was bewildered that Stanton would ask him to broker a seemingly illegal transaction. The files had never been declassified and were not Stanton's property to sell. The official began taking notes. When he and Stanton finished talking that night, the official summarized the conversation in a formal "Memorandum for the Record."

As described in the memorandum, Stanton said that he had the records of the 525th Military Intelligence Group, which tracked MIAs in Vietnam. Stanton said "he had obtained the records in Saigon in 1973 and had merely put shipping labels on the material and had it sent to his home."

Stanton claimed to have a wealth of documents. "He said the files included complete copies of the board proceedings, contained such things as photos and slides, as well as copies of letters that were written home," the official wrote. "He stressed the files were sensitive, and frequently contained information that had not been released to the families. Specifically said that some files contained photos of the men with Asian girlfriends, even though they were married, and this info had not been passed on to the [next of kin]."

The official gave his memorandum to the appropriate office, which promptly misfiled it. The memo was lost in the bureaucratic maze at DOD, and nothing was done to follow up on it.

Stanton carried on with his writings but did not sell the MIA material. He also developed a side career as an unofficial mentor to people researching the Vietnam War. A self-described "pack rat," he became well known as a source of valuable documents, photos, and maps that could not be found elsewhere. Even the military on occasion went to Stanton to provide material for various official histories.

In late 1991 and the spring of 1992, two researchers visited Stanton at his home in Bethesda, Maryland, and Stanton showed them his private trove of MIA material. The collection consisted of rare items, including a top secret, one-hundred-page booklet describing covert operations and POW rescues undertaken by MACVSOG. Stanton's collection included investigation files on several Army generals killed in air crashes in Vietnam. The files contained gruesome photographs that had never been shown to the men's families. Stanton also had an extensive accumulation of Vietnamese covert agent pay cards and, as the showpiece of his collection, roughly one thousand classified case files on American MIAs.

The two researchers realized they had seen highly sensitive material that should not be held privately. They contacted the FBI, and Stanton was soon under investigation to determine his role in the possession of classified documents.

I wrote about the FBI investigation in my exposé on Stanton. After the article appeared, the Pentagon's Defense Investigative Service and the Army's Criminal Investigative Division also launched inquiries. The National Archives, which suspected that Stanton might have acquired some of its holdings, began its own internal review and even combed through the published books of well-known historians to determine whether they contained material illegally supplied by Stanton. In this atmosphere of intense scrutiny, Stanton voluntarily surrendered almost half of his one thousand MIA files.

MIA families were outraged to learn that Stanton had hidden away such valuable material for nearly two decades. They protested that the files could have shed light on MIA cases in 1973, when it would have been far easier to track down the missing men. The families also wanted to know what had happened to the other six hundred case files Stanton supposedly still had. Green Berets were doubly angry, both because of the missing files and because one of their own had acted so badly.

Despite the fury surrounding the Stanton case, the episode has had little impact on MIAs. The four hundred returned files were set aside as evidence for a possible indictment and as a result have not affected the MIA list. In fact, with all its known shortcomings—misreported evidence, inclusion of dead men, and the like—the MIA list has been affected by little more than the occasional return of remains. Its basic form and function remain intact.

The main purpose, of course, is to record the names of missing men. But the list is also a reference tool. It serves as an index to extensive case files on individual MIAs and is coded to indicate which cases could most likely be solved by the Vietnamese. The code takes the form of five categories, which determine how certain it is that the enemy knew about each individual man.

Category 1 means the enemy had confirmed knowledge of an

MIA. This includes men who were identified by the enemy by name, as well as those who were identified by other reliable sources as having been in captivity. Category 2 refers to cases of suspect knowledge, where the enemy might reasonably be expected to know about an MIA. Category 3 describes cases where it is doubtful the enemy knew anything. Category 4 describes cases where the circumstances of disappearance are unknown. And Category 5 is for incidents in which there is no possibility the enemy knew anything.

The code was designed for internal use only. It was, in one sense, a bluffing guide; the rankings enabled investigators to determine which cases they could demand information on from Vietnam. But the category system fell into the hands of activists, who used it to exploit the MIA issue.

The activists learned about the system in 1979, in the course of receiving a much larger, unexpected bonanza: a seventy-nine-page working MIA list spontaneously declassified by DIA. The list had a broad scope, as described by its cumbersome title: "U.S. Citizens and Dependents, Captured, Missing, Detained or Voluntarily Remained in SE Asia, Accounted For or Unaccounted For, from 1/1/61 Through Current Date." Its release marked the first time the government had issued a comprehensive listing of persons who had vanished during the Vietnam War.

The document contained valuable information about each case, such as the exact map coordinates where an MIA disappeared and comments such as "Voice contact on the ground prior to capture" or "Seen in captivity by returned PWs." It also contained the category assignments.

The activists quickly realized that some of the categories could be interpreted in a way the government had not intended: to indicate which MIAs were possibly still alive. The activists assigned this meaning to categories 1 and 2, which indicate certain or reasonably certain knowledge by the enemy; and category 4, pertaining to unknown knowledge. The activists then began circulating reports that certain men from these three categories were indeed alive. The activists continued this practice into the 1990s, claiming to have information on dozens of living men from categories 1, 2, and 4.

One of the principal persons to exploit both the list and the category system is Senator Bob Smith, a New Hampshire Republican. An otherwise unremarkable lawmaker, Senator Smith has built his career on fanning the hopes of MIA families by telling them their loved ones might still be alive.

In 1992 Senator Smith scoured the DIA's list along with other government documents, including MIA case files and old interviews with returned Air Force POWs, and compiled a list of his own. The senator came up with 324 "Compelling Cases" of men he thought might have survived in captivity. An overwhelming number of men on the Smith list were from categories 1, 2, and 4, the same categories singled out by the activists as designating MIAs who might still be alive.

When he released his list, Smith emphasized that it was deliberately conservative and that the true number of survivors was probably much higher.

The MIA families and activists were grateful for Smith's efforts and embraced his "Compelling Cases" as if they were an investigative breakthrough. But Smith's contribution added nothing to the hunt for answers. His list only befuddled the issue even further, since some of his "Compelling Cases" are so conclusive it is difficult to imagine how the men involved could have escaped death. In at least five cases, the men didn't. The Smith list includes William R. Andrews, Vernon Z. Johns, Dale F. Koons, John M. Mamlya, and George C. McCleary, all of whose remains have been recovered and accepted by their families.

One of the cases in which Senator Smith sees compelling evidence of survival involves two airmen lost in Cambodia.

Captain Alan Trent and First Lieutenant Eric Huberth were the crew of a two-seat F-4D that was hit on May 13, 1970. The crew of a second F-4 also on the mission reported seeing Trent and Huberth's jet descend in a dive, then crash into a ridgeline. The downed plane was full of explosives and erupted into a fireball when it hit the ground. The wreckage was spread over a 1,500-foot area. The crew of the surviving F-4, as well as the pilot of a forward air control plane, said that no one had ejected from the crippled aircraft. There were no parachutes and no signals from the locator beepers the airmen carried. The witnesses agreed that both Trent and Huberth had gone down with their plane and had still been inside when it burst into flames. Senator Smith says one of the two somehow survived the fireball, was captured, and might still be alive.

In another of Smith's "Compelling Cases," a man radioed in his own death.

Captain Park Bunker was piloting a small single-seat O-1 observation craft when he was shot down over Laos on December 30, 1970. He radioed his position. His last transmission was "I'm hit at least five times. For all practical purposes I am dead."

Search-and-rescue teams found the body of an American pilot lying facedown about thirty feet from the plane. They logically assumed it was Captain Bunker. The body was riddled with gunshot wounds from the waist up and had a serious head wound. The rescue team tried to collect the body but was driven off by hostile troops. Senator Smith says Park Bunker might still be alive.

Another of Smith's "Compelling Cases" is that of Air Force Major John Carroll, shot down over Laos on November 7, 1972. Major Carroll crashed on a grassy ridge and immediately radioed his position. In the only transmission he made, Major Carroll reported that he was coming under small-arms fire from hostile forces and that he would stay with his plane, an O-1.

The first aircrew to look for him was repelled by additional small-arms fire surrounding the crash site. The pilot of the rescue plane reported seeing Major Carroll alive, but within a hundred feet of six or seven enemy troops.

A second rescue plane flew within twenty feet of the downed O-1. The crew reported seeing the body of an American pilot under the wing of Major Carroll's plane. The body appeared to be that of Major Carroll, who was the only pilot on the ground at the time. He was afflicted with a massive head wound. The man appeared to be dead. The rescue craft was driven off by ground fire. Senator Smith says Major Carroll, too, might still be alive.

One of the best known names on the Smith list is Air Force Captain David Hrdlicka, shot down over Laos in 1965. Captain Hrdlicka was known to have been captured, since he was forced to make a Pathet Lao propaganda tape. He was held in a cave in Sam Neua with Charles Shelton. At the time of the Paris Peace Accords, Captain Hrdlicka was believed to have died in captivity. In 1982 a Laotian security official reported that Captain Hrdlicka had indeed died, in 1968, of complications of malnutrition. The official, Colonel Khamla, said that Hrdlicka had been buried near the cave and that his gravesite had later been destroyed by U.S. bombing attacks.

Senator Smith and other POW activists helped convince the Hrdlicka family that David might have been alive as late as 1991. The family, which was already angry over previous ill treatment by the government, pressured the Pentagon to tell the "truth" about Hrdlicka—but the Pentagon had already told the truth. In April 1992, to satisfy the demands of the Hrdlicka family and Senator Smith, the government's Joint Task Force–Full Accounting dispatched a team to exhume Hrdlicka's gravesite in Laos.

Team members talked to local villagers who remembered the burial that took place in 1968. The villagers reiterated Colonel Khamla's story, that the gravesite had been bombed. Not surprisingly, the excavation team was unable to find the actual grave.

The Hrdlicka family, however, under the influence of Senator Smith and other activists, concluded that the U.S. government was somehow in collusion with Laos to conceal the truth about David. So despite the overwhelming likelihood that Hrdlicka is dead, the Pentagon dares not remove his name from the MIA list. Any attempt to do so would be interpreted as evidence the Pentagon has a "mind-set to debunk."

It is an interesting turnaround, a long way from the days when the Defense Department was a trusted institution to which men like Doug Hegdahl knew they could turn for help. It is a process worth examining, for the Pentagon's fall from grace is an integral part of the POW myth.

3

The DIA Office

In the predawn hours of March 28, 1991, Army Colonel Millard A. Peck slipped into the Pentagon undetected. He snaked through the corridors leading to the tightly secured headquarters of the Defense Intelligence Agency, taking care to avoid anyone who might recognize him. He wore rumpled clothing to make it seem as if he had pulled a Pentagon "all-nighter," so no one would notice his unusually early arrival.

As chief of the DIA's Special Office for POW/MIA Affairs, Peck had every right to come and go as he pleased. On this particular morning, though, he had assigned himself a secret mission, which he carried out in keeping with his Special Forces training. The mission would have tremendous impact, serving as the final discrediting blow against the much-criticized DIA. It would also revitalize the MIA issue to a greater degree than any other single act since the 1970s and pave the way for a series of pivotal hoaxes perpetrated the following summer.

Today Peck is humble about his achievement, disclaiming any deliberate attempt at controversy. But in retrospect, it is difficult to imagine how he would think his actions could have resulted in anything else.

On that morning of March 28, Peck nailed a five-page single-spaced indictment to the door of his own inner sanctum at DIA and then withdrew, intending never to return.

Titled "Request for Relief," Peck's memo was an explanation of why he wanted out after only eight months on the job. The letter rambled at length about "puppet masters" working behind the scenes and "high-level knavery" on the part of government officials involved in the MIA issue.

Unlike typical military memos, written in a flat, passive voice, this one was suffused with color. It was at times both accusatory and self-pitying, referring to Peck as a "whipping boy for a larger and totally Machiavellian group." The memo was divided into imaginatively labeled sections, such as "The Stalled Crusade" and the pseudo-Latin "Suppressio Veri, Suggestio Falsi." But if the memo was melodramatic, even silly in places, it also contained serious charges.

"It appears that the entire issue is being manipulated by unscrupulous people in the Government," Peck wrote. "This issue is being controlled and a cover-up may be in progress. The entire charade does not appear to be an honest effort, and may never have been."

Peck accused the DIA of having a "mind-set to debunk" live sighting reports. He complained that virtually all the analysis conducted had aimed at discrediting sources, with no follow-through on the information contained in the reports. Elsewhere, Peck charged that when dealing with the POW issue, government bureaucrats were willing to sacrifice anyone who was troublesome or contentious, including POWs.

"From what I have witnessed," Peck wrote, "it appears that any soldier left in Vietnam, even inadvertently, was, in fact, abandoned years ago, and that the farce that is being played is no more than political legerdemain done with 'smoke and mirrors,' to stall the issue until it dies a natural death."

Aside from matters of style and method of delivery, the

memo was odd in other ways. It was dated February 12, 1991, more than a month prior to its posting. In addition, large portions had been blacked out with a heavy felt-tip marker.

All this was left to the discovery of the first DIA office staffers to arrive at 7:30. As Peck later confided, the internal reaction to the memo was even stronger than he had anticipated. "It was pure pandemonium when they found it," one DIA staffer told me. "The deputy division chief just about fell over."

Alarmed by the fact that the memo was literally nailed to the door and by certain dramatic phrases Peck used to describe himself, some staffers worried that he might be suffering a mental breakdown; some suggested this might be a thinly disguised suicide note. Of particular concern were lines from a paragraph in which Peck called himself "one final Vietnam casualty."

But while the amateur psychiatrists were evaluating Peck's risk to himself, others were thinking in terms of broader impact. Within an hour of its discovery, the memo was on the desk of then–Defense Secretary Richard Cheney. Cheney recognized the memo as signaling a serious crisis. Peck was a former Special Forces officer who had taught at West Point and earned numerous awards for valor in Vietnam, including several Silver Stars and the Distinguished Service Cross. In the course of battle, Peck had once played dead, waiting for enemy soldiers to loot his body. When two had approached to steal his handgun, he had shot them both at point-blank range.

In short, Peck had perfect military credentials. If the memo went public, Cheney knew, the POW/MIA office, the DIA, the Pentagon, and Cheney himself would all suffer the consequences.

Cheney made three demands: first, that the DIA find out why the memo had been posted so long after it had been written; second, that he be given the original, unexpurgated version; and last, that all charges in the memo be answered by close of business that day. Cheney did not have to order spin control. Everyone knew what was at stake. Fearing the memo had been leaked to the press, the DIA was already planning its campaign to discredit Peck.

As serious as it was, though, the Peck crisis—or one like it—was inevitable, requiring only the right mix of circumstances and personality. Since the end of the Vietnam War, the POW office had been on a collision course with disaster, acting at cross-purposes with itself.

Beginning in 1966, the DIA was given the task of collecting data on Vietnam POWs. The agency effectively oversaw the individual services in that regard, making sure they placed a high priority on looking for POWs. The DIA was held in high regard for its expertise; the military branches all followed investigative procedures established by the DIA. Even the CIA deferred to its Pentagon counterpart in the matter of POWs. When the war ended, the services no longer tracked POWs or MIAs. The CIA, which judged that there was not enough evidence to support the continued analysis of POW reports, shifted its efforts elsewhere. The DIA emerged as the sole agency responsible for analyzing all POW/MIA data collected during the war and for collecting and analyzing all new intelligence. But the DIA was also inexplicably assigned a new responsibility, for family outreach. The same agents who had been valued for their skill at cold, dispassionate analysis were now assigned to work with the MIA families.

As the families will attest, the DIA outreach officers performed miserably. They displayed little sensitivity to the plight of parents, wives, and children awaiting word on their loved ones. Marian Shelton once told me she could feel the outreach officers' distaste in dealing with her. "It was like I was a skunk they had just run over," she said. "They had to get me out of the road, so they just picked me up by the tail and held me at arm's length."

Donnie Collins, wife of MIA Tom Collins, told the Kerry Committee what it meant to be "assisted" by the DIA: "I, as an MIA wife, was frustrated by knowing little, being left out of the loop, and it seemed at times being treated as the enemy, more feared by the Administration and military intelligence than the North Vietnamese whom we should have been unified against.''

"The complaints are legitimate," one former analyst told me. "The more active families were looked on as a hindrance. They would come to us with things like 'He was a strong man; if anyone could survive, it was my husband,' and expect us to take that as evidence. This stuff had absolutely no place in an investigation, and here we were, expected to nod solemnly and write it all down. We got to where we were pretty rude, even with the families who just wanted to know what was going on.''

Agents came under increasing pressure to be more sensitive in dealing with the families; but, as the former analyst told me, "We just didn't know how.''

The agents also didn't know how to deal with the rage directed against them as the result of a gag order sent down by the Johnson administration: the families were prohibited from talking to the press about the missing men. The official reason for this was that information revealed in the press could be used to harm the prisoners. The wives sensed they were being silenced in order to stop the public from becoming emotionally involved in the war. They suspected their outreach officers of trying to enforce the gag order.

For their part, the outreach officers continued to fumble human relations and in the process reinforced the image of themselves as malevolent agents of a conspiratorial government.

The reality was far less exotic. Within a few years of the war's end, the DIA's POW/MIA office had evolved into a decidedly humdrum part of the defense behemoth. Bureaucracy, politics, and public relations were as integral to the caseload as good old-fashioned police work. The office was inundated with questions from Congress, the press, and the general public. It became the butt of Pentagon jokes; POW analysts endured the snipes of

DIA colleagues who ridiculed them for chasing ghosts. The office that had once performed a vital wartime service was now mired down in a myriad of peacetime considerations.

Case officers were forced into the charade of treating all reports—even those that clearly did not pass muster—as if they might lead to the return of a live American.

In one instance, it seemed as if the smart-aleck colleagues were right when they joked about hunting for ghosts. A farmer in southern Vietnam approached the DIA with tales of strange goings-on in his village. A local woman was sitting up in bed each night, demanding in perfect English to be fed a plate of fried chicken. The farmer said that many years earlier, the body of an American serviceman had been buried underneath the woman's hut. The villagers believed the American's ghost was now homesick and had taken over the woman's body. The farmer wanted the DIA to pursue the case. Agents were not sure what was expected of them, but they went through the motions of checking the report before telling the farmer there was little they could do.

In another instance, the DIA went to great lengths to investigate a claim that was clearly the product of wild imaginings. An Amerasian teenager living in the United States said that in 1984 he had lived in a tunnel in Vietnam with some American soldiers who didn't know the war was over. The teenager embellished his story with obviously false details, including an elaborate description of a longhorn cattle ranch that had been carved out of the jungle. The boy's report was so outlandish his own mother said he was lying. Nevertheless, the DIA pursued the case with diligence. Agents spent several days at a hotel in New Hampshire, listening to tales of how the MIAs would tie themselves to trees each day and how they had accumulated a huge arsenal of American weapons and ammunition.

Ordinarily, the DIA would not have wasted time and money on the foolish youngster, but he had been discovered by Senator

Bob Smith, who demanded that the boy be interviewed. The DIA could not refuse Smith. The senator had a blackmail hold over the Pentagon, threatening to scream about a "mind-set to debunk" if the DIA ignored his orders. Ultimately, however, a polygraph exam of the boy showed deception.

But Senator Smith was not the only one involved in questionable live sightings. From 1975 onward, thousands of sources, mostly boat people and refugees, gave the U.S. government more than 15,000 reports on live Americans. Most of the stories were based on hearsay, describing incidents that had taken place years earlier; only 1,650 were based on firsthand information.

The DIA says that more than 70 percent of the 1,650 eyewitness reports pertained to persons not missing. The subjects included a defector named Robert Garwood; returned POWs; American civilians stranded during the fall of Saigon in 1975; and dead prisoners whose remains had already been returned.

Many live sighting reports described James Lewis, a civilian official arrested during the tumultuous period of April 1975. The Vietnamese who had witnessed Lewis's capture did not know he had been released after only a few months in captivity. Long after Lewis had gone on to new assignments, witnesses continued to tell U.S. authorities he was a POW. Each retelling of the story was treated as a separate live sighting.

Another subject of multiple reports was Herman McDonald, a former serviceman who voluntarily returned to Vietnam to find his wife and children. Hanoi held him in prison for a brief time in 1975 for violating immigration law. McDonald was then set free to search for his family and was deported in 1976.

One of the most frequently reported Americans, second only to defector Robert Garwood as the subject of sightings, was a commercial fisherman named Arlo Gay. Gay also had a Vietnamese family and was trying to get them out of Vietnam when he was arrested in April 1975. His captors carted him around to various prisons and showed him off to villagers. He must have been a major attraction at his many stopping points; even though Gay was freed in 1976, villagers continued to report him as a POW for another ten years.

The DIA also received information on people who weren't American. Amerasians, Soviets, Vietnamese-Algerians, Germans, Japanese—anyone who looked ethnically different was the potential subject of a live sighting. Villagers even told U.S. officials about a prisoner who turned out to be one of their own countrymen, a Vietnamese Army lieutenant colonel who was unusually tall and light-skinned. The colonel was captured after the fall of Saigon and was paraded through many villages. He joked to the peasants that he was an American pilot. The villagers took him literally and reported him as a POW.

The DIA analysts came to recognize the variations on each faulty MIA sighting and were quickly able to spot an Arlo Gay, for instance, or a black Amerasian. To the DIA, this was good analysis. Critics said it was evidence of a mind-set to debunk.

In 1983 the POW/MIA office was evaluated as part of a routine review by the DIA's independent inspector general. The IG concluded that the office was "overexposed to outside pressures" from Congress, activists, families, and the press. The IG's report validated the frustrations of analysts trying to juggle their caseloads and family outreach. But this was an internal evaluation whose results were not reported on the front pages of major newspapers. Among the families and an increasing number of interested outsiders, the DIA's reputation continued to worsen. Criticism focused on the handling of live sighting reports. Charges were made that important information was being lost because DIA interviewers were hostile to witnesses. Some suggested that the DIA's true mission on POWs was to collect and suppress all evidence.

So persistent were the allegations that two years after its first investigation, the inspector general conducted a second inquiry into the workings of the POW/MIA office. Again, the results showed nothing to substantiate charges of wrongdoing.

The inspectors said that there was "no indication that DIA interviewers used any procedures that intentionally downgraded, humiliated, embarrassed or abused the witnesses. There was no evidence to suggest that any truly knowledgeable witness could be discouraged by DIA methods from making information known."

The IG inspectors also found that the "outside pressures of the previous inquiry had only increased. Allegations of mistreatment were judged to be responses from individuals who had attempted to use the PW/MIA issue for their own purposes," the inspectors wrote. "There was evidence that DIA had been and continued to be manipulated on the PW/MIA issue by entities outside the U.S. Government."

The inspectors acknowledged that the office had serious public relations problems but said they were unavoidable under the current conditions: "There can be no improvement to the worsening situation until the policy and public relations interface is inserted between the DIA and the rest of the world."

Despite this exoneration by the inspector general, the DIA decided in early 1985 to conduct its own internal critique of the POW/MIA office. The findings echoed that of the IG regarding outside pressures. DIA inspectors also praised the office for the high quality of its analytic work.

In mid-1985 a Navy commodore, now-retired Rear Admiral Thomas H. Brooks, took over the POW office for a period of four months. He was surprised at what he found there. The number of staff analysts was much smaller than he had expected, and, on a more minute level, the filing system did not meet his standards. At the end of his brief tenure, Brooks wrote a memo that was sharply critical of office procedure. Brooks wrote that the DIA was sloppy in its handling of the POW/MIA issue and said there was an element of truth to charges of a "mind-set to debunk" live sighting reports.

In his 1992 testimony before the Kerry Committee, Brooks elaborated on his reference to the mind-set to debunk: "A certain degree of cynicism, I think, crept into our intelligence analysis. And it is human nature. We had been confronted with so many reports that were either deliberate fabrications or were grossly inaccurate that I think the analysis becomes cynical. . . . There is also a category of people at work surrounding the POW/MIA issue which I will categorize as professional predators."

His 1985 memo, however, contained no such elaborations, only a list of shortcomings and recommendations, including a reference to one of Colonel Peck's future cohorts, Congressman Billy Hendon. Hendon had previously worked as a consultant at the Pentagon and had used his connections to access DIA files. In his 1985 memo, Brooks warned that Hendon was about to make his own use of the files. The Pentagon must somehow work to "damage-limit Congressman Hendon," Brooks wrote. "It is clear that Congressman Hendon will be using our files to discredit us (and he will have lots of ammunition there)."

Indeed, Hendon had much in store for the DIA. But the agency did not heed the memo's warning and worked instead to damage-limit Admiral Brooks. The DIA dismissed the memo as poorly grounded, saying the author was not in any position to draw conclusions after only four months on the job. The memo was classified, in the hope of keeping it from public view; but its contents were leaked to selected activists, who spread word of a scathing internal indictment that was being covered up by senior brass.

Meanwhile, the House Foreign Affairs Subcommittee on Asian and Pacific Affairs began hearings in 1985, on reports of Americans being held captive in Southeast Asia. A former DIA director, Lieutenant General Eugene Tighe, Jr., testified that he believed Americans were being held against their will. When questioned by John McCain, who was then serving as a congressman from Arizona, General Tighe responded that his belief was based on reports that had crossed his desk over a period of years.

When I spoke to General Tighe shortly after those hearings, he told me he did not have definitive proof to back his statements, but he believed that about fifty Americans remained captive.

John McCain told me he had often heard reports of live American prisoners, but he was not convinced the reports were true. "However," he added, "when someone like General Tighe speaks, you have to listen."

McCain wrote to then–Defense Secretary Caspar Weinberger, asking that General Tighe be recalled to active duty so that he could reexamine the POW case reports. McCain believed that if Tighe were allowed to refresh his memory, and if he were given an update on live sightings, he would conclude that no live prisoners remained.

"I truly believe that unless Gen. Tighe is allowed to thoroughly review the current evidence that exists," McCain wrote to Weinberger, "his beliefs will continue to fuel the live sightings issue."

Weinberger replied that he appreciated McCain's suggestion but that such a move would be unnecessary. Lieutenant General Leonard Peroots, then-director of the DIA, had already offered General Tighe access to DIA case files.

Weinberger hoped to avoid the creation of yet another investigative committee. By having Tighe conduct an informal review, Weinberger told McCain, the burden would be placed "on Hanoi to resolve this question, something the proposals for commissions would erode by making the problem appear to be in Washington, rather than Hanoi."

The effort backfired. The informal personal review evolved into the formal Tighe Commission, which consisted of both former and active DIA and CIA officials, as well as former prisoners of war. Though the panelists concluded that there had been no government cover-up or malfeasance relating to POWs, they did charge that there was a "strong possibility" that prisoners were still being held against their will in Vietnam.

The activists took the conclusions a step further, claiming that General Tighe himself had said that men were actually being held. That the DIA was unable to find the POWs was taken as proof that the agency was actively engaged in a cover-up.

Over the next four years, the DIA continued to commission a series of internal reviews of the POW/MIA office. Analysts quipped that they had become so accustomed to the reviews, they couldn't work unless inspectors were hovering over their desks. Beneath the surface bravado, though, the analysts grew increasingly resentful of the implication that they couldn't do their job without oversight.

There was little to substantiate the need for repeated internal reviews. The various investigative teams were properly critical of inefficient office procedure, poor management, and insensitive dealings with families but found no indication of the more serious charges.

One investigator, Colonel Joe Schlatter, did at one time believe there was a mind-set to debunk, but he reversed his opinion later, after he became head of the POW/MIA office.

Nearly all the reviews noted that the recommendations of previous investigators had been duly implemented. The inspectors also repeatedly found that the analysts were hampered by the directives to work with individual families, Congress, the press, and leaders of the National League of Families. It is unfortunate these findings were ignored, for it is the last group's leader who eventually helped Colonel Peck bring on the crisis that would add great confusion to the already distorted MIA issue.

To understand how this came about, it is important to look

into the background of the individuals and organizations involved.

The National League of Families of Prisoners and Missing in Southeast Asia started out as a grassroots group aimed at drawing attention to the plight of POWs. The group was formed in the late 1960s by Sybil Stockdale, whose husband, Jim, was at that time the ranking prisoner held at the Hanoi Hilton. Jim Stockdale would eventually retire as a Navy admiral and would go on to become Ross Perot's running mate in the 1992 presidential race.

One of the first to join Sybil Stockdale's group was the family of Lieutenant Commander James Mills, who had been shot down over North Vietnam in 1966. Mills's father, Bus, and sister, Ann, were determined to learn what had become of the young aviator. Father and daughter were angry and aggressive. They became increasingly more active in the League. From 1973 to 1974, Bus served as its executive director. Ann was on the board of directors. In the late 1970s, Ann became executive director.

The job took Ann to Washington, D.C., where she transformed from an outspoken counterculture type into a savvy insider. League members who had known Ann in her California days were amazed that the woman who had once picketed the White House and organized protest marches was now hobnobbing with generals and other high-ranking officials.

Through her position as director of the National League of Families, Ann—now Ann Mills Griffiths—gained a charter spot on an obscure yet powerful committee, the Inter-Agency Group on POW/MIA Affairs.

The IAG, as it is called, is made up of representatives of the Joint Chiefs of Staff, the State Department, the National Security Council, the National League of Families, and the Secretary of Defense's International Security Affairs office. The DIA, notably, does not have a formal seat, although the chief of the POW/MIA office is allowed to attend meetings in an advisory capacity.

Since its inception in 1980, the IAG has set U.S. government policy on POW/MIA matters. The board operated under a cloak of secrecy. From 1981 through 1991, it kept no minutes of meetings; board members considered them a waste of time.

In this atmosphere of unaccountable authority, Ann Mills Griffiths forged a close relationship with retired Army Colonel Richard T. Childress, who served on the National Security Council. With Childress's help, Griffiths gained access to classified Pentagon material she had not been cleared for. Childress also helped her obtain an unprecedented perk for a civilian: Griffiths was given her own desk at the DIA.

Griffiths did not accept this incredible favor with quiet grace; rather, she abused it, assuming authority over the analysts. Before long she was handing out assignments, demanding that the agents drop whatever projects they were working on in order to carry out her orders.

The DIA wanted her gone. Try as they might, however, agency officials could not penetrate the bureaucracy that kept her in place. By 1983 Griffiths's power was such that the DIA inspector general was deeply concerned. The same report that exonerated the POW/MIA office also singled out Ann Mills Griffiths for criticism. The report described her as follows:

> Griffiths was to have visual access to . . . selected case files and reports, [but] her access to (and retention of) PW/MIA data became so pervasive . . . that the PW/MIA staff gave her and her assistant director weekly briefings on various topics of their choosing.
>
> Ms. Griffiths would exercise her contacts . . . who would order up DIA information for her. More recently, her entree to PW/MIA intelligence has been principally through a staffer on the NSC who . . . apparently supplies her with whatever she desires.
>
> While her direct access to DIA intelligence had been largely suppressed . . . she still had access through the IAG and her contact at NSC.

The report further stated that Griffiths's power to assign work to analysts had a "chilling effect" on them, interfering with their ability to pursue MIA cases.

Griffiths also wielded increasing power over the MIA families. She angered League members by preventing families from getting information on their own missing men—something the League had initially faulted the government for doing. At League meetings, Griffiths employed uniformed patrol squads, known to family members as "goons" or "Gestapo." The goons exercised strict control over who could use the floor microphones during question periods and the types of questions that could be asked.

In 1984 the League tried to throw off the yoke. At the families' urging, board members voted to fire Griffiths from her post as executive director. The effort failed when Childress threatened to withdraw all government cooperation with the National League of Families. Unhappy members eventually split off to form another support group, the National Alliance of Families for the Return of America's Missing Service Men and Women.

Griffiths continued to run afoul of various powerful people and institutions. When Senator Charles Grassley of Iowa wanted information on POW sightings, Griffiths tried to block him from getting it. She later attempted to keep classified material hidden from Senate staff investigators who had received the appropriate clearances.

No matter whom she angered, though, Griffiths forfeited nothing. She only gained power, and she began to jockey for a political appointment. She hoped that when the United States established diplomatic relations with Vietnam, the president would overlook all evidence of her poor diplomatic skills and she would be named ambassador. Until such time, she would remain at the DIA, where there developed what can only be described as a bad atmosphere. Griffiths wanted subservience, and the agents wanted her gone.

Into this setting came Colonel Millard A. Peck.

Mike Peck seemed like an excellent choice to head the POW office. He was a highly educated, combat-hardened officer who knew nothing about the POW issue. The idea was that he would bring his considerable mental powers and no preconceived judgments to bear on the matter.

But Peck's high IQ came with an even bigger ego. Peck keeps two diaries—one for plans, the other for accomplishments—and intends to bury them in a time capsule for the benefit of posterity. A bachelor who will only give his age as "forty-something," Peck takes pains to cultivate an image of himself as lady-killer. He makes it known that he keeps a string of gorgeous girlfriends who are all ignorant of one another's existence. In my first meeting with Peck, when he had just resigned from DIA, he was more interested in discussing his girlfriends than in talking about POWs. It was as if Peck, with his chest full of ribbons and his impeccable credentials as a war hero, wanted to make absolutely certain I knew he was virile.

While he worked at DIA, his lady-killer airs were viewed in different ways by different women. Some viewed Peck as harmless; Griffiths found him tiresome. She made no attempt to find common ground with Peck and abruptly dismissed his attempts at conversation.

For his part, Peck found it difficult to relate to the crop-haired, fiftyish, chain-smoking Griffiths. He was offended by her gruff mannerisms and her refusal to observe what he thought were social niceties.

The personality clash quickly devolved into a struggle to control the POW office. Peck seemingly had territorial advantage, in that he was the acknowledged boss and Griffiths's desk was in a different section of the DIA. But Griffiths soon concluded that Peck was incompetent. Shortly after Peck took over the POW office, Griffiths asked Cheney to fire him.

Spurred on by the struggle with Griffiths, Peck sought to raise his profile. He began granting press interviews. Going completely against the government policy that the United States assumed that some POWs remained alive in Southeast Asia, Peck made a startling comment to a reporter from a New Jersey newspaper. When asked if he thought any POWs remained alive, Peck answered, "Nah. They're all dead."

Peck used another interview to criticize the IAG and belittle the war in the Persian Gulf: "Big deal," Peck said. "We went in and beat up a third-world country. They're giving ticker-tape parades for guys who went in there and shot the enemy in the back. I fired more rounds myself in Vietnam than the whole Army did in the Gulf."

As if the press interviews didn't do him enough damage, Peck further enraged his superiors by aligning with activist Billy Hendon. Hendon, who knew the DIA analysts despised him, would saunter into the POW office and make a big show of collecting Peck. The analysts tried to dissuade Peck from meeting alone with Hendon. They were suspicious of the relationship and felt that at the very least it exposed the office to criticism.

Peck responded by staying where the analysts couldn't see him. Toward the end of his tenure, Peck was rarely at his desk. His absence was even noted by personnel in departments outside the DIA. Soon after Peck resigned, a Pentagon staff officer told me the chief's desk had long been vacant. "I go down there quite a bit, and in recent months when I went there, he wasn't in. I don't know where he was. He was just not there."

Tension surrounding Peck's continued absence was compounded by an internal crisis, created when several outraged civilian sources called the DIA to say they had been contacted by Billy Hendon. These sources had given MIA information to the DIA on the understanding that their identities would be kept secret. According to these sources, Hendon called them, seeking additional details on their MIA reports.

The POW office was both shocked and embarrassed. "The cardinal rule is, you never give sources away," one analyst told me. "You absolutely protect them."

The fact that the breach occurred on Peck's watch only further stoked an office rumor that Peck was about to be fired. Peck eventually deduced that he was in trouble, and in early February he requested a meeting with DIA chief Harry Soyster. Peck hoped to impress Soyster and presented a briefing that included charts, graphs, and a slide show.

Peck told me the presentation contained valuable suggestions in several key areas. A source close to Soyster said it was "gibberish." Despite their differences on the presentation's contents, both agree that Soyster was unmoved.

"Nothing happened when the show was over," Peck said. "Soyster sat there for a while. Then he said, 'Maybe we need to find you a new job.' "

Soon afterward, Peck wrote the memo dated February 12. On that date he delivered it to Soyster and another DIA official as they came out of a meeting, handing each a sealed copy of the complete memo. Peck then waited in the hall outside Soyster's office, expecting the DIA chief to respond. After a long wait, it became evident that Soyster wasn't coming out. Peck went home.

When Soyster finally contacted Peck several days later, it was not to address the memo but to discuss new job possibilities for Peck. That was when Peck decided to go public. He nailed the memo to his office door, he told me, as a way to get attention. He specifically wanted the press to pick up on his charges against Griffiths. As for the date he chose to post the memo, March 28—it was a symbolic date, the anniversary of the day he had joined the service.

After the memo went up, the Army wasn't sure what to do with Peck. He didn't know whether he wanted a new job or a discharge, so the Army gave him a temporary desk assignment that required no work. The activists spread word that Peck was under lock and key, living in a cell beneath the Pentagon's Navy Annex. One of the more vocal activists, Ted Sampley, called to tell me of Peck's imprisonment. When I called the Army to ask if it were true, my question was greeted with gales of spontaneous, hysterical laughter.

I met with Peck several times during that period, and he confided that he had decided to get out of the service. He thought he would go to South America and start a cattle ranch. Meanwhile, he said, the DIA was spying on him. Peck said the agency had set him up in a "honey trap": his newest and best girlfriend, he claimed, was a DIA agent. She had broken into his apartment, he claimed, and stolen the time capsule diaries. He knew it was this girlfriend because she was the only one who knew the diaries were kept in his gun case. Peck also claimed he was being followed.

When I asked about the specific charges he had made in his memo, Peck promised he could document every single one. He promised to give me the proof, just as soon as his discharge came through. He also promised the Kerry Committee that he would supply proof of a government cover-up.

Peck never provided anything. He did meet in closed session with the Senate committee's investigators but failed to impress them.

Peck emerged a hero from his tanglings with Griffiths and the DIA. To the activists, he is yet another martyr in the search for missing men. The reality is that Peck, who actually believed all the "POWs" are dead, seized on the MIA issue only as a last-ditch effort to keep himself out of trouble. In the process he caused serious damage—to families who trusted his claims that their men are still alive and to the sources he compromised via Billy Hendon.

Peck was aided by reluctant allies at the DIA. By keeping silent on the complaints about Peck, the DIA only enhanced his status and further contributed to the myth of live POWs. The agency also helped strengthen its nemesis, Griffiths, by allowing her to remain on record as the only one to say Peck should be ousted.

For all the high drama surrounding the Peck episode, little has changed in the way the Pentagon looks for MIAs. Agents continue to go through the motions of tracking down even the phoniest of leads. If a report comes in, the agents are not permitted to use the most basic police procedure, which is first to evaluate the source. No matter who submits information and no matter how poorly it is conceived, the agents are required to follow through. For this reason, agents handled with great seriousness a report from a Laotian citizen who wanted a reward for delivering a letter from an MIA, Air Force Major Albro Lundy, Jr. The letter was complete nonsense. It read, in part, "I am master (VN) people it's send to Mr. Bousy (Lao). Do you see it!" The author later identified his wife as "Marry Two Childrens" and gave other personal information, such as "Two my cars two my dogs and etc and they money in the B. Internation Washington D.C. 1 500 000 $ No 784529 U.S."

Political pressure is greater than ever before. The incident wherein Senator Smith forced investigators to talk to the imaginative Amerasian is but one example. "That kind of thing happens all the time," one agent told me.

Office work is further hampered by a steady stream of POW hoaxes. In 1992 Senator John McCain of the Kerry Committee asked Robert Sheetz, Peck's replacement as head of the POW/ MIA office, to describe the amount of time devoted to chasing down hoaxes.

"At times, Senator, I would tell you that that process literally precluded us from doing anything else," Sheetz answered.
"Essentially, what you're doing is dropping the work that would
probably have more payoff to chase after things that ultimately turn
out to be useless exercises."

4

The
Turncoats

Most of Washington was starting to shut down shortly after lunch on September 3, 1993. It was the Friday before Labor Day, and people were getting a jump on the holiday traffic. The casual atmosphere pervaded most of the Pentagon, as well—except for the POW office, where there existed the equivalent of Red Alert. For days, the office had been trading cables with a station in the South Pacific, and now came the urgent message: an American MIA had surfaced in New Zealand.

Late Friday afternoon, four agents were dispatched to Auckland. They returned Tuesday with disappointing news: the report was a hoax.

For the agency, it was a particularly bitter letdown. This report, which hadn't come via Senator Smith, Billy Hendon, or any other familiar but unreliable conduit, had been grounded in reality. It had held out the possibility of producing someone from the one genuine class of live MIA: the defectors.

There are roughly a half-dozen defectors currently living in Southeast Asia. The government has tracked them for years while simultaneously denying their existence. The Defense Department was allowed to implement this policy all on its own; from the

Nixon administration to the present, neither the White House nor the State Department has ever shown an interest in defectors.

The denial policy is a holdover from the war, when the Pentagon thought the antiwar movement would turn the defectors into a propaganda issue. But the original reason for hunting the defectors—to punish them—has changed. The Pentagon now wants the turncoats to help clear the books of MIAs. An accounting of defectors could greatly reduce the number of genuine unsolved live sightings. Of the ninety-nine MIA reports that are considered true mysteries, forty pertain to possible defectors.

The turncoat files date back to early 1967, when Marine First Force Reconnaissance units operating in I Corps found themselves battling renegade Americans. But if the Marines were the first to run into enemy brethren, they were certainly not the last.

During the war, there were hundreds of reports of Caucasians fighting alongside the enemy. Shocked young soldiers back from patrol gave breathless accounts of Americans in black pajamas hijacking jeeps at gunpoint, sniping at U.S. troops, or leading enemy assaults. At first, field commanders tended to dismiss the reports, thinking them the work of immature imaginations. But the frequency and consistency of the stories eventually made it clear that the unthinkable was true: American traitors were hard at work in the war zone.

The military launched an undercover assault on the defectors, compiling thick dossiers even on men who were only suspected of having crossed over. To understand the degree of scrutiny applied to possible defectors, it is useful to look at the case of Army Private, First Class Gustav Mehrer, who disappeared from his unit in Vietnam.

Mehrer was assigned to Bravo Company, 523rd Signal Battalion, 196th Infantry Brigade. In 1968 he was charged with possession of marijuana. Mehrer told friends he was afraid of the punishment to come, and he told his commander he would not serve any time in jail. He left his unit, unauthorized, on Christmas Day.

Mehrer was considered AWOL for one month. On January 24, 1969, he was reclassified a deserter. He likely would have kept that designation, except for a strange find two months later.

On March 8, a road-sweep team from the 46th Infantry came across two letters, conspicuously "mailed" on wooden spikes set out on Route 535. The letters were from Gustav Mehrer, praising the Viet Cong and explaining that he was now a "head," which was VC slang for Americans who switched allegiance.

One of the letters was unaddressed; the other was intended for a soldier buddy, Steve Rishell. The men of the 46th Infantry platoon laughed at the letters, brushing them off as Viet Cong–induced propaganda statements, no doubt signed at gunpoint. The platoon lost one letter but saved the one addressed to Rishell and turned it in to authorities.

Within days, the Army began an investigation to determine whether Mehrer had defected. Agents were dispatched to locate Rishell; others were tasked with gathering military, medical, and financial records on Mehrer.

One agent compiled a list of the soldier's known correspondents, complete with their addresses and relationships to Mehrer; another opened Mehrer's footlocker and wrote a detailed three-page inventory of its contents, including a list of book titles and their authors and publishers.

Investigators developed fourteen rolls of film found in the locker and wrote frame-by-frame descriptions of the pictures. Mehrer's mail was transcribed and analyzed.

There was nothing to indicate that Mehrer had Viet Cong sympathies, but the mail indicated a complicated personal life, one he might not wish to return to. Investigators thought it possible he had snapped under pressure and thrown in with the enemy. It wasn't until 1971, when former prisoners told of having been held

with Mehrer, that his status was changed to POW. He was returned during Operation Homecoming. Ironically, Mehrer later
testified for the prosecution at the trial of Bobby Garwood; in the
course of that testimony, Mehrer admitted he had collaborated
with the enemy while in prison, out of fear he would otherwise
be killed.

While the scrutiny given the Mehrer case may seem ridiculous in retrospect, it was ultimately put to good use. Through
investigating this and other cases, the military learned important
distinctions about defectors.

Unlike the deserters, who sometimes relied on underground
networks, defectors nearly always acted alone. They had no organized support and no sense of community with others of their
kind. They did, however, have a shared social or psychological
profile.

They were all enlisted men (this applies to deserters, as
well—in a 1972 Army compilation of more than seven hundred
known deserters, most came from the three lowest military pay
grades).

The defectors usually came from troubled backgrounds—
they had grown up in extreme poverty or suffered other forms of
hardship. Their problems carried over into the military. They
were usually tagged by disgusted comrades as the unit "bozo" or
"hothead" for fumbling assignments or erupting into violence
with little provocation. They had few friends and frequently got
into trouble.

Not all defectors fit the profile exactly, but their stories are
fascinating.

One who stands out is McKinley Nolan, "the Black Khmer."
He was the first American to openly defect and collaborate with
the enemy since 1954, when twenty-one American POWs refused
repatriation from Korea.

Nolan disappeared on November 9, 1967, after escaping

from the Army stockade at Long Binh, Vietnam. He was being
held on drug charges.

After breaking out of the stockade, Nolan ingratiated himself
with the local Viet Cong cadre. He began making propaganda
statements on Radio Hanoi and in leaflets. Nolan appealed to black
servicemen in particular to "oppose the dirty war," but he also
addressed his antiwar pleadings to American troops in general.

Little is known of Nolan's background, except that he was
poorly educated. His propaganda statements were virtually indeci-
pherable. His writing was so bad that even the Viet Cong recognized the problem. The Communists took Nolan's original
compositions to American POWs to be corrected before publication.

Nolan's motives for defecting are unclear. He is, however,
known to have had an Indochinese wife, and the couple had at least
one child. Nolan's wife worked as a cook for the Viet Cong in
camps that held American prisoners. Nolan also worked in the
camps, doing odd jobs. The prisoners often tried to talk to Nolan,
hoping to learn his story, but Nolan always walked away, making
it clear he wanted no contact with them.

In early 1973 Nolan and his wife had a falling-out with the
Viet Cong. It was possibly the culmination of long-standing ostra-
cism—some of the Viet Cong who also worked in the prison
camps were openly contemptuous of Nolan and his wife, considering them inferior. Whatever triggered the couple's estrangement
from the Viet Cong, the results were fairly serious. The two were
arrested in South Vietnam. They escaped and went to live with the
Khmer Rouge in southeastern Cambodia.

Nolan and his family lived on a coffee plantation near Memut
village in Kampong Cham province. They were housed in a section
of the plantation that served as a detention camp for civilian and
Cambodian prisoners. Nolan, who by then had taken on the name
"Buller," was assigned to work as a farmer. He and his wife lived

and worked apart from the prisoners and enjoyed a fair measure of what the Khmer Rouge regarded as personal freedom.

Another American, "Chaigar," lived on the plantation. He worked as a truck mechanic, and had a status equal to Nolan's. Chaigar was more than six feet tall, thin, and in his early twenties. He had soft, short red hair and many freckles on his face. He was probably a marine defector who led units from the North Vietnamese Army's 17th Regiment, which battled U.S. armored troops during the ARVN incursion into Laos. The freckle-faced marine was responsible for at least six American casualties in March 1971.

The relationship between Nolan and Chaigar is still a subject of debate. Intelligence analysts are still trying to determine whether they lived at the same facility by accident or because they had worked in concert. It is interesting to note that Nolan's son was also named Chaigar. If the boy was named after the American redhead, it could imply a previously unknown relationship between the two defectors. It also raises questions about Nolan's activities in Vietnam—was he really a solitary defector who limited his anti-American activities to propaganda statements, or did he team up with another turncoat and actively fight his own countrymen?

Whatever the answer, Nolan and the redhead were not seen together after 1974. Chaigar the defector remained on the coffee plantation after May of that year, when Nolan was transferred to another camp to raise vegetables.

No live sighting reports on Chaigar were received after 1974, and he is believed to have died while fighting the ARVN. Nolan, meanwhile, continued to work for the Khmer Rouge. In 1979 General Tighe told Congress that Nolan was possibly living in Southeast Asia. In the early 1980s, a North Vietnamese delegation told American officials about a defector known as "the Black

Khmer.'' Details of his appearance, including specific information about tattoos, led the Americans to conclude that this was McKinley Nolan.

Two others who remained in the Khmer Rouge agricultural system—whether by design or otherwise—are the military/civilian team of Larry Humphrey and Clyde McKay. Their little-known saga is unique even within the defector demimonde.

It began in March 1970, when two American civilians, McKay and Alvin Glatowski, hijacked a munitions freighter, the *Columbia Eagle,* and forced the captain to dock in the Cambodian port of Kompong Som. The men, who fancied themselves Marxist revolutionaries, intended the hijack as a protest against U.S. involvement in Vietnam. Both hijackers were crewmen on board the ship.

Once in port, McKay and Glatowski surrendered to local officials and asked for asylum. The request was at first granted, but the men were eventually placed under arrest. They were held on board a prison ship that was moored at a naval base across the river from Phnom Penh. They were joined on the ship by another American, Larry Humphrey, who had sought asylum in Cambodia after deserting from the Army in Thailand.

The would-be defectors lived well, considering their status. They had friendly relations with their guards, who allowed them to send out for food and alcohol, as well as English-language books and magazines.

After six months on the prison ship, the three were transferred to better quarters in Phnom Penh. Relations among the men had already deteriorated; McKay and Humphrey were secret allies in a plot that did not include Glatowski, who was showing signs of a mental breakdown.

In October 1970 the prisoners and their guards went to dinner at a downtown restaurant. Glatowski tagged along as Humphrey and McKay excused themselves to go the restroom. When Humphrey and McKay proceeded to climb out the restroom window, a surprised Glatowski followed suit.

The two plotters intended to join the Khmer Rouge and did not want Glatowski interfering with their plans. They quickly abandoned him and headed for the countryside.

The disoriented Glatowski tried in vain to get asylum in both Sweden and the Soviet Union. After two months in hiding, he gave up and turned himself in to the American embassy in Phnom Penh. He was shipped back to the United States, where he served five years in prison for his part in hijacking the *Columbia Eagle*.

Humphrey and McKay, meanwhile, made their way to the Sangke Kaong area of Kampong Cham province. They worked with the Khmer Rouge in several locations until at least 1974.

In 1986 Cambodian guerrillas from the KPNLF told U.S. officials that both Humphrey and McKay were completely assimilated into Communist Cambodia. The Americans were living in a remote area of Ratanakiri province in northeastern Cambodia, along the border with Vietnam. Both men now spoke fluent Khmer, were married to local women, and worked as farmers on small plots of land.

Yet another intriguing case is that of Michael Louis Laporte, a Navy medical corpsman attached to the Marines' First Force Reconnaissance Company.

"Doc" Laporte was well integrated into the service, although he was rumored to be exceptionally violent in combat. His background was notably unstable. He had spent his youth shuttling among feuding relatives, half siblings and stepparents. His stepmother once said that Laporte didn't feel he belonged anywhere.

His inner conflicts came to a head in Vietnam, when he was faced with a replay of the family separations that had marked his childhood. Laporte had secretly married a Vietnamese woman, and the couple had a baby. The twenty-four-year-old

Laporte signed up for an extended tour of duty on the expectation he would be assigned to Saigon, where his wife and child lived. In August 1967 Laporte learned he would not get the transfer. After that, his buddies noticed a complete personality change. He became withdrawn and sullen. He showed little interest in socializing.

His new mood did not seem to affect his willingness to fight. When his unit learned it would be required to supply nine men for an upcoming mission behind enemy lines, Laporte took pains to make sure his name was on the roster.

The mission, code-named Club Car, would not be an easy exercise. Military intelligence had found a Soviet missile launcher hidden in triple canopy jungle deep inside Vietnam's Happy Valley. This was home turf to the North Vietnamese Army's formidable 2nd Division. First Force Recon's job was to find the missile launcher, disable it, and get out fast.

At the premission briefing for Club Car, Doc and others in the "stick" were given stern orders to pack light; they would need a full measure of strength and energy, and no one was to be hampered with a heavy rucksack.

Despite this admonition, Laporte showed up for the September 5 jump with a pack so heavy his teammates had to push him up the ramp to board the waiting Caribou aircraft. When the plane was airborne, Laporte explained that he had packed extra blood and medical supplies, in case the group ran into trouble.

Others in the stick thought Laporte must have had a premonition, or at the very least a serious case of the jitters. All the way to the drop zone, he sweated so heavily that his camouflage makeup dissolved and had to be reapplied three times.

When the Caribou arrived over the drop zone, Laporte again seemed edgy. He repositioned himself several times, ensuring he would be the last to go.

As the men floated down over Happy Valley, they were

buffeted by sudden high winds. The skilled troops were able to keep their parachutes in a tight grouping—all except Doc Laporte, who maneuvered well away from the team. The other men were deeply unsettled. Laporte was heading straight into the wind. He couldn't have done so by accident. Given the force he was up against, Laporte would have had to work hard to move as he did.

Once on the ground, Laporte took cover. Then he opened fire on his own men. He vanished into the jungle.

The Marines wanted to believe Laporte was missing in action. They launched several search-and-rescue missions, hoping to find the lost medic. The men of Club Car insisted that Laporte was a turncoat. They too conducted a search—of Doc's personal quarters.

The men discovered that Laporte had left them a note, saying that Ho Chi Minh was right and they had no business being in Vietnam. The men also found Laporte's emergency survival kit, which he should have taken along on the jump.

Laporte's hooch maid said he had given her some of his personal belongings, explaining that he wouldn't need them anymore. The rest of his belongings were tucked beneath the blankets of his bunk, wrapped in packages and addressed to various members of his family.

Investigators later learned that the heavy rucksack Laporte had carried on the jump had been laden with morphine illegally scrounged from twenty-five different sick bay pharmacies. Both the investigators and the Marine buddies concluded that he could have only one use for so much morphine: to give to the Viet Cong.

For the next eight years, information on Laporte continued to come in. He was always seen traveling with the Viet Cong: not as a prisoner, but as one of them. The official verdict on Laporte is inconclusive, but his buddies believe he was a genuine defector.

Other defectors have been more difficult to trace. These are guerrillas who operated so smoothly they are known only by nicknames.

"The Phantom Blooper" was the most frequently sighted renegade of the war. He carried an M79 "Blooper" grenade launcher, which he used with a vengeance, mostly against Marines. There has been some speculation that he was a tall Viet Cong or North Vietnamese Army soldier; but Americans who have used the M79 say it is so difficult to operate that only a specially trained infantryman could use one with any degree of accuracy.

"Pork Chop" was so named for his muttonchop sideburns. He specialized in daring escapades, such as hijacking military vehicles while they were in use. He once broke into an ARVN armored vehicle compound and drove off with two American-made M113 Armored Personnel Carriers, one hooked up behind the other.

"Tex" spoke with a distinct Texas drawl and was an expert in explosives. He talked his way or broke into U.S. munitions depots, mostly in the III and IV Corps areas, and planted timed detonation devices. He was probably a Navy-trained EOD (Explosive Ordnance Division) man and is believed to have died after a 1969 shoot-out in Bien Hoa.

From 1967 to 1974, ground troops near the DMZ and along the Laotian border reported encounters with a two-man team known as "Salt and Pepper." One was white and the other black. The two were mainly known for stealing supplies and transportation equipment and were also involved in spreading anti-American propaganda. But Marine First Force Recon patrols also saw Salt and Pepper deep inside enemy territory, fighting alongside NVA units. They were wearing NVA uniform gear and using AK-47 rifles. In August 1974 Salt and Pepper were spotted leading an attack on ARVN troops near Quang Ngai City.

The descriptions of Salt and Pepper were so consistent that a military artist composed a wanted poster that was distributed throughout Vietnam. The DOD wanted them badly enough that it broke its own policy and had the sketch broadcast in the United States by ABC News. But despite the saturation of publicity, Salt and Pepper were never apprehended or identified.

Some ex–Army Special Forces officers thought they had solved at least half of the mystery in July 1992, after my first article on Shelby Stanton appeared. One former officer, who had seen the sketch of Salt and Pepper in *Soldier of Fortune* magazine, thought that Salt bore a remarkable resemblance to Stanton. Other former SF men agreed. Soon the rumor spread that Stanton was the elusive Salt.

But while a good case can be made for the resemblance, the rumor is more likely the product of angry soldiers seeking an explanation for Stanton's stealing Army records and lying about his military past. Stanton's own Army files show that he could not have been Salt, because he was not in Southeast Asia when the black-and-white defector team first became active. In addition, Stanton's whereabouts at other times can be accounted for, both in the record and through the personal recollections of men who served with him.

Meanwhile, by 1971, the defectors were causing enough trouble that the military devoted considerable effort to catching them. Army Intelligence placed a small unit in Da Nang, assigned to capture or kill two defectors known to be in the area. The team had many near successes but never caught a turncoat.

Ironically, the U.S. press erroneously reported in 1968 that a Marine First Force Recon unit had killed an American who was fighting alongside the enemy at Phu Bai. Although his name was not published at the time, the American was the most notorious defector of the Vietnam War, Marine Private Robert Garwood.

The Garwood story, in simple outline, is that Garwood was taken prisoner in 1965 and decided to join his captors. He worked for them in the POW camps and fought alongside them in the field. He was released from captivity in 1967 and elected to remain in Vietnam as a Communist. In 1979 he slipped a note to a foreign businessman in Hanoi. "I am American in Vietnam," read the note. "Are you interested?"

Garwood maintains he wrote the note at his first opportunity for escape. It is far more likely he made the move because he thought Vietnam was about to go to war with China, and he didn't want to fight.

In any event, the note led to Garwood's return to the United States, where he was convicted of assault on a POW and collaboration with the enemy.

Over the years, Garwood has attempted to clear his name through various projects designed to show him in a sympathetic light. The most recent was a 1993 ABC television movie, *The Last Prisoner,* starring Ralph Macchio, of *Karate Kid* fame.*

Macchio was a cute but miscast Bobby. The former defector would more properly be played by Tommy Lee Jones or someone similarly used to portraying villains, for it is important to recognize that Garwood was a genuine defector who knowingly harmed his fellow Americans. His alleged information on POWs must be viewed in light of his campaign to rehabilitate himself.

The truth about Garwood is most eloquently presented by those who knew him in Vietnam.

Ken Majeski was fresh out of boot camp in August 1965 when he was assigned to the motor transportation section of the 3rd Marine Division, stationed just outside Da Nang. "One of the first things I was told when I got there was to watch out for a guy named Garwood," Majeski told me. "He was almost thoroughly

---

*The film has an interesting place in the annals of POW lore. Its producer, Robert Emr, had connections with several POW/MIA extremists and fringe operators, including Scott Barnes and Jack Bailey. Emr and his son were murdered execution-style in 1991 near Garden Grove, California. The murders have never been solved. In 1992 Bailey's assistant, Tommy Mahan, gave me a news clipping of the incident, across which he had scrawled, "Got his karma. Guess Scott will too."

disliked by everyone in the unit. They said he was a liar, a thief, and totally untrustworthy. He was a pretty sleazy character, before all these other events took place. That was a big thing in a Marine unit. That he was tolerated at all, that people weren't regularly beating the hell out of him, is an indication of the attitude among marines that he was 'one of ours.' "

Garwood took little pride in his work as a motor pool driver and performed poorly. He was often in trouble for "goldbricking," or goofing off on the job.

Garwood had a Vietnamese girlfriend, with whom he sometimes stayed in Da Nang. If he could find someone to cover for him, he would go into town to meet the girlfriend, then return the next morning.

The other marines did not understand Garwood's actions. "They thought he was pretty stupid for being so regular, so predictable," Majeski told me.

The morning of September 29, 1965, Majeski returned from night guard duty to find the entire motor pool in an uproar. Garwood was missing.

In Garwood's subsequent version of events, he was captured the night of September 28 after getting lost on assignment to pick up an officer. According to Garwood, he was taken prisoner after a heated gun battle, during which he was shot in the arm. To this day he shows scars as proof of the bullet wounds, although there is evidence to suggest that they are the result of a childhood hunting accident.

The Marines say Garwood had no assignments the evening he disappeared. He was supposed to spend the night on base, but he told the dispatcher to cover for him while he went to visit his girlfriend. He stopped by the Da Nang Hotel around dusk and ran into three of his tentmates, Private, First Class John Geill, Private, First Class Allen Braverman, and Lance Corporal Gary Smith. He told them he was planning to make a "skivvy run," slang for a sexual encounter. An unpublished photograph of Garwood taken shortly after his capture shows that he was indeed in his skivvies.

Garwood was absent at bed check that night, but no one reported him. The alarm didn't go up until the next morning, when he wasn't at formation.

"Two guys went to the girlfriend's house to get him," Majeski said. "The girl and her clothes were all cleaned out. Garwood wasn't around. A day or so later they found his jeep burned out."

For the next few weeks, Marines kept going to the local graves registration office looking for Garwood's body. Back at the motor pool, the men were starting to think they might never learn what had become of the unit outcast. Then, on December 3, troops from the 3rd Regiment found Garwood's signature on a propaganda leaflet posted on a gate near Da Nang. Garwood's colleagues thought it a fitting discovery. "The guys joked they were surprised it took him that long to cross over," Majeski said.

But if the men in the motor pool thought Garwood a likely defector, the Marines felt he might have signed the leaflet under duress. The "Fellow Soldier's Appeal" improperly stated that Garwood was a chaplain's assistant; additionally, the signature looked as if it might have come off a rubber stamp. Given these factors, the Marines used caution and classified Garwood as a POW.

The Marines spent nearly two years hunting for Garwood and were able to track his progress through various camps in South Vietnam. The reports grew less and less heartening: Garwood was in the camps not as a prisoner, but as a Viet Cong cadre.

In January 1968 two POWs released from a camp in the South said they had seen the missing marine. Army Private First Class Jose Ortiz-Rivera and Marine Lance Corporal Jose Agosto-Santos both said Garwood was now an officer in the North Vietnamese Army. Agosto-Santos and Ortiz-Rivera said they had attended a ceremony in May 1967, during which Garwood had been freed. Garwood had been offered the chance to return home but chose instead an NVA commission. He had changed his name to Nguyen Chien Dau, meaning "brave freedom fighter."

The Marine Corps immediately sent through an order to reclassify Garwood from POW to deserter. They withdrew the paperwork at the last minute. The corps repeated the process three more times during the war, eventually deciding to let the POW classification stand. Marine officials were convinced Garwood had defected but were afraid of bad publicity. Instead, they froze his rank at Private First Class, denying him the automatic promotions usually awarded to POWs.

Six months after the returned POWs gave their shocking news of Garwood, the "White VC" was spotted by Marines from the First Force Reconnaissance Company.

Eight men from the Dublin City team were coming off a mountain south of Phu Bai on July 13, 1968. The group stopped to rest by a stream near Hill 273. They filled their canteens with water, then sat down to eat a lunch of C rations. After thirty minutes or so, Lance Corporal Perry Gordon stood up to readjust his gear and in doing so happened to glance across the stream. He froze at what he saw. Not more than twenty-five feet away was a white man, staring back at him. The man looked American, but he was dressed like a Viet Cong scout.

The lone Caucasian carried a Communist AK-47 rifle. He wore a red sash across his body, indicating that he was a liberated prisoner. Other Viet Cong emerged at his side.

Gordon and the white VC continued to stare at each other; then Gordon sensed something subtly—almost imperceptibly— different in the other man's manner. He yelled, "My God! He's going to shoot me!" and dove for his rifle.

Gordon and the other man exchanged fire. The white VC

collapsed into the stream and started to get up. "Help me! Help me!" he yelled. He had an American accent.

The other marines and the rest of the Viet Cong squad joined in the fray. Gordon fired the rest of his magazine into the enemy American, and the marines scattered into the bush. Later, the First Force Recon patrol was ambushed and its nineteen-year-old point man, Private First Class Curtis Brown, was killed.

Back on base, five of the surviving patrol members looked at hundreds of photographs of possible MIAs. Four picked out Robert Garwood, and the fifth chose a civilian who looked very much like Garwood. All five gave a physical description that matched Garwood's height, weight, age, and coloring.

One of the marines on that patrol told me there was no question who it was and what he was doing.

"I am one hundred percent certain it was Bobby Garwood," said Paul Olenski, now a computer engineer living in Chicago. "For one thing, we had never heard of Garwood and never knew his name until 1987. The MIA book they showed us was three inches thick. It had missing Americans, Australians, French, civilians, and some ringers set to fool us. There were no names, no indication of uniforms, and almost all were head shots. It was definitely Garwood."

The First Force Recon team thought it had killed the renegade marine. A search unit tried and failed to find the body, and the official report listed the white VC as a "probable KIA." The Marines continued to carry Garwood as a POW but were now almost certain he was dead.

Garwood now denies he was in the firefight. But in 1969 he bragged to a POW, Army Sergeant Willie Watkins, that he had been in a gun battle against American troops and that only he and one VC had survived.

The Marines came to realize that Garwood was still alive

when POWs returning after 1969 spoke angrily of the defector "Bobby." The former prisoners said Bobby had gone to Moscow for a time for political indoctrination. They told unsettling stories about his actions in the camps. It wasn't until the court-martial in 1980, however, that the Marines learned the extent of Garwood's betrayal.

Jose Agosto-Santos testified that Garwood's true nature was widely known in the camps: "There was no doubt in the mind of any of the prisoners that Garwood was on the Viet Cong side. He was secretly called 'the Traitor' or 'the Snake' or 'the Son of a Bitch.' "

Garwood was known to sneak through the compound, eavesdropping on the prisoners. Anything he heard was sure to be reported to the camp commander.

Dr. F. Harold Kushner told naval investigators of one episode when Garwood had spied on him and another POW. "I recall an incident in the summer of 1969 when Harker and I were digging a bomb shelter and in the process were talking to each other in a very negative term about the camp commander. Garwood was hiding under a hootch nearby and apparently overheard our conversation unbeknownst to us and reported it along with some fabrications."

As punishment, Harker's and Kushner's already meager rations were reduced for a number of weeks.

While digging another bomb shelter, a group of POWs were discussing life in Fascist POW camps as opposed to life in Communist camps. The men agreed the Communist camps must be "ten times worse." Garwood reported the conversation, and the men were taken before a camp assembly, where they were beaten with rifles.

The POWs also held Garwood responsible for the deaths of some of their fellows. Some were killed after Garwood informed on their plans to escape; others died from "give-up-itis" resulting from their treatment by Garwood.

In the summer of 1969, five starving POWs decided to supplement their monthly ration of one ounce of meat by eating the camp cat. The men were caught before they had a chance to cook the animal. Garwood led the interrogation. Finally, one POW, Russ Grissett, said he had killed the cat by accident. Grissett, who came from the same Dublin City team as Olenski, had hoped Garwood would minimize the incident; instead, Grissett was dragged from the compound and severely beaten. Garwood helped beat another prisoner involved. Grissett was then strung up by his wrists overnight, as were the four others.

"After that, Grissett seemed to change and went into what I believe was a severe depression where he would just sit on his bunk all night and day," said Robert Lewis III. "A couple of months later, as I recall, Grissett died in camp. I believe that Grissett's death was directly related to this incident and the treatment he received from Garwood."

Another POW, First Sergeant Williams, was already physically weak when he was slapped and ridiculed by Garwood during a political indoctrination.

"This had a very adverse effect on Williams's morale," said Francis Anton. "He later said to me that he did not understand how one American could do that to another American. Williams had exhibited high morale up until that point, always being very outgoing. After this incident his morale decreased visibly and he never seemed to recover. Within several months he died with the usual symptoms of those who had given up and died for no apparent physical reason."

The former POWs had no sympathy for Garwood. "If he had stayed a prisoner like the rest of us I wouldn't hold anything against him at all," said James Strickland. "I think he has let down this country. I can never forgive him for being on their side. He should have stayed in Vietnam.''

Garwood now denies any wrongdoing. In the ABC movie, Ralph Macchio as Bobby sat doe-eyed through testimony that had been rewritten to sound like petty complaints. The presentation so outraged John McCain that he issued an angry statement on the Senate floor. At the real trial in 1979, however, Garwood didn't attempt to deny or paraphrase the accusations; he only tried to excuse himself.

He said he had been tortured into cooperating with his captors. He said the torture sessions had caused him to develop a mental illness that erased his ability to tell right from wrong and that his actions had been no worse than those of other Americans who had not been charged.

But the evidence was overwhelming. In all, eighteen returned POWs provided sworn testimony that Garwood had been a clearheaded, willing defector.

It was a sensational case for its time. The pretrial publicity was so inflammatory that at one point Garwood and a detractor squared off in a fistfight near Camp Lejeune, North Carolina. Garwood pummeled his opponent so badly, the man was sent to the hospital.

So complicated was the case that it dragged on for nearly two years, becoming one of the longest in the history of military law. The 1981 conviction was something of an anticlimax. For collaboration with the enemy and assault on an American prisoner, Garwood was demoted two pay grades to the entry-level rank of private and was denied his fourteen years of back pay.

The publicity surrounding the trial brought Garwood an unexpected bonus, a public relations benefit so lucrative he abandoned the mental illness claim and instead took up the mantle of a mysterious, all-knowing intelligence operative. The key to Garwood's new persona was the rapidly spreading POW/MIA movement. The activists were enamored of Garwood. They saw in him living proof that the United States had lied when it said that no Americans had remained in Vietnam after Operation Homecoming. If Garwood had been kept behind, the activists reasoned, so, too, had other Americans. The activists threw in a conspiracy angle to explain why the Marine Corps had prosecuted Garwood so vigorously. The activists said that Garwood had inconveniently returned from the dead, thus proving the government's duplicity.

The activists conveniently ignored cases that disproved their theory. Vito Baker, a comparatively apolitical defector, was at one time assigned by the Vietnamese to work in the jungle alongside South Vietnamese Army POWs. He was deported in the purge of 1975/76. Baker was accused only of desertion and returned to the United States without incident.

Garwood and the activists enjoyed a perfect partnership. The activists supported Garwood, and Garwood gave the MIA issue a whole new urgency. All Garwood had to do was continue to maintain his innocence—and talk about POWs.

And talk he did. Suddenly, after two years of silence on the subject, Garwood said he had seen hundreds of Americans held captive in Vietnam after 1973. He claimed he had seen twenty POWs at a camp in Bat Bat in the fall of 1973; twenty-two POWs planting vegetables on the Rock River in the Bat Bat camp in March 1975; six POWs loading a truck at a warehouse in Gia Laim in July 1975; thirty POWs getting off a train at Yen Bai in July 1977; thirty POWs on an island camp in Thac Ba in 1977; seven POWs in Hanoi in 1978; and more.

Garwood told his stories over the course of many years. The details always varied and were sometimes at odds with previous versions.

In my own conversations with Garwood, he never seemed embarrassed or discomfited by the contradictions. Repeated requests for explanation went unanswered. If I asked him something

directly, he would simply draw his serpentine face into a tight
smile and wait until I went on to the next question. He would not,
for example, give details on the POWs he had supposedly seen
because, he claimed, it would endanger their lives and the lives of
his informants in Vietnam.

Garwood comes across as a man with enormous faith in his
own charisma. He assumes he can persuade people on the strength
of his charm. Perhaps he does have that ability. His supporters have
included Ross Perot, Senator Smith, and, appallingly, the daughter
of a POW he betrayed in Vietnam. This last alliance is particularly
disturbing, since returned POWs say the man died as a result of
Garwood's actions.

Garwood has gained some of his support by claiming the
government never debriefed him on his knowledge of POWs. But
Garwood was debriefed, on March 29, 1979, by Marine Captain
Michael Shanklin. Two attorneys and Garwood's father were also
present. The interview lasted nearly two hours and involved a lot
of back-and-forth regarding hearsay stories Garwood had picked
up in Vietnam. But the entire session can be summarized in the
following exchange.

> *Shanklin:* Do you know of your own knowledge of any
> Americans now alive in Vietnam? Not what you heard from other
> people, but of your own knowledge.
> *Garwood:* No.
> *Shanklin:* Have you seen any living Americans in North Viet-
> nam since the time that you were brought to North Vietnam from
> South Vietnam in 1969 or 1970 or thereabouts?
> *Garwood:* No.

The DIA continued to meet with Garwood from time to time
to discuss new claims. The reason, as one analyst explains it, was
that even a stopped clock is right twice a day, and Garwood was
right once. He told the agency that another defector, Earl Weath-

erman, had not died in captivity as was generally thought but had
faked his own death and remained in Vietnam. This correlated
with other information the DIA already had. Garwood could not
have learned about Weatherman unless he had firsthand knowledge of the case.

Garwood, who is openly contemptuous of the DIA, agrees to
the meetings for his own reasons, which are the key to his continued involvement in the MIA issue. He hopes to get his conviction reversed so he can collect his back pay, which would amount
to hundreds of thousands of dollars. His attorney, Vaughan Taylor,
told me he would begin proceedings if someone would donate the
legal fees.

Garwood has been the source of tremendous misinformation
on MIAs; nevertheless, he has provided some measure of benefit.
In 1991 the DIA hired an analyst whose sole assignment was to
study the Garwood case. In June 1993 the analyst completed a
ten-volume report, which concluded with a six-page summary of
the lessons learned.

Among those was the caveat that all defectors might one day
return home. One of the reasons the Garwood case had gotten so
out of hand, the analyst implied, was that the Marines had assumed
Garwood would never come home. They had thought they would
never have to deal with him and were unprepared for his sudden
return.

The agency would do well to take the warning to heart. Two
decades after the war, reports on turncoats now number in the
thousands. Significant sightings took place after the January 1973
cease-fire. It is entirely plausible that the next emergency trip to
New Zealand or some other far-flung port will turn up another
Bobby Garwood.

5

The Government Cabal

By the late 1960s, there had been considerable testimony—by human memory bank Doug Hegdahl and other returned POWs—that the Communist Vietnamese were torturing the life out of American prisoners. This fact was of course extremely distressing to MIA families in particular, but also to President Richard Nixon and members of the American Red Cross, all of whom were outraged that Hanoi was ignoring Geneva Convention rules governing the humane treatment of POWs.

Nixon, the families, and the Red Cross all began to act as POW advocates in three significant areas.

First, Nixon placed POWs high on the list of points to be addressed in the ongoing peace negotiations in Paris. Nixon instructed U.S. peace delegates to insist that the prisoners be returned. Through his negotiators, Nixon declared he would not withdraw troops from Vietnam unless Hanoi met the conditions regarding POWs.

Second, MIA wife Sybil Stockdale, whose husband, Jim, was the ranking prisoner in the Hanoi Hilton, formed the National League of Families of Prisoners and Missing in Southeast Asia. League members aggressively sought better treatment for the prisoners and carried on Nixon's tactic of putting pressure on

Hanoi. At one point a group of wives even went to Paris and personally confronted the North Vietnamese delegation.

The Red Cross, for its part, tried to force Hanoi to comply with the Geneva Convention rules pertaining to POWs. As the Red Cross repeatedly stressed, North Vietnam had been among the nations that had signed the Geneva accords in 1949 and as such was bound to abide by them. The relief agency continually asked Hanoi to provide a full accounting of the POWs; to allow them to receive mail; to permit prison inspections by the Red Cross; and to cease all torture.

These combined efforts by the administration, the wives, and the Red Cross helped focus national attention on the POWs, but they were undermined by activists from the American antiwar movement. These "peace" activists took it upon themselves to visit North Vietnamese prison sites, where they made appalling declarations that the American POWs were war criminals and were not being mistreated in any way. Actress Jane Fonda even allowed herself to be photographed at the controls of a North Vietnamese antiaircraft gun, pretending to shoot down American planes.

Former prisoners have told me that in the wake of the activists' and Jane Fonda's visits, the torture increased exponentially, and the POWs realized they would have to somehow spread the word about what was happening to them.

Thus the POWs themselves became activists. While appearing at forced press conferences, during which the Vietnamese claimed the POWs were happy and well treated, the prisoners sent coded messages to the outside world. Some posed for pictures while making obscene gestures with their fingers. Others took even riskier routes. Jeremiah Denton, later a Republican senator from Alabama, blinked out "torture" in Morse code. Navy pilot Richard Stratton pretended to be brainwashed by making a series of profound bows to his captors.

Stratton told me he was "worked over pretty good" in retaliation for the bowing episode, but he succeeded in creating an uproar in the United States. Grassroots concern for the POWs spread across the nation. A California radio personality, Robert K. Dornan, came up with the idea of showing support through the wearing of POW bracelets. Each tin or copper bracelet was engraved with the name and date of loss of one prisoner; the bracelet's civilian owner was to wear it until the POW came home and then present it to him. Dornan, who later became a U.S. congressman, told me 5 million Americans purchased and wore the bracelets.

Meanwhile, the original POW advocates—Nixon, the wives, and the Red Cross—continued to promote the prisoners' cause. The issue was so pressing that in November 1969 the House Foreign Affairs Committee was moved to convene hearings on the inhumane treatment of American POWs.

The hearings did not lead to conclusions, recommendations, or even a final report; but they did serve as a forum for interested persons—mostly family members, veterans, and government officials—to air their concerns. They gained so much attention that the Foreign Affairs Committee held three more sessions, in 1970, 1971, and 1972. Collectively, the hearings established that Hanoi was not being forthright about the number of POWs being held; that the Communists were continuing to torture the men; and that the Nixon administration was relentless in its efforts to gain both a full accounting of and decent treatment for the prisoners.

At the same time as these various hearings were being conducted, the United States and Communist Vietnam continued their ongoing peace talks, during which the two sides tried to reconcile their radically differing views on what constituted fair negotiating points. A major difference was that the United States considered POWs to be a humanitarian issue; Hanoi did not. Philip Habib, who assisted Secretary of State Henry Kissinger during secret negotiating sessions, later described his shock at learning that Hanoi sought to link POWs with war reparations:

"In one of the first lists of negotiating points put forward by the North Vietnamese, the Communist side bracketed the release of prisoners with what they described as 'U.S. responsibility for war damage in Vietnam' in a single numbered point. . . . I know of no instance in which an adversary so openly treated this humanitarian problem in this way."

The United States responded with a monumental effort to separate the issues. The task was not easy. The Americans took the stance that prisoners must be released regardless of whether Vietnam received aid or not. Hanoi maintained that the aid should be given regardless of what happened to the prisoners. During the course of these talks, Kissinger repeatedly stressed that even if he did favor reconstruction aid, he was not in a position to offer it. Only the U.S. Congress could authorize such funds.

In early 1973 the U.S. and Vietnamese delegates finally reached a peace settlement. The United States had been forced to make many concessions; but in one key area, Kissinger's team prevailed. The POWs were to be returned without linkage to postwar reconstruction funds.

The peace agreement was announced on January 23. Richard Nixon told the American people, "Within sixty days from this Saturday, all Americans held prisoner of war throughout Indochina will be released. There will be the fullest possible accounting for all of those who were missing in action." Four days later, on January 27, the belligerents signed "An Agreement Ending the War and Restoring Peace in Vietnam." It was official: the war was over. The United States would withdraw its troops, and Hanoi would return all captives during a phased program code-named Operation Homecoming.

Before the operation got under way, Nixon made a gesture that eventually would be accorded great and sinister significance.

On February 1 he dispatched a letter he had written to the Vietnamese premier, Pham Van Dong, discussing U.S. aid to Vietnam. Nixon couched the letter in language that underscored his lack of final authority on the matter. Instead of making a concrete offer, he wrote a softer version of what he was prepared to give: "preliminary studies indicated" it would be "appropriate" for the United States to contribute reconstruction aid "in the range of" $3.25 billion over a five-year period.

The Vietnamese did not interpret this as a literal offer. As Kissinger had already told them, the matter would first have to go through Congress. The Vietnamese were prepared to wait for the money. They proceeded as planned with Operation Homecoming.

The process was completed on March 28, 1973. On March 29 Nixon announced, "All our American POWs are on their way home." In all, Operation Homecoming had netted 591 returnees, including 25 civilians.

Publicly, the U.S. government was satisfied. Dr. Roger Shields, head of the Pentagon's POW/MIA Task Force, announced, "We have no indications at this time that there are any Americans alive in Indochina."

Privately, though, U.S. negotiators and the DIA wondered why only 591 came home. An additional 1,321 servicemen were still missing in action; what had happened to them?

The United States began pressing Laos and North Vietnam for answers, but none were forthcoming. The DIA also conducted extensive interviews with men returned in Operation Homecoming to see if they could resolve the fate of any of the MIAs. Some of the returnees said they had indeed seen some of the missing men in captivity, but most were reported as having been very sick and likely dead. The MIA list was revised downward to reflect a total of 1,284 names.

In May 1973 the House Foreign Affairs Committee convened new hearings to determine whether live POWs had been held back by North Vietnam. Among the witnesses were former POWs, most of whom testified that they thought it unlikely that any Americans remained in captivity.

Over the next two years, the United States continued in vain to pressure Hanoi for news of the missing men. The issue took on mounting importance, and in September 1975 Congress formed the House Select Committee on Missing Persons in Southeast Asia to investigate the MIA problem. The committee was known as the Montgomery Committee, after its chairman, G. V. "Sonny" Montgomery.

The investigation, which lasted fifteen months, concluded that some deserters and defectors possibly remained in Southeast Asia. But, it found, "no Americans are still being held alive as prisoners in Indochina, or elsewhere, as a result of the war in Indochina."

Members of the National League of Families were shocked. They were certain that POWs must still be alive. The League compiled an official twenty-five-page critique of the Montgomery Committee's final report. The League accused the commissioners of being predisposed to conclude that there were no prisoners. In addition, the League demanded an investigation of Nixon's offer of $3.25 billion in reconstruction aid to North Vietnam; the League also requested the sworn testimony of Henry Kissinger on the subject.

It was at this moment that the postwar POW movement began. People who had once been advocates became activists, turning against the very men who had been most determined to secure the release of all American prisoners: Richard Nixon and Henry Kissinger.

The activists developed and promulgated a theory that Henry Kissinger had secretly promised the aid to Vietnam but had never intended to make good on his promise; he was merely tricking his opponent into laying down arms. According to the theory, Hanoi had anticipated the ruse and was secretly holding back hordes of prisoners as collateral for the promised funds. Later, when Kissinger failed to keep his word, Hanoi kept the men, intending to hold them hostage until the money was paid.

The activists then claimed that the phony offer was Nixon's idea and that Nixon and Kissinger were covering up the fact that they had made a secret, illegal offer to Vietnam. The activists added that Nixon and Kissinger knew that POWs remained alive, had willfully abandoned them, and were hiding that fact from the American people.

The theory did not make sense. Ever since the war had ended, Hanoi had consistently said it did not have any more POWs than had been released in Operation Homecoming. Why would Hanoi hold as hostages men it claimed not to have?

Furthermore, there was no cover-up by Nixon and Kissinger. They were not concealing the existence of live POWs, nor were they hiding the fact that they had offered money to Vietnam.*

Nevertheless, the activists were so persistent in their claims about POWs that in February 1977, just a few months after the Montgomery Commission issued its final report, the new president, Jimmy Carter, formed his own Presidential Commission on Americans Missing and Unaccounted for in Southeast Asia. The panel was chaired by United Auto Workers President Leonard Woodcock. Panel members sought to obtain a full accounting of MIAs and to secure the return of all recoverable American remains. They also went to Vietnam and Laos and met with Communist leaders to learn what they could about any possible POWs.

In its final report, the Woodcock Commission concluded:

*The matter of postwar aid to Vietnam did not even originate with the Nixon administration. President Lyndon Johnson first raised the issue on April 7, 1965, in a speech at Johns Hopkins University. The matter was frequently brought up throughout the remainder of Johnson's term and was discussed during Nixon's, as well. There was certainly nothing secret about the possibility of sending aid to Vietnam.

"There is no evidence to indicate that any American POWs from the Indochina conflict remain alive." The activists responded that President Carter had obviously joined Nixon and Kissinger's cover-up.

There ensued more congressional hearings, plus a series of official delegations to Vietnam and Laos. The investigations continued over the years. None came anywhere near finding evidence of a single live POW. Still, the activists insisted that the men remained captive.

The activists' claims might have died down eventually, if not for the boost they received during Ronald Reagan's terms in office. Reagan never accused Nixon and Kissinger of wrongdoing, but he did take it on faith that POWs were being held in Vietnam. His constant talk of finding the men not only made it acceptable to believe in POWs but also encouraged Republican leaders to take a similar line.

In 1985 the POW issue took a decidedly bizarre turn. More and more conservatives began to espouse a POW conspiracy featuring Nixon and Kissinger; but at the same time, prominent Republicans were also backing the rehabilitation of Nixon, who had been in disgrace since resigning the presidency in 1974. Nowhere was the Republicans' schizophrenia on the matter more apparent than in the Washington, D.C., publishing arena. For example, while editors at the conservative *Washington Times* were treating Nixon as a celebrated elder statesman, journalists across town at the *Conservative Digest* were going after the former president with a gusto reminiscent of the Watergate investigators'.

Republican antipathy for Nixon came into the open in December 1985, when *Conservative Digest* published a POW exposé authored by former New Hampshire governor Meldrim Thomson.

Thomson rehashed the old war reparations story, with added details about Hanoi's motives for continuing to hold the prisoners. According to Thomson, Vietnamese officials had kept back prison-

ers because they feared that the men who returned during Operation Homecoming would talk about the systematic torture they
had endured in captivity and that Nixon would retaliate by refusing
to pay the promised $3.25 billion. Hanoi would then offer to
return the remaining prisoners in exchange for the money.

Again, the theory did not make sense. Thomson did not
explain how the Vietnamese could exploit collateral they claimed
they didn't have. He also neglected to consider that the United
States already knew the extent to which POWs had been tortured.
From the 1960s on, escapees and released captives had given
detailed descriptions of what went on inside the prison compounds
of Southeast Asia. Vietnam was well aware that it could not
pretend it had not tortured the prisoners.

Thomson also sidestepped other pertinent issues. He made
no mention that Hanoi was responsible for living up to the agreement it had signed that it would release all prisoners during
Operation Homecoming. Thomson did not even touch on the
notion that Hanoi was at fault for holding back prisoners. Instead,
he directed his wrath at his own government.

Thomson wrote with righteous indignation: "It is a blot on
our national honor that Secretaries of State under four Presidents,
and a host of sycophantic aides, have deceived the people of the
United States about Americans still being held as Prisoners of War
in Southeast Asia."

In January 1986 the Senate Committee on Veterans Affairs
responded to the charges from Thomson and others and convened
yet another inquiry into the POW situation. From January through
August, the committee held seven open hearings to determine
whether or not prisoners remained alive in captivity. Throughout
most of 1986, there was a constant stream of witnesses coming to
Washington, either to appear before the committee or to prepare
their testimony. In this semicarnival atmosphere, new theories and
rumors flourished.

Activist Ted Sampley personally created several when he issued a commemorative ''fact sheet'' marking the twenty-fifth anniversary of the capture of Charles Duffy, the first American listed as missing in action in Vietnam. In it, Sampley said that Hanoi was indeed holding back prisoners for cash. But, he added, Hanoi had other motives for keeping POWs. They included the following:

· Hanoi was holding the men as security against renewed military intervention in Vietnam.

· Hanoi needed Americans to translate the repair manuals for the high-technology equipment abandoned in Vietnam.

· Hanoi was using Americans as torture subjects for international terrorist training camps.

· Hanoi was keeping the men as reminders that it had beaten the powerful United States.

Sampley also listed some reasons why the United States was denying the existence of POWs. One was that the Defense Intelligence Agency would have to be disbanded if the POWs came home. According to Sampley, the DIA had concocted a massive cover-up in order to preserve its reason for existence. He neglected to consider that POWs constitute only a minor portion of the workload undertaken by the DIA.

Sampley implicated the news media as well, explaining that the press should have realized in 1973 that POWs remained in Vietnam. Sampley said that the same reporters who had bungled the POW story in 1973 were now in positions of authority at various newspapers; in order to conceal their past ineptitude, these journalists were now suppressing the truth on POWs.

Another rumor that surfaced in 1986 involves thousands of ex–Green Berets known as the Black Cowboys, who supposedly remained in Vietnam when Saigon fell in 1975. Their mission had been so sensitive that it could never be revealed, and therefore their existence had been kept "off the books." None of these soldiers ever returned from Vietnam, and none has appeared on the official MIA lists.

In 1986 there also arose a "secret repatriation" theory, in which POWs had been returned to the United States under assumed identities. The supposed motive was to prevent the public from learning that the government had lied about the POWs.

That same year, one of the activists' own heroes, Lieutenant General Eugene Tighe, headed the Tighe Commission, which specifically looked into the question of a cover-up. The general made his findings clear: "We have found no evidence that anyone in DIA (or anywhere else in the U.S. government) has intentionally covered up anything about the POW/MIA issue." Similarly, the Senate Veterans Affairs Committee had concluded that it was unable to find any proof that POWs remained alive in Southeast Asia.

Nevertheless, new myths continued to emerge. One that gained a large following was that many soldiers in Vietnam had contracted a sexually transmitted disease so deadly it could devastate the American populace. In order to avert an epidemic, all the infected men had been shipped to a secret island and were officially classified as either MIA or KIA/BNR.

In time the activists implicated Nixon, Kissinger, Gerald Ford, Carter, Reagan, George Bush, the CIA, the DIA, the State Department, the House of Representatives, and the U.S. Senate as participating in some part of a POW conspiracy. Bush, who had been head of the CIA during part of the Vietnam War, was singled out as being particularly culpable for concealing the truth about POWs and for perpetrating dirty tricks against the activists. Several claimed that Bush had personally set out to "get" them while he was president. William Cook of Sacramento, California, said that after he had revealed the existence of live POWs in Cambodia, President Bush had ordered his military pension and Social Security checks stopped.

In 1991 the public's concern about live prisoners intensified, and in response the U.S. Senate formed a panel to look into every aspect of the POW issue. Under the direction of the committee chairman, Senator John Kerry, members first tried to determine whether POWs had been held back after Operation Homecoming; and, if so, whether U.S. officials knew about it.

A string of high-powered witnesses, among them Henry Kissinger and former defense secretaries Melvin Laird and James Schlesinger, appeared before the committee and testified on the events surrounding Operation Homecoming. The witnesses had differing opinions on whether North Vietnam was holding back prisoners.

After listening to the various statements, the Kerry Committee concluded that it could not determine whether men were in fact being retained in Vietnam; but the activists seized on the testimony from the witnesses who believed men were being kept back and juxtaposed it against the 1973 statement by Richard Nixon that all the POWs had been returned. According to the activists, that made Nixon a liar.

The Kerry Committee then examined the notion that Nixon and Kissinger had deliberately abandoned POWs and that they had orchestrated a cover-up to conceal the fact.

Again, prominent witnesses were called to testify. Several pointed to the obvious. Any cover-up, if it existed, would have had to start in the waning days of the Nixon administration. It would have been a poor time to begin a complicated plot, when Nixon himself was thoroughly distracted by Watergate and unable to concentrate on most other matters.

Other key links for a POW cover-up did not exist. In a six-month period in 1973, for example, there were four different secretaries of defense and three different heads of the Central Intelligence Agency. One of the former CIA directors, James Schlesinger, said he had spent 90 percent of his tenure trying to determine whether the CIA had been involved in Watergate.

Lieutenant General Leonard Peroots, former director of the DIA, testified that a conspiracy would have had to involve, at the outset, hundreds, perhaps thousands, of military personnel, from the lowest privates on up through four-star generals and admirals, as well as civil servants ranging from entry-level GS-1s through cabinet appointees. To preserve such a conspiracy for more than twenty years would have involved adding scores of new confidants with each incoming administration. By the 1990s the number of conspirators would have been in the millions.

General Vessey commented on the likelihood that American servicemen would participate in a cover-up of POWs: "American soldiers, sailors, airmen and marines are not conspirators. It's hard to keep military secrets long enough to get the operation going along without the enemy knowing what's going on. Even at the time when we were at low ebb, we still had one-hundred-and-some-odd people involved, and those rotated. Many of them rotated every two or three years. So I'd say the prospect or probability of a conspiracy being kept without it being blown wide open is almost zero."

General Vessey said that during his entire military career, including his tenure as chairman of the Joint Chiefs of Staff, he had never seen any evidence of a conspiracy or cover-up.

Admiral James Stockdale also declared that he had never seen any evidence of a conspiracy. "To go into it as a venture, you'd be a fool because there are so many possibilities of leaks and so forth."

Other witnesses gave similar testimony. Henry Kissinger bristled at the mere mention of a conspiracy: "There is no excuse, two decades after the fact, for anyone to imply that the last five presidents from both parties, their White House staffs, secretaries of state and defense, and career diplomatic and military services either knowingly or negligently failed to do everything they could to recover and identify all of our prisoners and MIAs.''

The Kerry Committee properly concluded that the United States had not willingly abandoned men in Southeast Asia and that there had been no government conspiracy to conceal their existence. The activists then charged that all of those who had testified against the existence of a conspiracy were themselves a part of it.

In early 1993 the activists hoped to take advantage of Bill Clinton's perceived ignorance about Vietnam and educate him on the misdeeds of his predecessors. But the activists soon became suspicious of the new president, after ''discovering'' that his spokesman on POW/MIA affairs, Winston Lord, had served as deputy to Henry Kissinger during the Paris peace negotiations.

Then, in February 1994, Clinton did something that was interpreted as being on a par with the infamous ''secret offer'' Nixon had made to Hanoi twenty years earlier. In the face of strenuous opposition from those who believed that the long-standing economic embargo against Vietnam was the United States' only leverage regarding POWs, Clinton lifted the embargo.

That was all the proof the activists needed. Now Bill Clinton, who had literally no history in Vietnam and who in fact had gone to great lengths to avoid serving in the Vietnam War, had become part of the government cabal that sought to conceal the truth about POWs.

6

Presumptive Findings

During Operation Homecoming, MIA wife Kay Bosiljevac was overjoyed to learn from the Air Force that her husband, Captain Mike Bosiljevac, would be among those returning from captivity. The Vietnamese had not placed Mike's name on the list of men to be released, but circumstances led the Pentagon to conclude he would come home, anyway. Mike, an F-105 weapons officer, had been shot down over North Vietnam very late in the war, on September 29, 1972. He and his pilot, Lieutenant Colonel James O'Neill, had ejected safely from their jet. They had landed uninjured, within a half mile of each other. Both men had been taken prisoner, and Mike's capture had been reported by Radio Hanoi. Since he was known to be alive and since the North Vietnamese were thought to be less ill disposed toward POWs in the face of impending peace, no one doubted Mike would be among those released.

The atmosphere in the Bosiljevac home was highly charged that spring, when the first American prisoners stepped into the embraces of their loved ones. Kay's excitement was heightened by the return of James O'Neill, who reported that while he was in prison, a guard had told him that Mike was in good health. Kay had every reason to believe that she, too, would soon be racing across an airport tarmac, her arms outstretched.

But the expectation dragged into wondering and finally into dread. In the end, Operation Homecoming came and went with not a word of Mike Bosiljevac. Kay was devastated.

The Pentagon was puzzled and angry—not just about Bosiljevac but about hundreds of others who also did not return as expected. The United States asked Vietnam to explain all the cases but was particularly insistent about Bosiljevac. He had been imprisoned only a few months. There was no way his captors could have lost track of him. Yet that is precisely what Hanoi claimed they had done. Repeated demands for information on Mike were met with infuriating protestations of ignorance. Hanoi insisted it had no knowledge of Captain Bosiljevac or his whereabouts.

The Pentagon had little recourse but to keep asking for information on Mike Bosiljevac. It was less sure of how to handle the plaintive cries for help from Kay. Air Force officials met with her but could offer only condolences. Kay was relentless, pressing for information the service was unable to give out. The officials came to view her as a less sympathetic version of Marian Shelton.

In June 1980, eight years after he disappeared, Mike Bosiljevac was declared dead. To Kay, this was the ultimate betrayal. Her husband had been known to be alive and in good health in 1973. The Vietnamese were known to have lied about him; they had claimed they had no knowledge of Mike, despite having announced his capture on Radio Hanoi. How could the U.S. government simply write him off now, with the stroke of a pen?

Other families were asking the same question. President Jimmy Carter had campaigned in part on a pledge to account for all the MIAs. His promise had been quite specific. During a campaign debate with President Gerald Ford, Carter spoke with rousing determination: "We need to have an active and aggressive action on the part of the president, the leader of his country, to seek out every possible way to get that information which has kept the MIA families in despair and doubt." Carter was equally determined when explaining why the United States should not normalize relations with Vietnam: "We will account for the MIA-POWs before we reestablish any relationships with Vietnam, and you can depend on that."

Within months of his inauguration, Carter began living up to his word in a way the families found perverse. Carter was having all the men declared dead.

This was accomplished under the euphemistic process of "status review," in which an MIA's case file was examined in order to update his status. In practice, though, anytime a file was opened to conduct one of these reviews, the MIA was reclassified with a presumptive finding of death, or PFOD.

The idea was to solve the government's MIA problem and also to allow the families—wives in particular—to get on with their lives. The only problem was, the wives were not as complacent as the government seemed to want them to be. They did not go along with the government's position that they, as young women, should stop mourning their husbands and start looking for replacements. The women wanted their husbands back; failing that, they wanted a verifiable accounting.

The wives saw the PFODs as a way for both the United States and Vietnam to forget the men had ever existed. If the United States closed its books on the missing men, Vietnam would have an excuse to follow suit. Hanoi would not feel obliged to account for men known to be dead.

The move to implement status changes did not originate with Carter. In January 1973, after the Paris Peace Accords were signed, the Pentagon wanted to issue PFOD rulings on men who had vanished under circumstances that suggested they were dead.

The National League of Families protested vehemently, saying it was too soon to make such findings. The League thought information might yet be forthcoming from Vietnam, Laos, and Cambodia. In July 1973 the League helped five families file a class action suit in U.S. District Court in New York to stop the status reviews. The court immediately issued a temporary restraining order prohibiting the government from making any status change that was not requested in writing by an MIA's primary next of kin. But the court's final ruling, in March 1974, was far less supportive of the families. Instead of stopping the PFODs entirely, the court merely ordered that the families could attend the status change proceedings.

Over the next three years, the families continued to fight the status reviews and enlisted staunch allies in Congress, notably Congressman John Rhodes and Senator Barry Goldwater. The reviews were suspended and restarted many times. When Jimmy Carter took office in 1977, though, a court stay prohibiting the process had expired, and the new president made clear his intent to resume issuing PFODs.

Despite Carter's desire to be rid of the MIAs, some White House personnel kept seeking genuine answers. Michael Oksenberg, who served on the National Security Council, recalled that his office had acted in apparent contradiction to the official policy. "The reclassification process had no impact on our resolve to pursue this issue," Oksenberg said.

Others who worked for Carter had their own pressing concerns about the status reviews. At the Pentagon, officials feared that Vietnam could exploit the MIA listings by offering information on missing men in exchange for favors. A memo dated May 26, 1977, from the secretary of defense, stated that in the long run the United States might be forced to make concessions to Hanoi if the Pentagon continued to carry the men as missing in action.

Nevertheless, it was the families who felt the impact of the PFODs. They again turned to the courts for help. In *Hopper v.*

Carter, a suit filed by MIA father Colonel Earl P. Hopper, the families demanded that the government abandon the status changes until after it obtained a "true accounting" of missing men. This time the court did not issue a temporary order in support of the families; the case proceeded at its own pace, and Carter pressed on with the status reviews.

It was a time of bitter confrontation. By then the wives deeply mistrusted the government. The Pentagon, in a moment of sheer ugliness, accused the wives of wanting to maintain the MIA classification only so they could continue to collect government benefits.

The wives did enjoy a certain measure of security as long as their men were listed MIA or POW. Depending on what each MIA had specified in his military benefits forms, his wife received either all or part of her husband's monthly pay. All wives of POWs or MIAs retained their right to free military housing, and all dependents had access to free medical care, the post exchange, and other privileges.

In the case of a serviceman's death—even a presumptive death, with no body or evidence—his wife lost the monthly pay and housing benefits. She received a $50,000 life insurance settlement plus a lump sum totaling six months of her husband's salary. The family was allowed to keep its medical, dental, and PX privileges.

To counter the accusation that they were holding out for a life of ease at government expense, the families offered to give up their benefits. In return, they wanted the government to stop making wholesale status reviews. None of the families opposed a status change, even to PFOD, that was made on the basis of new or genuine evidence. Their understandable complaint was against the policy of men being declared dead for the sake of convenience.

Despite concessions by the families, though, Carter was determined to complete the accounting as quickly as possible.

Under his direction, officials went through the motions of review-
ing each case, but the result was the same as if they had spent a
single afternoon with a set of rubber stamps. By 1981, when
Carter left office, all the MIAs were accounted for: 1,100 were
already listed as Killed in Action/Body Not Recovered; 1,485 were
assigned a presumptive finding of death. Charles Shelton would be
the only one restored to the status of POW.

As per the court instructions issued in 1974, the families had
been allowed to attend the status reviews. Those who did so had
no illusions that they could influence the outcome.

Navy Captain Harley Hall, a crack aviator who had flown
with the Blue Angels precision flight team, had been shot down
over Quang Tri province in South Vietnam on January 27, 1973.
Ironically, it was the same day the United States and Vietnam
exchanged their lists of prisoners. Harley's backseater, Lieutenant
Commander Phillip A. Kientzler, who was captured and held for
a few weeks before being released during Operation Homecoming, said his guard had told him Hall was dead. But Navy Intelligence told Harley's wife, Mary Lou, that her husband had been
captured. The Navy said the National Security Agency had evidence Hall had been taken to a camp on the Laotian border.

Harley Hall's case came up for status review in 1980. The
Navy notified Mary Lou in case she wanted to attend.

"I did not want Harley declared dead," Mary Lou told me.
She said she had evidence he might still be alive. "I knew going
in that I wasn't going to make a difference in the outcome of the
status hearing. I knew what they were going to decide. But I went
anyway. You have to go. I gave a good fight."

The review board's inclinations were by that time so well
known that Mary Lou considered it a victory just to have fought
the government. "I left and felt good," she said.

Her fight also brought another small victory. Most of the
status changes were signed by the individual service secretaries

immediately after the review boards made their recommendations. Mary Lou was so persuasive that Harley Hall's status change was not signed until a year after his case was reviewed. The board had recommended a PFOD, but the paperwork remained at the Pentagon until President Carter had a chance to install his own Navy secretary, who signed the certificate.

Not all the wives had the satisfaction of fighting back. The wife of a serviceman missing in Laos wrote of her experience with the PFOD process in a letter that was read before the Kerry Committee. After her case officer said that her husband would be coming up for status review, the woman wrote, she announced her plans to attend the hearing. The case officer discouraged her.

"He said, 'Oh, you don't need to come. It's just a hearing. We will let you know about it.' I said, 'You are talking about killing off my husband legally. The way you've talked to me so far, I don't trust you.' "

The case officer asked if he could do anything to help. The woman asked him to make reservations for her at the inexpensive base visiting quarters, but the case officer told her she would have to stay in a motel.

"They closed my husband's case and declared him killed in action as of August 17, 1979. He was such an honest, straightforward man; he would not be pleased with the situation I've been placed in all of these years."

Carol Hrdlicka, whose husband, David, was lost in Laos in 1965, testified to the feelings of helplessness brought on by the charade of the automatic status changes: "In 1977 the Air Force Casualty Office contacted me and advised me that they were going to review David's case, and unless I had any new evidence that he was alive, they were going to declare him dead. I then stated that I had no evidence since I was not allowed access to intelligence. Why is it that the burden of proof is always on the families?"

The question was particularly poignant for the family of Navy

Lieutenant Ron Dodge, who was shot down over North Vietnam on May 17, 1967. Dodge was known to have landed safely on the ground. He radioed his wingman, saying he was surrounded by enemy troops and would try to get away. Radio Hanoi later broadcast that Dodge had been captured alive.

Four months later, a picture of Dodge appeared in an issue of *Paris Match* magazine. His head was swathed in bandages, and his uniform was in tatters. His dog tags still dangled from a chain around his neck. His left arm was in the grip of several hostile hands, as if a crowd had got hold of him. His shadowed, anguished face bore scant resemblance to that of the confident airman who had earlier been photographed standing next to his jet; but his wife, Janis, knew without a doubt that it was Ron.

Soon after the picture was published, Ron was featured in an East German propaganda film, *Pilots in Pajamas.* He was depicted walking through a village, escorted by North Vietnamese guards.

Given this evidence that her husband had been held for at least a short period, Janis did not understand why his name had been left off a list of prisoners issued by Hanoi in 1969. Janis asked the Navy to press for information but was told that the service preferred to wait.

In 1971 Janis enlisted the aid of Ross Perot, who bought her a ticket to Paris. There she repeatedly tried to get an audience at the North Vietnamese embassy and finally resorted to an ambush of sorts. She waited outside the site of the Vietnam peace negotiations and confronted Le Duc Tho and Nguyen Co Thach as they walked toward their limousines. Janis showed them the *Paris Match* picture and asked what had become of Ron. The two officials said they didn't have Ron Dodge. Janis insisted they must know something. At the very least, she said, they could tell her what had become of him. Tho and Thach professed that they had never heard of Ron.

Back in Washington, the Navy gave Janis the appropriate lip

service. They had no new information on Ron; they were proceed-
ing through proper channels; they would continue to press Hanoi
for an answer; they would let her know when they had more
information.

In February 1979 the Navy had something more to say, but
it was not what Janis wanted to hear. Ron Dodge was coming up
for status review. If Janis wanted him retained as an MIA, she had
to prove he was alive. To Janis, the request was completely
unreasonable. As she told the Kerry Committee in 1992: "The
government, with all of their resources, did not have to prove him
dead."

In 1981 Hanoi inexplicably returned Ron Dodge's remains.
Janis's fourteen years in limbo were over, but she had to wait
another eleven years for the next bit of information. In 1992 the
Vietnamese gave Senators Kerry and Smith a document stating that
Ron Dodge had died after only five days in captivity.

The Navy, as it turns out, was right to have assumed that Ron
Dodge was dead. But the assumption was made in such a way as
to arouse both mistrust and resentment.

It is of course misleading to imply that all the families were
against the status reviews. On the darker end of the spectrum, a
few wives were just as glad to be relieved of men they no longer
wanted. Some were anxious to legitimize their lives with new
boyfriends. It was better to be a widow than to be a woman who
had divorced a man while he was missing or captive.

Other families wanted the reviews for other reasons. In his
testimony before the Kerry Committee, Oksenberg, the former
NSC official, spoke of being deeply moved by the plight of a
woman whose pilot husband was missing in North Vietnam. The
woman came to see Oksenberg during one of the intervals when
status reviews were suspended. She begged to have the reviews
reinstated.

"She told me she was desperate," Oksenberg said. "She

explained that she had lived in suspended animation for, I think, six or seven years. She wanted to know whether the United States government thought her husband was alive or dead.''

The woman was plagued with guilt that news of her husband's death would bring its own form of relief. As such, she was afraid even to ask the Pentagon if it had new information; she felt that such a request on her part might result in her husband being reclassified, from missing to dead.

''She wanted to remain faithful to her husband as long as there was any hope, and she would do nothing to destroy that hope,'' Oksenberg said. She wanted the government to make its own assessment, unbidden: ''She requested that the government change its policy and implement an automatic review of all cases, including that of her husband.''

For the most part, though, families resented having the status reviews thrust upon them. They were outspoken in their opposition and in return were derided by a government that unfairly lumped them in a category with the far more hostile antiwar protestors.

Ironically, the families used another Carter initiative—the Freedom of Information Act—to help battle the government. Using the FOIA, families were able to get information they couldn't otherwise obtain. But the documents they received aroused even more suspicion; they would arrive with large portions blacked out under the guise of national security or the Privacy Act. In all likelihood, the censored parts contained information that would have compromised confidential sources; but the families thought the censorship concealed information vital to them.

One of the wives who made extensive use of the FOIA was Kay Bosiljevac. Among her first batch of FOIA-released documents was an Air Force file that had nothing to do with Mike. The file was all about Kay. It portrayed her as a hysterical, pushy wife who badgered the Air Force to distraction. Kay's case officer had assigned himself the role of psychologist and had written notes describing her state of mind. He had diagnosed Kay as unstable and denigrated her for refusing to accept assurances that all was being done to find her husband.

But if the Air Force thought Kay was pushy, the network of families saw her as an aggressive, resourceful investigator. Beginning in 1973, she scraped together funds and began to travel in search of Mike. Her quest took her to Laos, Thailand, and France, which, the families joked, were safer than the government corridors in Washington. Along the way, Kay learned much that kept her going.

In October 1973 the chargé d'affaires at the North Vietnamese embassy in Laos told Kay that Mike was alive and in good health. The chargé said Mike would be released only after the U.S. government fulfilled each of fifteen policy conditions pertaining to international relations. The exchange was likely a ploy on his part, but it was the first and last time anyone from the Hanoi regime had made such a statement. After that one strange revelation in Laos, officials from Hanoi resumed saying they knew nothing of Captain Bosiljevac.

Later, a U.S. official confided to Kay that Mike might have been sent to a third country, most likely the Soviet Union. An investigator for Task Force Russia, a Pentagon office researching whether Americans from any war had been shipped to the USSR, told me a handful of POWs had been "loaned" to that country by North Vietnam. All of them were highly trained in cutting-edge nuclear or electronic weaponry. Mike Bosiljevac fit that profile and was most probably one of them.

In the fall of 1987, Hanoi released what it said were the remains of Mike Bosiljevac. The DIA demanded an explanation: how could Vietnam now claim to be returning the remains of a man it had long disavowed any knowledge of? Hanoi had nothing to say, other than to repeat the statement that this was Mike Bosiljevac.

And indeed it was. Army pathologists and an independent forensics expert hired by Kay confirmed the identification. In 1988 Mike Bosiljevac was finally buried.

Kay never learned how her husband died, or when, but she harbors great resentment toward the people she thought were supposed to help her. She summed up her views before the Kerry Committee: "The U.S. government position was to wear the families down and eliminate us through frustration and attrition. So they wouldn't ever have to deal with the problem. The 'presumptions of death' are a pretty good example."

But the governmental wrongdoing goes beyond cavalier treatment of the families and a rubber-stamp approach to human tragedy. During the Carter administration, the White House received information that could have helped Kay and scores of others gain a more realistic perspective on the fate of the MIAs.

In 1979 a Vietnamese mortician who had worked for Hanoi defected to the United States. The government was at first suspicious, and both the FBI and DIA investigated him. Both agencies confirmed his identity. The mortician had good, verifiable information. He knew things about Bobby Garwood and other defectors that were true but had never been publicized.

The mortician told a fascinating story. He said that in 1975 and 1976 he had processed the remains of 452 American servicemen. The remains were stored in a Hanoi warehouse. The mortician gave detailed information that matched what Army pathologists already knew about Vietnamese processing techniques. By 1992 the mortician's claims were well established. Seventy percent of the remains returned from Vietnam bore the characteristics he had described and showed evidence of long-term storage. More important, Hanoi reversed its earlier protests that the mortician was lying and admitted he had told the truth.

In retrospect, it is clear the mortician could not have solved individual MIA cases. But he had much to contribute toward their resolution. The families would have been well served to learn that their missing men might be among the hundreds stored in Hanoi. But the mortician's report never reached the families until the PFODs were completed and the next of kin had learned to mistrust the government.

The withholding of the mortician's report is an example of the presumption that took hold in the Carter administration, that the slate was best wiped clean as quickly and as thoroughly as possible.

To this day, Carter stands out to the families as a symbol of government knavery. He is an example of an American president who inherited the POW issue, yet wound up reviled for his part in the so-called cover-up. Sadly, he has only himself to blame. In his zeal to solve the MIA question, Carter raced headlong into a public relations disaster. Worse yet, he fostered suspicions that have only grown with the passage of time.

7

Scandal in Paradise

If the families hoped to get any resolution by actually receiving the remains of their loved ones, they were in for another shock. Sometimes years after holding funeral services, families learned they had not in fact buried their own men. The scandal erupted full force in 1985, following a field investigation in the southern Laotian village of Pakse.

American officials had gone there with a team of Laotian combat engineers assigned to help sift through the detritus of an old crash site. The group was looking for remains of the thirteen crewmen of an AC-130 gunship that had burst into flames and plowed nosefirst into the jungle on December 21, 1972. Witnesses described the episode as both gruesome and fantastic. The plane had been loaded with ammunition, which continued to explode for hours after the crash.

No one expected to find whole skeletons at Pakse. The investigators thought that all on board the plane had probably been consumed by fire. Any bones that hadn't been thoroughly destroyed, they reasoned, were most likely charred beyond recognition. The true purpose of the excavation was not so much to retrieve remains as it was to establish cooperation between the U.S. and Laotian governments.

Given these conditions, the Americans were surprised to find the crash site literally covered with bone shards. Over the course of a painstaking excavation, investigators counted more than 65,000 fragments. The pieces were gathered and shipped to the Army's Central Identification Laboratory in Hawaii (CILHI).

When the Pakse bones arrived at Fort Shafter in the spring of 1985, the CILHI staff was overwhelmed by the volume of material that was virtually dumped in the office lobby.

"It was quite obvious that what we had on our hands was a complete mess," said a civilian who worked at the CILHI at the time. "The temptation was to come right out and say so. But that was not an option. Our assignment was to roll up our sleeves and get to work."

The laboratory first set out to cull the most usable material. The staff divided seven hundred of the largest fragments into piles representing the thirteen men on board the plane. According to the civilian employee, the main goal was to create thirteen piles, with little or no regard for scientific integrity.

"It was an impossible assignment from the start," the worker said. "We weren't dealing with neatly broken parts that fit together like a puzzle. We had thousands of little chips, like crushed shells, that were supposed to correspond with specific individuals. It couldn't be done."

The lab did it anyway.

"We made what we thought were likely matches, according to texture, color and location. That's how we came up with the thirteen 'men.'" The combined remains weighed in at just under three pounds.

The lab announced that it had positively identified the remains of the crewmen. This meant that the CILHI was able to state identity based solely on information gleaned from the remains.

The fragments were shipped off to the next of kin for burial. Before the families could take possession of the remains, however, they were required to sign documents accepting the Army's work.

MIA wife Anne Hart was told to expect a package containing what was left of her husband, Air Force Lieutenant Colonel Thomas T. Hart III. Anne was skeptical. For years, MIA families had complained about the identifications made by the CILHI. The families knew the CILHI often based its conclusions on circumstantial evidence. Anne wanted to make sure that any remains she buried were actually those of her husband. She decided she would not sign any papers until she knew for certain she had Tom. But the Pentagon would not allow Anne to examine the bones unless she first signed for them.

Having spent much of her adult life as a military spouse, Anne knew not to engage the Pentagon on its own terms; any challenge made within the system would only drag on for years and end in predictable defeat. So she stepped outside the system and obtained an order from a civilian court allowing her to get an independent expert opinion before accepting the remains.

Armed with the court order, a noted forensics expert was waiting for the Pakse remains when they arrived from Hawaii at the Oakland Army Base in California. Dr. Michael Charney, then-director of the Center of Human Identification at Colorado State University, unwrapped the Hart package. It contained a five-inch bone fragment and six small shards.

Charney was disgusted. "What we're talking about here is a bone from which they claim you can tell race, age, height, weight, and handedness," he told me. "There's no way those bones proved those things, yet CIL said they did." Charney also found that the lab report established height based on bones that weren't there. "Now we're going beyond scientific sloppiness," Charney said. "Now we're talking scientific fraud."

Questions were raised about other Pakse cases, as well. Donald Parker accepted the remains of his uncle Sergeant James E. Fuller only to find himself in possession of twenty-eight bone chips and a CILHI wristband bearing Sergeant Fuller's name. Parker took the remains to his county medical examiner in Portland, Oregon, and learned that the chips yielded no information other than the fact that the bones were human.

Parker went to several other anthropologists, including Dr. John K. Lundy, head of the Division of Forensic Studies at the Oregon Health Sciences University. Dr. Lundy also concluded that most of the chips were of human origin; some could be identified according to which part of the skeleton they had come from; and a few looked as if they might have come from a male. Dr. Lundy could not tell whether the bones were those of Sergeant Fuller.

A couple in Georgia was given two dozen badly charred bones identified as their son, an Air Force captain. Dr. Charney reviewed the case file and concluded there was no way to tell even if the bones belonged to a single individual. The family, which has shunned publicity, decided to accept the remains rather than turn their son's body into "a battlefield for the experts."

Anne Hart, who had already been successful using civilian courts against the Pentagon, filed suit challenging the CILHI identification process. A District Court judge in San Francisco dismissed the suit, claiming he had no jurisdiction; but Anne's new initiative brought attention, and with it, more stories.

MIA wife Kathryn Fanning contacted Dr. Charney because she was suspicious that the handful of bones she had already buried might not be those of her husband, Marine Major Hugh Fanning. Kathryn had been given the remains in 1984 and was told they had been identified through skull and dental analysis. Kathryn accepted that explanation until 1985, when she learned that her casualty assistance officer had hidden Hugh's forensic report in his own home.

Kathryn realized something must be seriously wrong; but, like Anne Hart, she knew not to make direct demands on the Marine Corps. Circumventing the military defenses, she pleaded her case before the casualty officer's wife. The wife relinquished the forensic report.

It was immediately clear why the casualty officer had hidden the report. It showed that, contrary to what Kathryn had been told, neither teeth nor skull had been used to identify Major Fanning.

Kathryn obtained a court order of her own, allowing her to exhume Hugh Fanning's grave. The coffin was pried open to great suspense. Once open, it proved Kathryn's fears well founded. The coffin did not contain a skull or teeth—only fragments of bone.

Dr. Charney and another expert, Dr. Clyde Snow of the University of Oklahoma, analyzed the remains and found that while they were human, they yielded no other information, including the race or age of the victim.

"It was another case of out-and-out fraud," said Dr. Charney. "The Army flat-out lied."

Word spread among the families. Soon, Dr. Charney was being called upon to examine other cases processed by the CILHI. "In most of the remains I looked at, identification was not possible," Dr. Charney told me.

The families learned from one another that problems with the CILHI went back for more than a decade.

One of the earliest was the case of Navy Corpsman Mark V. Dennis, who disappeared on July 15, 1966. The Navy told the Dennis family that Mark had died on that date in a helicopter crash. Mark's remains were returned and buried. Four years later, family members read a *Newsweek* magazine story about American POWs in Southeast Asia. The family was certain that Mark was in one of the pictures.

Mark's brother, Jerry, exhumed the remains. Anthropologists were unable to say who was in the coffin, but it certainly wasn't Mark. The body was seven inches shorter than the six-foot Mark Dennis. In addition, the coffin contained a phony dog tag that identified its wearer as belonging to the Church of Christ. Mark's tag had said "Protestant." Chemical tests showed that whereas both the body and the dog tag had been burned, they were done so at different times and at vastly different temperatures.

The Dennis family asked the Navy to rescind the identification. The service refused, and the family enlisted the help of its congressman, Bill McCollum, Jr. The Navy told McCollum the Dennis case was one in which "reasonable men may be expected to disagree": it was all a matter of deciding how much weight to give certain evidence and how to interpret it.

The Navy apparently had decided to ignore the physical evidence of the short skeleton and the phony dog tag and instead had gone with the CILHI's conclusions based on circumstantial evidence. The official identification remained intact.

The Dennis family's ordeal was typical of that undergone by others. The shoddy work at CILHI was invariably backed by the services, which in turn shielded the CILHI from even the most legitimate and compelling protests. In 1985 Anne Hart found herself living a version of the Dennis case.

Armed with statements from Dr. Charney that the Air Force's "Thomas T. Hart" was not her husband, Anne refused to accept the remains. The service tried to force her hand. A female assistant secretary of the Air Force wrote Anne a letter that began soothingly, assuring Anne that the identification of Tom "was thorough, painstaking and accurate." The letter closed with a threat: if Anne did not accept the remains by November 13, 1985, the Air Force would bury "Tom" with full military honors at Arlington National Cemetery.

Anne sued, charging the service with the misidentification of her husband. This time the suit was not dismissed. Finally, even the Pentagon realized there was a problem. The Army commissioned an independent review of the CILHI.

Three forensic specialists were called on to conduct an on-site inspection. The chairman was Ellis R. Kerley of the University of Maryland, a member of the team that had identified the remains of Nazi war criminal Josef Mengele. The other two investigators were Lowell Levine, a forensic odontologist who had also been on the Mengele team, and William R. Maples, curator of physical anthropology at the Florida State Museum at the University of Florida.

The experts spent three days inspecting the laboratory and the case reports on thirty sets of remains, including those of the Pakse victims. In February 1986 the team released the results of its investigation.

In the case of the Pakse remains, the team wrote that it had found no mistakes; but it also said that there was no scientific basis for eleven of the thirteen identifications. In other cases examined, the team could neither prove nor disprove the CILHI's conclusions.

Later, Dr. Maples said that the team had been generous in its findings. "We didn't have any bones available, just the paperwork, and in some cases only Xerox copies of the X rays. We said 'We found no mistakes.' We can't look at a rather poor presentation of material and disprove it. We gave them a certain benefit of the doubt."

How, then, could the CILHI have made such insupportable identifications? "The conclusions were based on presumptive evidence," Dr. Maples told me. "But they were not labeled as such. They were described as being made on scientific evidence."

The team report said the laboratory had made identifications based on prior knowledge of the occupants of an airplane, rather than on evidence contained in the bones.

As for the laboratory itself, the team evaluated the facilities as being somewhere between inadequate and barely adequate. One of the inspectors later told me privately, "It would be an insult to have to work under those conditions."

The team report made the lab sound more like a hastily constructed field facility than the world-class processing center touted by the Army. The laboratory lacked the most basic amenity, hot water, which meant, among other things, that the staff could not process its own X-ray film. The X-ray equipment itself was in poor condition, hard to use, and offered little shielding to protect the technicians against the effects of radiation. The lab also had no mobile body tables, forcing the staff to move remains from place to place on antiquated canvas stretchers. During the mid-1980s, bone fragments from twenty-five different sets of remains were shattered when they bounced off the canvas stretchers.

The investigating team's report concluded with the stinging recommendation that because so many questions had been raised regarding the work at the CILHI, the lab should reopen all recently processed cases.

Despite the condemnatory tone of the report, however, it also contained a seemingly discordant endorsement that the operation of the laboratory was "above reproach."

An explanation may be found in the relationship between the team chairman, Dr. Kerley, and the CILHI's then–chief anthropologist, Tadao Furue. The two had been close friends since they had met in 1954. Furue had been best man at Kerley's wedding, and at the time of the CILHI review, Kerley was a sponsor for Furue's pending membership in the Physical Anthropology Section of the American Academy of Forensic Sciences (AAFS).

But while Furue may have been a good friend and even a pleasant boss, he was not qualified to run the CILHI. A native of Japan, Furue had first gone to work for the U.S. Army in 1951, as an assistant to doctorate-level anthropologists identifying Korean War dead. Over the years, Furue had continued to work for the Army as a civilian contractor. In 1977 he had been hired full time as the chief scientist at CILHI.

While at the CILHI, Furue had developed what he called his "morphological approximation technique" of identification. This special method, he said, allowed him to draw scientific conclusions about an entire skeleton, even if only portions of bone were available. The precise workings of the technique remain a mystery. Furue never submitted the method for peer review in a professional journal, a standard practice among anthropologists and other scientists. According to Furue, the Army would not allow him to publish his methods, which he said involved classified work; but the Army claims it never stopped Furue from publishing and would in fact have encouraged him to do so.

Furue was widely assumed to have a Ph.D. in anthropology. He was frequently identified in person and in print as "Dr. Furue." When he sought to join the American Academy of Forensic Scientists, however, his résumé raised eyebrows among members of the admissions board. Furue had inflated his high school diploma and bachelor's degree into bachelor's and master's degrees.

Furue's application was still under review during the academy's 1986 annual convention. Dr. Charney, who by now was engaged in a personal crusade against the CILHI, took some of the Pakse bones to the gathering. He asked his colleagues to evaluate Furue's work on a set of twenty-seven bone chips that had been identified as belonging to James Fuller.

The scientists who looked at the Fuller remains reacted with a mixture of scorn and horror. They termed Furue's work both sloppy and ridiculous. One of the anthropologists, Dr. George Gill of the University of Wyoming, said that if one of his own undergraduate students had invented Furue's morphological approximation technique, Dr. Gill would have given him a failing grade.

Confronted with the weight of opinion marshaled against him by Dr. Charney, Furue withdrew his application to join the AAFS. The Army, meanwhile, retained Furue as head of the CILHI and issued a series of statements endorsing his professional qualifications. Despite what Dr. Kerley's team had recommended, the Army did not reopen any of the CILHI cases.

Privately, some of the team members agreed to examine the records on Thomas Hart. Dr. Kerley's conclusion was unequivocal: "These remains cannot be identified." So was Dr. Maples's: "The identification of Lt. Col. Hart is not positive. It is not even probable."

Other families continued to call on Dr. Charney to examine Furue's work. In 1986 alone, Dr. Charney reviewed twenty sets of remains processed by Furue. Charney was able to confirm the identities in only two cases; the other eighteen, he charged, had been deliberately falsified.

The Army then launched its own very quiet criminal probe into wrongdoing at the lab. Agents from the Criminal Investigation Division (CID) found three expert witnesses eager to cooperate.

Drs. Peter Miller, John Lundy, and Samuel Strong Dunlap, all civilian anthropologists employed by the CILHI, felt themselves ethically compromised by their work there. They knew that the "morphological approximation" technique, which was still being used, had no scientific validity. This and other unscientific practices had caused them to conclude that the entire lab had no credibility.

Dr. Dunlap wrote to Anne Hart, telling her she had been right to doubt the identification of her husband: "The inescapable conclusion is that there is a very high probability that these identifications [on Tom and others] were fraudulent."

Aided by the anthropologists, the Army CID began to build a case against Furue and others at the lab. The investigation gathered momentum until Army Secretary John Marsh inexplicably ordered the investigation stopped. On July 8, 1986, the CID special agent in charge told Dr. Dunlap there would be no further inquiry at the CILHI. As an aside, the agent said it was the first time in his seven years at the CID that he had seen an investigation stopped.

Dr. Dunlap pleaded with Marsh to reconsider. In a letter of which he also mailed copies to President Ronald Reagan, Defense Secretary Caspar Weinberger, Congressman Les Aspin, and others on Capitol Hill, Dunlap wrote that he hoped the stopping of the investigation would alert Congress to conduct its own inquiry into the CILHI.

Dunlap got his wish. Under pressure from the families and their anthropologist advocates, notably Dr. Charney, Congress conducted hearings on the lab. Not surprisingly, the lawmakers found the facility wanting in a number of areas. The Army agreed to implement several recommendations, one of which was a direct challenge to Furue: the lab would have to begin using scientifically accepted methods and not the mysterious, ill-defined "morphological approximation technique."

Furue was allowed to stay on, but he resigned in 1988, citing poor health. He died shortly thereafter.

The Army reorganized the CILHI, bringing in three Ph.D.-level anthropologists and two who were in the process of completing their doctorates. The service also added two odontologists and an archaeologist and placed the lab under the direction of a chief anthropologist who was an Army lieutenant colonel.

"It was intended to put some science where there had just been hocus-pocus," a lab employee told me. "I think the Army looked on this as 'sunrise for the CIL.' "

Indeed, a 1991 examination by the General Accounting Office found that despite a few organizational glitches, the lab had successfully instituted the required reforms. Facilities and equipment had been upgraded. In-house checks had been introduced to minimize the margin for error. A world-renowned, board-certified forensic anthropologist was now the scientific director. And, most important, the morphological approximation technique had

been dropped in favor of scientifically recognized methods. All
seemed well.

Then, in 1991, the front pages of newspapers all across the
country carried what has since been nicknamed by the DIA the
"Three Amigos" picture. The photo purported to show three
MIAs alive and in captivity, holding a sign that bore a coded
message. The picture has since been proved a hoax, but its release
prompted one of the men's wives to tell a story that once again
raised the specter of an incompetent CILHI.

When the photo was first published, the Vietnamese government protested that it had returned the remains of one of the men,
Air Force Colonel John Robertson, a year previously. Robertson's
wife, Barbara, confirmed that the Air Force had contacted her in
March 1990 to say that it had her husband's remains. The Air
Force Mortuary Service wanted to know how it should dispose of
them.

"I told them to do nothing until Dr. Charney had looked at
the remains and made a determination," Barbara said.

The mention of Dr. Charney's name was enough to prompt
the Air Force to commission its own review of the Robertson case.
It turned out that the remains were not even human. Barbara was
summoned to Washington, D.C., where a casualty assistance officer had the unhappy task of revealing that John Robertson's
"bones" were in reality a piece of rock, part of an airplane, and
a portion of bone that had come from either a cow or a horse.

Both the Senate and the GAO feel that the main complaint
about the CILHI today is that identifications are made with such
care that they are slow in coming, leaving a backlog of nearly a
thousand cases. But the situation that precipitated the Pakse crisis
still exists. The remains connected with these cases at CILHI reveal
little scientific information. Most of the sets comprising so-called
skeletons are woefully incomplete; only a minute portion, about
1 percent, of the skeletons represent more than three quarters of

an individual. Most of the remains stored at CILHI are tiny bone fragments less than two centimeters in diameter.

But the greatest problem at CILHI is the legacy of mistrust affecting people such as Anne Hart, Barbara Robertson, and the Fullers. The Robertson case, in particular, casts doubt on the entire CILHI reform program, leaving no room for errors that might otherwise have been forgiven.

The documented bungling of CILHI has not only disrupted MIA families' lives but has also helped seal the case against the U.S. government for its woeful mishandling of the MIA issue. The combined government failings have in turn paved the way for con artists and charlatans to exploit the tragedy of men who are missing in action.

PART TWO

The True Conspiracy

How the POW myth has been actively encouraged by unscrupulous profiteers

8

Enter
the Hero

As soon as the Communists captured their first American prisoners in Vietnam, the United States began launching rescue raids. The character and frequency of the missions are the stuff of many a barroom boast. One former Army colonel, military writer Fred Caristo, has said that he personally took part in more than two hundred failed official missions. Caristo's claim, while dubious, is but part of the lore created by men who say they organized, participated in, or analyzed what would amount to a constant flow of rescue missions.

The true number of military raids conducted throughout the war is something of a mystery, partly because many were informal or poorly documented. What is known for certain is that the success rate was depressingly low. In forty-five rescue attempts conducted by the Special Forces from 1966 to 1970, for example, only one man was actually recovered, and he died soon afterward. Between 1964 and 1973, only thirty-seven Americans escaped or were rescued from prisons in Vietnam and Laos.

A Navy SEAL team stormed a Mekong Delta camp and freed some South Vietnamese prisoners in November 1970, but that success was overshadowed by a failed raid the same month on the Son Tay camp in North Vietnam.

In that famed episode, Colonel Arthur "Bull" Simons led a handpicked Special Forces team on a mission to retrieve upwards of a hundred prisoners. The rescuers hit the ground running, killing twenty-five guards before realizing the compound held no captives. The POWs had been moved out only days earlier.

It was a risk that had been calculated into the mission. Rescue raids involved innumerable pitfalls, not the least of which was faulty intelligence. But the U.S. military was willing to take a chance. So, too, were a handful of private citizens.

Beginning around 1970, a number of latter-day knights errant set out to accomplish what the U.S. military, with its considerable resources, could not.

In September 1970 a convicted car thief and Army deserter, Bobby Joe Keesee, hired two Thai pilots to fly him over northeastern Thailand. Keesee pretended to be scouting a movie site but was really planning to rescue POWs. Once airborne, Keesee hijacked the single-engine plane, forcing the pilots to land in North Vietnam. Keesee's ill-conceived plan was foiled when he himself was taken prisoner. He was brutally tortured by his captors, who refused to believe he was not an American spy. Keesee was released in March 1973.

Also in September 1970, a Dutch journalist, Johannes Duynesveld, set out to retrieve two photographers captured the previous spring. Duynesveld was looking for Dana Stone and Sean Flynn, the son of actor Errol Flynn. The two photographers had been taken prisoner while riding motorcycles into a hostile section of Cambodia. Duynesveld went after them on a bicycle. He was captured after three days and killed a few months later.

The only successful private effort was a 1970 mission on behalf of CBS News. In that operation, CBS hired indigenous mercenaries to recover the remains of four employees killed in an ambush in Cambodia. The network said nothing publicly of the mission. The entire episode was kept secret for eleven years, until the details were revealed in a 1981 court case.

After the war, POW rescue missions lost their urgency and faded from public consciousness. But in 1979 the concept resurfaced in a spectacular fashion, when the Son Tay raid's Colonel Simons was credited for rescuing two of Ross Perot's employees being held captive in Iran. The rescue made instant heroes of Perot and Colonel Simons. Perot and the colonel, who has since died, are still recognized for their part in the mission; but contrary to popular myth, neither Perot nor Colonel Simons had a hand in freeing the imprisoned employees.

The truth was uncovered when *Reader's Digest* assigned one of its writers, Nathan Adams, to write a book about the adventure. Adams was given free rein at Perot's Dallas office. Perot was apparently unprepared for the meticulous research that goes into *Reader's Digest* projects. From his place inside the Perot sanctum, Adams uncovered the unsettling truth: Colonel Simons had indeed planned to rescue Perot's employees. But in a replay of the Son Tay scenario, the colonel's plans had been circumvented. Before Simons had had a chance to carry out his mission, a rampaging mob had stormed the jail and released all the prisoners, including the American civilians. Once free, the Americans simply walked to the hotel where they knew their would-be saviors were staying.

"I have the utmost respect for Ross Perot," Adams told me. "His group had planned a prison assault, but it just didn't happen."

Reader's Digest said nothing publicly but quietly dropped the book. Novelist Ken Follett later wrote about the Iran rescue mission in his best-selling *On Wings of Eagles*. Long before the book appeared, however, the rescue was much admired by the activist community. Among those who knew of it was retired Army Lieutenant Colonel James "Bo" Gritz.

Gritz has most recently been in the news for his short-lived 1992 presidential bid, as well as for his role in persuading white separatist Randy Weaver to surrender after a shootout with federal marshals in Idaho.

At best, Gritz is an inveterate publicity hound who thrives on excitement and theatrics. He is also a genuine war hero who seems determined to be a legend. On his résumé, he portrays himself as the quintessential secret operative who has barely had time between missions to take the knife blade from between his teeth. He boasts that he was the inspiration for the main characters in the films *Rambo, Uncommon Valor,* and *Mission MIA.* He says he is a certified hypnotherapist and is fluent in Swahili and Mandarin. He has five objectives: to restore constitutional sovereignty; resist global rule; return the POWs; win the war on drugs; and revive integrity and accountability within government (in that order).

But if Gritz at first comes across as an amusing egotist, he is also a charismatic leader gone wrong, a man who has toyed with human lives while in pursuit of his goals. In the process, he has earned a dubious distinction, a place of note among the charlatans whose claims have so distorted the MIA issue; for it is Bo Gritz, American hero, who is directly responsible for constructing much of the framework that supports the POW hoax today.

MIAs have long been a part of Gritz's life. His father, a pilot for the Army Air Corps, disappeared while flying a mission in World War II. Gritz's mother was also absent from home, working as a wartime ferry pilot. Young Bo was raised by his grandparents, who encouraged his military fantasies. His grandmother sent him on nightly make-believe missions with his father and read to him daily about the exploits of fictional air commandos. Little Bo took on a soldier's mantle; old family photographs show him in military uniform from the time he was a toddler.

At age fourteen, Bo used the proceeds from his father's $10,000 life insurance policy to attend military school in Virginia.

There his fantasies came true. He did well at Fork Union Military Academy, rising to cadet corps commander in his senior year.

Gritz's graduation picture shows a heartbreakingly handsome teenager who could have gone straight from school to a career in Hollywood. Instead he chose the Army, where he found his niche in the newly formed Special Forces.

Gritz was smart, daring, and inspiring. His exploits were rewarded with an enviable array of decorations. He became a celebrity among his peers. But even then, his reputation was controversial.

In 1966 Gritz led a raid into Cambodia in search of the black box from a downed U-2 spy plane. The raid was carried out at the request of President Johnson, who was afraid the Soviets might acquire the secret codes contained in the black box. As Gritz tells it, he arrived at the crash site and found that the box was gone. He followed sandal tracks to a nearby NVA camp, then led a guerrilla assault and recovered the black box.

Other Green Berets say there was no firefight—that Gritz found the black box at the crash site and returned it without incident. For his efforts he was awarded a Bronze Star for meritorious service, without the Valor device.

The military community is divided on the topic of Gritz. Former General William C. Westmoreland portrayed Gritz as a hero in his 1976 memoir, *A Soldier Reports.* Others insist Gritz does not have the war record he claims and that he has not been awarded all the medals he displays on his uniform.

Gritz's twenty-two-year career ended in 1978 under mysterious circumstances. According to Gritz, the late General Harold Aaron, while deputy director of the DIA, asked Gritz to retire and lead private rescue missions into Indochina. After General Aaron died, Gritz circulated a letter from the general implying Gritz was associated with the DIA; the FBI determined the letter was a forgery.

Pentagon sources tell me the real reason Gritz retired was that he was pressured into leaving by superiors who felt he had "done a Colonel Kurtz," meaning he was uncontrollable, like the character in the Joseph Conrad novel *Heart of Darkness*.

Whatever the reasons for Gritz's retirement, it came soon after the supposed rescue in Iran. Gritz lost little time in contacting Perot and asked the Texas businessman to fund a private POW rescue mission run by Gritz and Colonel Simons.

The request was not as audacious as it may sound. Perot had been funding secret private rescue attempts since 1975. He would eventually finance about twenty failed raids and would become one of the more persistent MIA activists. He phoned the Nixon White House so frequently with news of POWs that the administration thought he was obsessed; an aide finally told him to "Goddamn stop calling." Later, Perot would pledge $2.5 million to the Reagan Library and renege on $2 million in retaliation for Reagan's supposed lack of interest in POWs. But even Perot made some sensible decisions in the course of his obsession. After meeting with Gritz, who flew to Dallas on money supplied by Perot, the billionaire declined to fund the project.

Gritz left Texas empty-handed but arrived home with a strange boast. Gritz said that Perot had given him an assignment from DIA Director General Tighe to rescue POWs. Gritz described the assignment as a "quasi go-ahead" from the U.S. government.

A small portion of the story was true. Gritz had recently acquired a "quasi go-ahead," but not from General Tighe. The assignment had come from one of Gritz's old Special Forces buddies, who was now working for the Army's secretive Intelligence Support Activity.

In the early 1980s, the ISA was what was left of the Foreign Operating Group, formed in 1979 to plan the rescue of American hostages held at the U.S. embassy in Tehran. The ISA had conducted several successful missions the world over. By 1981 the unit had run afoul of Pentagon bureaucrats, who viewed it as a rogue operation that deemed itself accountable to no one. In 1982 Deputy Secretary of Defense Frank Carlucci ordered the ISA disbanded. The organization was salvaged when it was reorganized into a more controlled—and controllable—entity. But at the time Gritz was in the market for a mission, the ISA still enjoyed considerable autonomy. One of its members, code-named Shipman, was Gritz's old buddy from the Special Forces. It was Shipman, acting on his own, who provided the ''quasi go-ahead'' that would prompt Gritz to organize his first POW rescue mission, Operation Velvet Hammer.

The underpinnings of Velvet Hammer were formed in late 1980, when Loh Tharaphant, an ethnic Vietnamese living in Thailand, approached American agents about POWs being held in Laos. Tharaphant's tale was persuasive enough to prompt a spy plane reconnaissance flight. The resulting picture of ''Fort Apache'' was intriguing but inconclusive. It showed a large facility with walls, fences, and two guard towers. It had standing figures whose shadows seemed to indicate they were taller than Asians and sitting figures who did not squat like Asians. In addition, the picture had what appeared to be the symbols ''B'' and ''52'' stamped out in the grass. A copy of the picture was given to the ISA.

In February 1981 the United States dispatched a covert team to reconnoiter the site. No Americans were used on the mission, just Thai and mainly Laotian operatives. Tharaphant briefed the team, explaining how to reach Fort Apache and where to spot the Americans.

But after a lengthy, risky stakeout, the team found no evidence of POWs. The camp looked as if it had been deserted for some time. The DIA suspected a setup and asked Tharaphant to take a polygraph test. He failed several tests, and the DIA dismissed him.

There still remained the question of Fort Apache. The DIA believed it was most likely a former reeducation camp, temporarily invaded by Tharaphant while he was staging the photograph. As for the so-called B-52 figures, expert analysts decided they were not deliberate but were naturally occurring shadows.

Nonetheless, the ISA's Shipman believed the photo showed a POW camp. He called his friend Bo Gritz and surreptitiously gave him the classified Fort Apache picture. Gritz wanted to organize a private rescue raid. Shipman said he could arrange funding from ISA.

News of Gritz's impending mission eventually reached the DIA's Admiral Allen Paulson, who was assistant vice director for collection management. Paulson was no fan of Gritz, thinking him an unstable glory seeker. Paulson would later tell Congress that the best thing Gritz could do for the POW issue would be to find another activity. When Paulson learned that the ISA had actually given money to Gritz, he was furious. He declared that Gritz was not to receive any government cooperation. He also asked that Gritz return the Fort Apache picture. Gritz refused. The "quasi go-ahead" was now officially countermanded, but Gritz was determined to carry on.

Gritz got out his old Special Forces directory and called on former comrades to join in a POW rescue. Gritz offered each man $7,000 to participate in Operation Velvet Hammer. The respondents thought they were part of a secret government project.

Gritz assembled his team at a cheerleading camp in Leesburg, Florida. In addition to the combat veterans, Gritz also recruited some unconventional rescuers, including a psychic and a hypnotherapist; but the strangest participant by far was Ann Mills Griffiths of the National League of Families. Griffiths has since dissociated herself from Gritz, but at the time the two were close allies. Lofty rhetoric notwithstanding, Velvet Hammer got off to a ludicrous start. Gritz invited two reporters to witness the training for the clandestine mission. He admitted the journalists only after threatening to kill them if they compromised the mission by reporting the story too early.

Inside the cheerleading camp, Gritz told his team they would raid the Fort Apache compound in Laos. He explained that he had a reconnaissance photo of the camp but refused to show the picture to anyone. A description of the prison was instead provided by the psychic, Karen Page, who saw the camp layout in a vision. Page said she intuited that the compound contained a building in an area surrounded by barbed wire. She said the building sat atop an underground tunnel that held a row of cells. Each cell door had a dog tag attached to it, identifying the POW inside. She was not able to read the names on the dog tags. Page said the prisoners spent their days digging up bamboo shoots near the edge of the jungle.

The team members could not believe their own senses. The Son Tay raid had been rehearsed meticulously, using exact replicas of the prison compound. Now Gritz was planning an attack based on psychic visions and a single aerial photo only he had seen.

Oblivious to the doubts that were already afflicting the team, Gritz told his men they would set up a base at the Nana Hotel in Bangkok. There would be a forward operating station at Nakhon Phanom. The men would use state-of-the-art equipment, including covertly obtained experimental devices, to swoop down on Fort Apache. Central to the mission was an item that had not yet been tested in combat, an inflatable rubber aircraft.

The team members grew even more dubious as they pictured themselves hiding in the jungle under cover of darkness, fervently pumping air into the untested plane.

The rest of the mission sounded as if it might have been

cooked up by little Bo as he sat on his grandmother's knee. Once the POWs were in hand, the team would send word via its series of relay stations to the base commander at the Nana Hotel. The Nana commander would notify Griffiths, who was on standby in Washington. Griffiths was then supposed to call her contacts at the DIA, who would tell the president to order the Seventh Fleet to dispatch helicopters to rescue the entire group of raiders and prisoners. To preserve secrecy, none of the agencies involved would know anything of the rescue until Griffiths made her call to Washington.

Training for Velvet Hammer consisted of morning and evening exercise sessions, plus group hypnosis and church services. Gritz was the preacher, telling the assembled he had been ordained by God to rescue POWs. The team members were his disciples. In one session, Gritz told his men they would all be issued cyanide capsules, which would be wired to their teeth. If they were captured or tortured, Gritz explained, they could simply bite down on the capsules. Gritz tried to energize his men with talk of their forthcoming victory parade up Fifth Avenue in New York. He rhapsodized about having a book, and then a movie, detailing the success of Operation Velvet Hammer. He was so enthralled with the idea of having his own *Wings of Eagles* glory, he allowed two more journalists to enter the camp. Again under threat of death, the reporters were told they could not write their stories before the mission took place.

Fortunately for the Velvet Hammer team, the journalists decided to risk their lives and break the embargo. Otherwise, Gritz might have found a way to get his people to Laos, where they surely would have run afoul of someone.

The mission fell apart in stages, commencing in March 1981. Gritz had confided to reporters that the operation was being funded with $300,000 from Federal Express. That corporation first learned of its own involvement when reporters called to confirm the contribution. Two team members sent to collect the money quit the mission when confronted by the wrath of an angry corporate executive.

Fearing the mission had been compromised, Gritz announced that he was moving the encampment to a nearby hunting lodge. Once there, Gritz grew even more spiritual, holding services that required the men to join hands and sing hymns. Five more members quit.

MIA father George Brooks, the chairman of the National League of Families, visited the new camp. His son, Nicholas, had been shot down over Laos in 1970. When Brooks arrived at the lodge, he learned that none of the team members had been paid. Brooks wrote a check for $20,000, to be used for the families of team members who had quit their jobs to participate.

Three days after Brooks's arrival, *The Orlando Sentinel Star* ran a front-page story on Operation Velvet Hammer. Gritz canceled the mission.

Most of the remaining team members were stranded in Florida, with no funds to get them home. George Brooks once again pulled out his checkbook, providing plane tickets for about twenty men.

Twelve years after the fact, Brooks was still angry about Operation Velvet Hammer. He told the Kerry Committee that an "extremely convincing" Gritz had "hoodwinked" him into believing that Gritz knew where prisoners were being held in Laos and that Gritz could get them out. Brooks said he wasn't specifically upset about spending $30,000 on Gritz, because that was only a tenth of what he had spent in the search for his son. "But," Brooks said, "I do believe that this committee has a responsibility to investigate and, where necessary, prosecute these incredible liars."

At the time, though, no one thought to prosecute Gritz. He quickly recouped his losses and went on to develop another rescue

mission. Its official title was Operation Grand Eagle. Gritz also
gave it a secret code name, BOHICA (Bend Over, Here It Comes
Again). It was a curious choice for a name, although perhaps it
applied to the handful of Velvet Hammer veterans who signed up
to participate.

This time Gritz claimed backing by the CIA. Former Laotian
general Vang Pao and Congressman Robert Dornan of California
both thought the mission was legitimate and pledged initial support. Dornan realized he had been fooled when, at Gritz's request,
he asked CIA Deputy Director Bobby Ray Inman why the funds
had not yet arrived. In a replay of the scene at Federal Express,
Inman replied that this was the first he had heard of his agency
supporting a civilian POW rescue mission.

Operation Grand Eagle ended on the spot. It would later
resurface in legend when one of its participants, Scott Barnes,
would write *BOHICA,* a book describing how he had been ordered
to kill American POWs.

Gritz threw himself into forming another mission, Operation
Lazarus. This time he intended to collect his own funds and call
in the government once the POWs were in hand.

Gritz bought a charter from the United Vietnam Veterans
Organization and used his new affiliation to solicit tax-exempt
donations. Gritz named his group the ''POW/MIA Never Forget
Chapter.''

Gritz then found a new group of sources, some of them
chosen specifically for their enmity to the CIA, which Gritz said
he no longer trusted. One such associate was General Phoumi
Nosavon, the former deputy premier of Laos. Phoumi was well
known for his shady maneuverings, but he claimed to have a large
army at his disposal, and Gritz seemed to think Phoumi would rent
him the troops.

Gritz recruited two other disreputable helpers, Loh Tharaphant of the Fort Apache episode and professional POW hunter

Jack Bailey. Others on the roster included holdovers from previous Gritz missions, plus two young MIA daughters, Lynn Standerwick and Janet Townley. The women were to be used as United States–based communications links.

Gritz intended to circumvent the DIA, the CIA, and any other agency that might try to foil his operation. He would tell only the president of the United States about the new mission. But Gritz did not know President Reagan, so he looked for a middleman to approach him. Gritz found his perfect contact in actor Clint Eastwood. Gritz showed Eastwood the forged letter from General Aaron and outlined the plan to raid Fort Apache. Eastwood signed on; he gave Gritz $30,000 and agreed to talk to Reagan. Eastwood's assignment was to convince Reagan to send in rescue helicopters from the Seventh Fleet. Gritz then wangled a meeting with actor William Shatner, who bought the book and movie rights for $10,000.

Litton Industries also gave $50,000 for Gritz to spend on Litton equipment, such as night vision goggles and field radios. Gritz purchased the equipment, including fourteen of Litton's highly sophisticated communications devices, worth more than $1 million. The so-called IDT boxes, about the size of a hardcover book, emitted coded transmissions to other IDT boxes. They were designed for use in nuclear war, but Gritz thought they would come in handy for his POW raid.

Gritz packed up his goods—the IDT boxes, the night vision goggles, a polygraph, and more—and led his group to Thailand.

Through a series of mishaps, Gritz wound up grossly unprepared for a cross-border foray. Phoumi Nosavon and his son, Phoumano, swindled Gritz out of $6,000, and Nosavon reneged on the offer to rent Gritz his army. Jack Bailey, who was paid $5,000 for the use of his boat, never got the boat into working order. Eastwood did not tell Reagan to send in the rescue helicopters. A contact who was supposed to supply guns apparently lost the key to the locker that held the weapons. And, finally, the $27,000 payroll for the men of Operation Lazarus mysteriously disappeared.

The payroll problem had serious repercussions for the men's families. One family was evicted for nonpayment of rent, and other similar tales began coming in from the United States. The Lazarus men grew restless.

When it seemed as if this mission, too, might end before it started, Gritz decided that his team would set out anyway. Despite objections from his followers, Gritz insisted they embark on a sixty-five-mile trek through dense jungle, armed with only three weapons for nineteen men. They were to meet with a hastily hired band of Laotian mercenaries and proceed from the rendezvous point to the still-unnamed rescue site.

Two days into the trip, Gritz's team was ambushed. One of the Americans, Dominic Zappone, was captured. The men of Operation Lazarus wanted to get him back, but Gritz—who finally had a genuine prisoner to rescue—ordered a retreat. The men took off at a dead run for Thailand. They encountered even more trouble. One man impaled his foot on a tree branch. Others were swept away and nearly drowned while trying to swim the Mekong River.

Back in Thailand, Gritz and his men holed up at a house owned by Tharaphant. There they learned that Zappone was being held for ransom by troops loyal to Phoumi Nosavon. He would be released in exchange for $17,500.

After another series of unfortunate incidents, Gritz returned to the United States. He told no one of Zappone's capture but instead began raising money for his next mission, Operation Lazarus Omega. But Gritz was out of luck: this time the funds were not forthcoming.

Then Litton Industries came looking for Gritz. There had been some misunderstanding over the IDT boxes, and now Litton

OPERATION HOMECOMING

American prisoners were released from captivity in the spring of 1973, during Operation Homecoming. The men, who were fed, washed, and shaved for the occasion, were overjoyed to leave Vietnam.

The United States was, in turn, delighted to have the men back.

HANOI HILTON

The men who returned from captivity told horrifying stories of torture and deprivation suffered in camps and in prisons such as this, the infamous Hoa Lo Prison, nicknamed the "Hanoi Hilton" by inmates.

Today, POW activists capitalize on the old horror stories, which help sell a wide assortment of POW paraphernalia.

THE DESERTERS

Over the years, many men who were thought to be POWs in Indochina were actually defectors who voluntarily remained with the enemy. Some deserted from the French Foreign Legion in the late 1940s and served with the Communist Combatants Internationaux. These are Viet Minh propaganda photographs.

FIGURE 10. SKETCH OF REPORTED COLLABORATORS "SALT" AND "PEPPER"

During the war, the United States tried in vain to capture reported collaborators "Salt" and "Pepper," whose identities were never learned.

American serviceman McKinley Nolan joined the Khmer Rouge and was known as "the Black Khmer."

The notorious U.S. Marine Private Robert "Bobby" Garwood, who returned to the United States and was convicted of collaboration with the enemy and assault on an American POW.

In this never-before-published photograph, Garwood is shown after his initial capture by Communist troops. Note that he is not wearing his marine uniform. Garwood has claimed his forearm was seriously injured at the point of capture, during a firefight.

The men of the Dublin City Team of the Marines' First Force Reconnaissance thought they had killed Garwood in the course of a firefight with Viet Cong guerrillas. The Marines said Garwood was fighting alongside the Communists.

During trial in the United States, a number of former POWs testified against Garwood. Francis Anton (left) said that the POWs had been ordered to bow to Garwood. David Harker (right) said that Garwood hit him after an incident wherein starving prisoners killed the camp cat.

THE ACTIVISTS

Among the first and most influential
POW activists was retired Army
Lieutenant Colonel James "Bo" Gritz.
In his graduation picture from Fork
Union Military Academy, Gritz looks as
if he could have conquered Hollywood.
Instead, he chose a career with the
Green Berets, and later helped form the
POW movement. The charismatic Gritz
recruited volunteers for a private rescue
mission of prisoners supposedly held at
"Fort Apache" in Laos (below). A secret
reconnaissance team dispatched to the
site by the CIA found the camp
deserted. The satellite photograph used
by Gritz as the basis for his mission
remains classified, but the Pentagon
provided this line drawing.

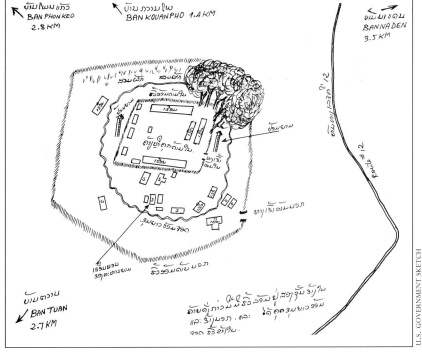

Gritz appeared before Congress to discuss his POW findings, but had nothing tangible to report.

AP/WIDE WORLD PHOTOS

Another early activist was Bobby Joe Keesee, who said he was going to rescue POWs. Instead, he was captured and held prisoner himself. Upon release, he kissed the American flag.

AP/WIDE WORLD PHOTOS

At one point, *Soldier of Fortune* publisher Bob Brown set up a secret camp, code-named Liberty City, and hired Laotian mercenaries to help find American prisoners.

Brown says he has spent a fortune hunting POWs but has found nothing.

Army Colonel Millard "Mike" Peck quit his job as head of the Pentagon's POW/MIA office, promising to reveal evidence of a government coverup on POWs.

Bob Brown and his associates set out with activist Jack Bailey for an ill-fated cruise aboard Bailey's boat, the *Akuna*. The group was looking for pirates and POWs. Although Bailey seemed confident at first, the trip ended in disaster when the *Akuna* broke down at sea and had to be towed back to harbor. The group did not find any pirates and heard nothing of POWs.

Bailey was involved in circulating this photo, supposedly of American MIA Donald Gene Carr. The man in the photo turned out to be German national Gunther Dietrich (below), who assured the Carr family he was not their missing relative.

Former Green Beret Captain Mark Smith said he had evidence of live Americans in captivity. The "evidence" was a tape that was offered for sale by a British entrepreneur who supposedly burned it in anger when his name was revealed in print.

Joe Jordan spent Memorial Day 1994 near the Vietnam Veterans Memorial in Washington, D.C., selling POW paraphernalia at a booth run by fellow activist Ted Sampley. Jordan and Sampley together acquired a set of grisly Vietnamese photographs depicting mutilated American war dead, and displayed them to MIA families.

wanted them back. The company sent one of its ranking executives, former POW Leo Thorsness, to collect the boxes from Gritz. The streetwise Gritz immediately realized that his luck had been restored. He admitted he had lost one of the boxes in Laos but said he would return the remaining thirteen for $50,000. Litton balked. Gritz upped the ante. He placed an ad in the *Los Angeles Times,* offering a "one-day only discreet sale" of the high-tech communications devices. Litton caved in, paying $40,000 for the IDT boxes.

Operation Lazarus Omega was in business. The Thailand team now included the two MIA daughters, Standerwick and Townley. When another team member, Vinnie Arnone, questioned the wisdom of taking two blond females along on a covert mission, Gritz responded that he could not exclude them. According to a report in *Soldier of Fortune* magazine, Gritz told Arnone that the two young women needed "Lawrence of Laos."

Lazarus Omega was yet another comedy of errors. Gritz used part of the operational funds to hire a transvestite prostitute to visit Arnone in his hotel room. He also ordered another mission participant, "Dr. Death," to make poison darts for the rescuers to use. In addition, he forced one of his Laotian operatives to take a polygraph test over the misuse of $700 and staged what may or may not have been a fake attempt on the man's life.

One of the mission's most bizarre episodes was a ceremony held in honor of Loh Tharaphant. On this occasion, Gritz awarded Tharaphant the Legion of Merit. To authenticate the award, Gritz gave Tharaphant a certificate signed by President Richard M. Nixon and General Creighton Abrams. Tharaphant did not seem to notice that his 1983 award had been signed by a president who had left office a decade earlier and a general who had commanded ground forces in Vietnam in 1968.

Zappone, meanwhile, was released from captivity, not because Gritz paid his ransom, but because Zappone found an explosive device, hung it around his neck, and threatened to kill himself and his captors if he were not freed.

All these antics notwithstanding, Gritz was single-minded in his intent to carry out the plans for Lazarus Omega—or so it seemed.

After much fanfare, Lazarus Omega finally got under way when Gritz departed Thailand, allegedly headed for a secret site in Laos. But Thai military authorities have reported that Gritz and his small band of mercenaries actually hid in a series of houses owned by Tharaphant. The day the men supposedly crossed into Laos, they were in reality holed up in a rock quarry owned by Tharaphant.

While the team was in hiding, the *Bangkok Post* ran a front-page story describing Gritz's mission in Laos. Other stories followed in both the *Post* and other Thai newspapers. Based on information contained in the articles, Thai authorities believed that Gritz had smuggled in illegal radio equipment. Thai agents raided one of Tharaphant's "safe houses," where Lynn Standerwick and another mission participant, Lance Trimmer, were staying. The agents found spy-quality radios and arrested the two Americans. Tharaphant posted bond on the promise that the two would turn themselves in a short time later.

Still at the rock quarry, Gritz then wrote a letter announcing that he had uncovered evidence of POWs. In the letter, Gritz confessed he had been working covertly with both the DIA and the despised CIA. Gritz gave the letter to a native courier and told him to deliver it to the Bangkok correspondent for the *Los Angeles Times*. Gritz told the courier to say he had brought the letter all the way from the secret camp in Laos.

On the day when Standerwick and Trimmer were supposed to surrender in Bangkok, Gritz himself showed up. Gritz was allegedly just in from a treacherous journey through Laos; but photographs taken of his surrender depict a freshly scrubbed, pressed, clean-shaven man.

Jim Coyne, who was on assignment for *Soldier of Fortune,* was there when Gritz was booked for illegal possession of high-powered radio equipment. "He was very pale, and his arms weren't scratched," Coyne told me. "He looked like he had been inside a house for a year."

The trial was a showcase for Gritz. He had his old Class A Army uniform, with its dazzling array of ribbons and badges, flown in from the United States. When the Thai police would not permit him to wear it, Gritz arranged for Tharaphant to carry it into court.

Gritz and his crew were found guilty but received suspended sentences on the understanding that they would leave Thailand immediately.

Back in the United States, Gritz became the center of a media whirlwind. He appeared on national television, stirring excitement with his promise to produce pictures of POWs held captive in Laos. Gritz said the pictures were contained on some undeveloped rolls of film.

Suddenly, Gritz was a national hero, the only man alive willing to rescue America's POWs, even though he had abandoned the one man he knew for a fact to be a captive in foreign hands, Dominic Zappone. Nor was it widely known that among his peers, Gritz, the "consummate Green Beret," was viewed as a bumbling fool. He had already been expelled from the Special Operatives Association as a result of his slapstick private forays into Southeast Asia.

While the hoopla was at its most frenzied, Gritz was invited to Washington to present his POW evidence at a hearing before the House Subcommittee on Asian and Pacific Affairs. It was to be Gritz's finest moment.

The first to discredit Gritz was the State Department's Richard Armitage, who testified on the contents of two bags of bones recovered by the Lazarus team. The team had given the bags to the U.S. embassy in Bangkok, saying they contained the remains of American POWs. Laboratory analysis had shown that the bags held animal bones and the remains of two Indochinese.

The worst indictment came from Gritz himself. Under intense questioning by committee members, most notably the chairman, Congressman Steve Solarz, Gritz finally admitted that he had no POW evidence. The photographs had not turned out. He had used the wrong camera setting.

In the end, though, the Lazarus Omega debacle was nothing more than a temporary setback. Gritz continued to make his case to the families, persuading many that he had proof their loved ones were alive. He vowed he would return to Southeast Asia. He would eventually make good on the promise, but not before his failed forays would inspire others who viewed him only as Bo Gritz, American hero.

9

Rescue
Fever

Gritz's escapades should have served as object lessons in the futility of private-sector forays. Instead, they fulfilled a folkloric purpose, underscoring the notion that if the system was corrupt, man himself was still noble. To the activists, this meant that if the U.S. government was willing to abandon POWs, citizen heroes would have to retrieve them on their own, even if they did so in violation of the Neutrality Act.

Gritz inspired even those who thought him a buffoon. Bob Brown, who devoted one entire issue of *Soldier of Fortune* magazine to lambasting Gritz, was spurred to action after a 1981 visit from three angry Gritz alumni. Fred Zabitosky, Earl Bleacher, and James Monaghan enlisted Brown's help in persuading MIA father George Brooks to stop funding Gritz. But the three alumni also gave Brown the idea that he could run a better operation than Gritz had. Brown decided to give it a try. Zabitosky and company joined him; unlike Gritz, Brown was both wealthy and generous, if somewhat eccentric in his spending habits (he once used a platinum American Express card to buy me a muffin and a cup of coffee). Also unlike Gritz, Brown actually paid salaries.

Brown established a secret base in Communist Laos, code-named Liberty City. The base was located west of the Mekong, near the border with Thailand. It was like a miniature colonial outpost, with a comfortable headquarters tent and Western amenities. Brown was a considerate commander. He did not want his men to personally haul in months' worth of necessities or exhaust themselves making supply runs into Thailand, so he arranged for a delivery service, manned by indigenous runners who were unfazed by the thin mountain air.

Brown and his fellow Americans set up shop as intelligence analysts, sifting through reports brought in by paid informants. The searchers fanned out over portions of Vietnam, Burma, and China. They returned with information that ranged from obviously bogus to enticingly plausible. When one agent returned with news of ten to fourteen Americans held within striking distance, it seemed as if Liberty City might actually produce results. The agent said he would arrange a rescue in exchange for $200,000. Brown gave him a down payment of $500, ostensibly to cover expenses. The informant retreated into the jungle and was never heard from again.

Brown did a good job of keeping his operation covert. The Laotian authorities never learned of its existence. But the Thai government was deeply concerned about trouble with Laos and was afraid Vientiane would hold Bangkok responsible for Brown's illegal project. The Thais pressured Brown to close Liberty City, and he complied after five months. He folded the tents in November 1981.

Brown continued his active pursuit of POWs until 1984, spending more than $250,000 in the process. I recently asked him what he had gotten in return for all his money.

"Nothing," he said. "We were out a quarter of a million dollars and came no closer to a POW than when we started out."

But the effort was not a total loss. In the course of searching for POWs, *Soldier of Fortune* writer Jim Coyne met a Hmong tribesman who said he had saved a sample of some mysterious yellow powder that had been dropped over his village from a Soviet MiG-17 aircraft. The tribesman said the powder had killed or sickened many people. He gave some to Coyne, who turned it over to U.S. authorities. The powder turned out to be a component of a deadly poison. It was the first time the United States had evidence that chemical weapons were being used in Laos.

Not all the private missions were as productive. Most continued in the farcical tradition of Bo Gritz. One such group was the Private Delta Force, named for the Army's Delta Force commandos. The PDF was organized in 1985 by a former Army Ranger, Mike Van Atta.

An advertising salesman who doubles as a Eucharistic minister at his parish church in New Jersey, Van Atta takes a distinctly nonpastoral approach to finding POWs. On the pages of his newsletter, *The Insider,* Van Atta appeals to the "Rambo faction" activists, interspersing his exposés with vindictive phraseology and violent imagery. In one edition he excoriated a favorite target, Chuck Trowbridge of the POW/MIA office. After outlining Trowbridge's latest outrage, Van Atta wrote, "Carlos Norman Hathcock II should be invited to remove Trowbridge, if the system fails to remove him."

When I first met Van Atta, I thought he might be just a harmless Walter Mitty who had read too many espionage novels. He spoke as if he himself were a spy, referring often to his "agents" and his "network." I began to suspect him of being paranoid when he developed a literary "legend" for himself. Fearing that the legitimate intelligence community was monitoring his writings, Van Atta created the literary persona of Joyce Cook. Her main purpose was to bombard various intelligence agencies with FOIA requests for government files on Van Atta. Joyce unwittingly gave away her true identity because she used the same post office box Van Atta did, and because she precisely mimicked Van Atta's frequently unintelligible style of writing.*

When Van Atta came up with his plan to form a private rescue team, he showed from the start that he was more likely to compromise any sort of covert operation than to complete one.

Like his predecessor Gritz, Van Atta emphasized that his private mission would be conducted in complete secrecy. Then he went public. Instead of inviting the press to his secret training ground, though, he placed an ad in a veterans' newspaper run by fellow activist Ted Sampley.

"Join Private Delta Force" read the prominent display ad, which included a picture of a rugged, M-16-toting commando. "Any person or group may apply and join the Private Delta Force. Train to infiltrate a target, perform recon at a POW camp, execute a rescue, excavate a crash site and move at night."

In case any potential team member missed the notice, Van Atta also sent a recruiting announcement to readers of *The Insider*.

Van Atta warned what the training would be like. "The physical requirements to navigate this course have been called 'training for a triathlon' and 'mountain aerobics' by those who have already participated."

In other words, this wasn't for weekend warriors. Yet that is precisely who it was designed for. The training would be held in Breezewood, Pennsylvania, every week from 6 P.M. Friday until 3 P.M. Sunday. The registration fee was $50. Anyone who didn't meet the physical requirements could sign on to provide intelligence, logistic support, financial aid, or the all-inclusive "moral support."

Six men were eventually selected for Private Delta Force. The group then needed a mission.

---

*In one letter to the DIA, Van Atta wrote, "The US Hanoi office as reportedly by U.S. officials there was monitored by electronic easdropping [sic] of all conversations and surveillance of all activity was constant."

Van Atta at first thought he would pursue a rumor that a Pathet Lao soldier had recently seen two POW camps along the Vietnam–Laos border. There were supposedly fifty-one men in one camp and thirty-two in another. Van Atta calculated it would take ninety-six men and 105 aircraft to rescue the men in a Son Tay–type raid. He also talked about sending in a parachute team, utilizing HALO (high-altitude, low-opening) drops fifty miles from the prison. At first he was enthusiastic about the mission. After a few sessions with his bank ledger, though, Van Atta decided that a rescue at this particular campsite was best left to the professional military. He focused his attention instead on a report of Americans held in caves in Laos.

This report was more to Van Atta's liking. The POWs were allegedly housed five to a cave, with a Soviet T-96 tank backed into the mouth of each cave. The Private Delta Force had studied the T-96 and discovered an "Achilles armor plate," through which the tank could be disabled.

Van Atta added about twenty more men to his team. The group continued to rehearse on weekends, using live booby traps and pyrotechnics.

By December 1985 the team had raised about $10,000. Van Atta realized he needed more money, but he was proud that his mission was being taken seriously. He boasted to contacts that Senator Jeremiah Denton, a former POW, had talked about Private Delta Force during a closed session on Capitol Hill. Van Atta didn't seem to understand that Denton had mentioned it only because someone was eventually bound to; Van Atta had delivered flyers describing the team to every member of Congress.

Van Atta planned his rescue for some time around Easter 1986. In January, just a few months before the raid was to take place, Van Atta decided he needed an additional seventy men. He took out more ads. In a move reminiscent of Gritz's actions during Velvet Hammer, Van Atta then called me to talk about his upcoming secret mission. He put me in touch with one of his team members, Don Mallen of Pennsylvania. I wrote about the mission in *The Washington Times.*

"We are preparing, in all its ramifications, to exploit the opportunity to rescue some live Americans held in Southeast Asia," Mallen told me. "We have an airlift capability. We have all the physical capabilities. No option is closed to us."

Colonel Chuck Allen, who ran the real Project Delta commandos in Vietnam, laughed when he heard of the impending raid. "I don't think they could rescue a sack of potatoes," he told me. "It's just a plan to put money into someone's pocket."

Even fellow activist and supporter Ted Sampley seemed to scorn the project. "It's not a fantasy thing you can do, like Rambo," he told me. But Sampley, mindful of the need to be politic about another activist, was quick to add that Van Atta was working from good intelligence. "They're not flakes involved in this thing," he said.

After all the hype, the rescue fizzled out a few months later. The team had not raised enough money by the time the rainy season started in Southeast Asia. Van Atta canceled the mission and did not reschedule for the following year. He said nothing more about the prisoners guarded by T-96 tanks.

Meanwhile, Gritz had made good on his promise of returning to Southeast Asia. In January 1985 he launched Operation Brokenwing, so named because it was meant to rescue a POW who had only one leg. Gritz managed to keep this mission relatively low key. He did not announce it to the press ahead of time, nor did he personally engage in any of the usual ill-fated shenanigans. Still, the operation was a fiasco.

As Gritz explains it, he organized the mission after learning about POWs from an exiled Laotian general, Kong Le. According to Gritz, Kong Le "gave" Gritz three POWs in exchange for Gritz having spirited Kong Le out of Laos to his new home in Paris. As

Gritz tells it, Kong Le arranged for the men to be freed by Pathet Lao defectors. This time there would be no need to call in the Seventh Fleet. All Gritz had to do was wait for the POWs at a prearranged point along the Mekong.

Gritz describes Operation Brokenwing as a dizzying sequence of pacts, betrayal, and murder, all culminating in a midnight rendezvous on the banks of the Mekong. On the appointed night, Gritz and his team were all in place when suddenly the POWs began talking on the radio. Gritz picked up his high-powered goggles and confirmed that the prisoners were indeed coming.

There came a last-minute snag. A powerboat appeared out of nowhere and ran down the prisoners' dinghies. Fortunately, the POWs survived, but they were forced to turn back. The rescue was on again the following night, but this time someone sent a rocket attack against Gritz as he crouched in the underbrush. After that, Gritz says, the mission had to be canceled because the media found out he was in Laos.

Another private group slipped into Laos a year later. The original plan, as formulated by Gritz alumnus Vinnie Arnone, was to enter Vietnam via China, sneak into Cam Ranh Bay, capture some high-ranking Soviet officers, and hold them for ransom in exchange for American POWs. Arnone wanted to trade the Soviets for four Americans. Two of the men Arnone planned to retrieve, Donald Long and Charley Moley, were not listed as missing in action. A third, Alfons Bankowski, had been killed in 1961. Only Thomas Daffron, who had disappeared in 1970, was genuinely missing.

The kidnap did not take place. Arnone and his rescue team wound up in Laos around December 10, 1985.

In mid-December, the U.S. station in Bangkok picked up a radio transmission out of Laos, from the Pathet Lao to Vietnamese troops. The Pathet Lao said they were chasing Caucasians. One of the men, probably Arnone, was reported shot and wounded. He

and another captured American were taken to Vientiane and inter-
rogated.

I was the first reporter to learn of the episode, nearly a
month after it happened. Yet when I began making calls to determine what had taken place, virtually every POW activist I talked
to was already familiar with the details. Each put his own particular
spin on the episode. Van Atta said he had been asked to go on the
mission. Tom Burch, of the Vietnam Veterans Coalition, implied
it was an official DIA operation. Earl Hopper, of Task Force
Omega, hinted at being involved when he said he could neither
confirm nor deny anything.

John LeBoutillier of Operation Skyhook was adamant that
Ross Perot had funded the mission. Perot told me he had not been
involved and that he was "absolutely against that type of operation."

The men were released when Laotian officials realized that
the CIA operatives they thought they had captured were nothing
more than a pair of renegade civilians.

Another former Gritz associate also surfaced that year, not to
run a new rescue mission, but to present a unique interpretation
of an old one. He is one of the most curious characters on the MIA
scene, Scott Barnes. Congressman Bob Dornan, the California
Republican, once told me Barnes "was like a phantom who keeps
popping up." That has certainly been true in terms of my own
experience.

Barnes gained national prominence in 1992, when it was
revealed that he had provided the information that caused Ross
Perot to withdraw from the 1992 presidential race.

POW insiders were amazed that Perot had actually listened
when Barnes claimed there were plots afoot to disrupt Perot's
daughter's wedding. Even within the credulous POW movement,
Barnes is widely dismissed as deluded, paranoid, or an outright
liar. *Soldier of Fortune* once ran an article describing him as "My

Favorite Flake.'' Even Bo Gritz, who allowed Barnes to join Operation Grand Eagle, holds Barnes in contempt. In his privately published book *A Nation Betrayed,* Gritz wrote of Barnes: "He was devoid of any special operations talent other than his ability to lie with a straight face.''

Barnes has alternately claimed to have been a fighter pilot, a Special Forces operative, a CIA hit man, a DEA informant, and much else. He did serve a short enlistment in the Army but never left the United States, and he was kicked out of the service when he accused his commanding officer of conspiring to traffic drugs.

Barnes was also a California police officer but was fired from various jobs on charges ranging from brutality to lack of credibility. At one point in his career, Barnes decided to join the staff of Congressman Bob Dornan. Barnes neglected to check with the congressman first.

"I've never met the guy myself,'' Dornan told me. "But he came by my office in D.C. and picked up a business card from a staff member. Then he had copies made up with his name on them. I was very prominent at the time. I was the chairman of the House POW/MIA Task Force. He went around Bangkok with this fake business card, saying he worked for me.''

My own experience with Barnes began in 1986, when he showed up at *The Washington Times* with BBC producer David Taylor. Barnes carried a video that both he and Taylor insisted I watch right then, in their presence. The tape contained explosive information about Operation Grand Eagle, they said; they could not loan it to me, nor would they allow me to copy it.

We proceeded to a private viewing room and set up the VCR. Taylor posed rigidly in his chair, notebook in hand, prepared to take my questions. Barnes would not sit still. He bounced constantly, watching me watching the show.

The tape depicted a groggy, supine Barnes on the receiving end of an intravenous drip administered by an attentive, hovering

Taylor. The IV supposedly contained sodium amytal, a potentially fatal narcotic. Barnes and Taylor said the drug was truth serum, although pharmacologists say the substance is much better suited to enabling deceit: it reduces one's inhibitions, so that even a normally truthful person can lie with impunity.

In his drug-induced state, Barnes recounted being asked by the CIA to look for POWs in Laos. He said he had found the POWs and had then been instructed to "liquidate the merchandise"; when he refused the order, another agent punched him in the stomach. "And it hurt, too," Barnes said.

The tape proceeded with much similar material.

When the tape was over, Barnes elaborated at length. He explained it had been he, not Gritz, who had been the central figure in Operation Grand Eagle, a.k.a. BOHICA. He said the mission had been undertaken by the CIA, in collusion with the ISA. He said I would not be able to confirm this because all relevant government documents had been destroyed. Barnes said that while on the mission, he had seen CIA agents planting yellow rain that would later be attributed to the Soviets. But the big news was that Barnes had seen POWs in Laos in 1981.

"Beyond a shadow of a doubt, they're over there," Barnes said. "I've seen them."

He said BOHICA had actually been a reconnaissance mission to confirm or deny reports of American POWs.

"I confirmed it," Barnes told me. "They were being held in a compound with other prisoners. Two U.S. POWs were visible. The rest were peasants or locals. The rescue was set to go. Then the boys were told to stand down. The mission was aborted."

Barnes said he could not reveal who exactly had given the order to abort. "For some unknown reason, someone super high up ordered it. You'll learn real soon who these people are. You'll find something shocking."

Over the next few weeks, Barnes called me at work and at home to report unnerving developments. The government was after him. His life was in danger. And then the government was after me. They were planning to "get" me for working on the POW story. I had been put on a special list at CIA headquarters. My phones were being tapped.

This latter claim was made during a late night call to my home and was particularly persuasive because as soon as Barnes told me I was being tapped, there emerged from the phone a series of mysterious clicking sounds. Barnes heard them, too, exclaiming, "There! Did you hear that? It's from the switching mechanism they put in your basement!" I later came to believe that Barnes himself produced the clicks on his end of the line.

Barnes called another night, again quite late, to announce that a particular naval officer was plotting to hide on a Washington, D.C., rooftop, and shoot Barnes with a high-powered rifle. Barnes hinted that I might also be on the hit list for knowing too much. A few days later, special agent Don Thompson of the Naval Investigative Service showed up at my office to ask about the assassination threats reported by Barnes. I told him I had not been threatened.

Over the course of about a year, Barnes and Taylor pushed hard for me to write an article presenting Barnes's version of events. One of their chief tools of persuasion, they thought, was Barnes's 1987 book, *BOHICA*. The book's cover touts it as an exposé of "the most heinous cover-up of the Vietnam saga!" The book is far less than it seems; of its roughly 800 pages, about 250 are devoted to a quick sketch of the heinous cover-up. The rest comprise what must be the largest appendix in publishing history. It appears to be a photocopy-style presentation of Barnes's entire scrapbook, including newspaper articles and employment documents. The most intriguing part of the book, from my own point of view, was the section containing Barnes's photocopied address book. This I examined closely, to make sure my own phone number had not been reproduced.

A few years later, while attending Nick Rowe's funeral at Fort Bragg, I saw several copies of the book on prominent display at the Special Forces gift shop. The clerk there told me that the book was not in great demand but that it sold at a slow, albeit regular, pace.

For a period in the late 1980s, Barnes and most of the other self-appointed commandos retreated into silence. As it turned out, the silence was only a lull. Then the private operatives staged a comeback.

Among the first to reappear was Mike Van Atta, who had spent the days since Private Delta Force in relative quiet, churning out his newsletter but otherwise causing little harm. Around 1990 he toned down his rhetoric and joined a relatively moderate group that sought to learn whether POWs were being held in the Soviet Union. He traveled to Moscow and met with officials who promised to think about American MIAs.

The publicity surrounding the Moscow trip revitalized the old Van Atta. The tall tales came back, wilder than before. Suddenly Van Atta, the former enlisted Army Ranger, made a whole new series of revelations about his past. He claimed to have been in charge of intelligence operations inside the Soviet Union and Cambodia. He said he had provided the Pentagon with Soviet agents assigned to look for POWs in the USSR. He boasted of having arranged a prisoner swap that had resulted in two American POWs being transferred to the Soviet Union. He said he had been caught spying in Cambodia and had escaped with the help of the Soviet ambassador and the U.S. mission. His local newspaper in Chatham, New Jersey, published a profile of Van Atta, describing him as having ties to the Defense Intelligence Agency and the State Department.

Van Atta also revived the forays, dropping the rescue missions in favor of the more elegantly named "research teams." These he dispatched into Vietnam, Laos, Cambodia, Russia, and Cuba. Van Atta said he gave the DIA full details after each mission.

In April 1993 Van Atta wrote to General Vessey, claiming that one of his research teams had found live POWs during a recent trip to Vietnam. Van Atta said his men brought back a DNA sample and other evidence uncovered through "ingenuity and cleverness" after being imprisoned, chased, and set up for arrest on false drug charges.

The DIA and the State Department were extremely interested in Van Atta's letter to Vessey. The DIA wanted more information on the live POWs. The State Department wanted to know about the imprisonment, however brief, of American citizens. The DIA repeatedly asked Van Atta to elaborate on the Vessey letter, but Van Atta could not answer the simplest of questions, such as how many Americans the team members had seen in Vietnam. Nor could he provide the DNA sample.

DIA officials were angry that Van Atta had wasted agency resources with his obviously bogus claims; but they also assumed that he was sufficiently embarrassed to go into retreat. He was not. Van Atta was soon back in touch, asking the Pentagon for updated secret maps of Indochina and "something like cooperation, off the record" for his next foray, a 1994 incursion into Laos to find David Hrdlicka.

This particular operation had the latest status symbol in the activist community: the direct participation of an MIA family member. David's wife, Carol, was to be one of the team members. The mission did not go as planned. Van Atta lost face when Carol became disillusioned with him and withdrew. But other new-style missions played quite well off the family angle. In 1991 two men who were serving on the POW Task Force of Arkansas Governor Bill Clinton recruited men and money by using the star power of MIA brother Kenneth Carr.

Ken told me he had been contacted in September 1991 by the leaders of Team Falcon, who had said they would help rescue Ken's missing brother, Donald Carr. Although Ken himself had contributed less than $2,000, others had supplied at least $60,000 for the failed mission.

Afterward Ken regretted having joined the group. "I just went on my emotions," he told me, "and that's what they were counting on to get me involved."

The 1990s also saw the resurrection of Scott Barnes, this time recounting his BOHICA tale in *Kiss the Boys Goodbye,* the POW conspiracy book coauthored by Monika Jensen-Stevenson and her husband, William Stevenson.

During his silent phase, Barnes had found work as a private detective. An MIA family hired him to investigate their daughter's new boyfriend, who turned out to be Bobby Garwood. Barnes investigated the Emr filmmaking family, whose members were rumored to have been murdered over something pertaining to POWs. On one of his cases, Barnes, the former police officer, set up an illegal wiretap. He was charged and convicted.

Barnes told anyone who would listen that the conviction was a setup. He said the government was trying to force him to shut up about BOHICA. Few believed him, but one prominent activist, Marian Shelton, was so moved by his plight that she adopted his cause as her own. Barnes told me that "Miriam" had become his best friend. Whether her best friend actually knew her name or not, Marian mortgaged her home to pay Barnes's legal fees and sent out Christmas cards asking her friends to "pray for Scott."

It was Barnes and two MIA daughters who discovered Marian's body after she killed herself in 1990. Barnes told me that while at the scene, he had first answered a phone call from President Bush, then dialed 911. After that he had phoned Ross Perot to tell him Marian was dead.

Some Barnes-watchers have suggested it was the Shelton

phone call that had forged the Barnes-Perot bond and led to Perot's use of Barnes as a confidential informant.* Regardless, Perot should have been the break Barnes was waiting for. The eccentric billionaire was just the person to send Barnes back into Laos to recover the POWs he claimed he had seen during the course of Grand Eagle/BOHICA. But Barnes never made the proposal.

It would have been a perfectly logical request. Perot had often said publicly that POWs could be bought back from captivity. I myself quoted him as saying buybacks were "doable" at only $25,000 per man. The price for Barnes's two Americans would have been $50,000—a paltry sum for Perot, especially in light of the money he put up for the most financially ambitious POW scam ever perpetrated.

---

*Whatever the source of the trust, it was ill placed. After Perot withdrew his 1992 candidacy, Barnes filed suit alleging an array of misdeeds perpetrated against him by Perot. Nothing came of the lawsuit.

10

For a Small Price . . .

In the summer of 1985, Bob Brown gave a party in his hotel suite in the Georgetown section of Washington. It was a typical *Soldier of Fortune* gathering that brought together people connected with Brown's various ongoing projects. The guests of honor were leaders of the anti-Communist Miskito Indians of Nicaragua. Bob was giving them an invisible-to-radar, Kevlar-coated speedboat for use in their efforts to force the Sandinistas out of power.

One of the party guests was a volatile ex–Special Forces officer named Mark Smith. Smith had intended to make the Army his career but had never made it past the rank of major. After being passed over twice for promotion to lieutenant colonel, Smith had received a routine discharge. As Smith told it, though, the military had gotten rid of him because he knew too much about POWs.

Smith had been a POW himself. He had been captured on April 7, 1972, and released less than a year later, during Operation Homecoming. He had been held in IV Corps, in the South, and had at one time been in camp with the defector McKinley Nolan. The DIA had been quite interested in what Smith knew about Nolan and had quizzed him for every conceivable detail. The agency soon lost interest in Smith, who nevertheless continued to pursue information on MIAs. He would eventually become a key figure in the MIA issue.

I saw a foreshadowing of Smith's role myself, the night of Bob Brown's party.

Smith spent the first part of that evening discussing the case of Thomas Hart (whose wife, Anne, was in the process of exposing the problems with the remains identified by the Army's Central Identification Laboratory). Smith said Hart had survived his crash in Laos, traveled north about 150 miles, and there trampled his initials into the elephant grass. Smith was emphatic that Hart was still alive and punctuated his story with shouts and angry gestures. At one point he got so excited while talking about the elephant grass that he punched himself on the leg and sloshed liquor on a nearby guest.

Smith then tried to get hired on as a mercenary for the anti-Communist Miskitos. He tried to impress their leader with his savagery. "I like the garrote," he told her. He wrapped his hands around an imaginary wire and pantomimed its use. "It gets the job done." Then he laughed aloud. "There's nothing I like better than killing commies," he said. "I love the smell of commie blood in the morning."

When I remarked to Brown that Smith seemed to have an abundance of bloodlust, Brown hinted there would soon be something to write about.

Not long after the party, I was indeed doing what Brown had predicted. So, too, were a host of other journalists. In September 1985 Smith and another retired Green Beret, Sergeant Melvin McIntire, filed suit claiming that the U.S. government had suppressed evidence of live POWs. The defendants were President Reagan, Defense Secretary Caspar Weinberger, Secretary of State George P. Shultz, and DIA Director General Leonard H. Perroots. The two litigants aimed to enforce the century-old Hostage

Act of 1868, which requires the president to do everything short of declaring war to secure the release of U.S. citizens held captive abroad.

The suit assumed a significant role in the annals of MIA activism. It galvanized the issue, drawing disparate players together in a single unified cause. Before being dismissed as unfounded, the suit would be joined by a Who's Who of MIA activists, including Marian Shelton, Anne Hart, and Kathryn Fanning. Affidavits would be supplied by Dr. Michael Charney, Bobby Garwood, and Bo Gritz. The suit would also rally Ross Perot and prompt him to pledge an unprecedented $4.2 million to fulfill its goals. And, last, the suit would boost the careers of two highly successful MIA opportunists, Senator (then Congressman) Bob Smith of New Hampshire and former Congressman Billy Hendon of North Carolina.

The events leading up to the suit began in 1982, when Mark Smith and McIntire were assigned to a Special Forces unit in Korea. As part of that unit, the two soldiers made regular visits to Thailand to participate in exercises with the Thai Special Forces.

McIntire, who served as the detachment's medic, set up an intelligence operation in Thailand. He recruited ten native agents to collect information on POWs. This was entirely his own doing; if his superiors knew of the network, they ignored it.

McIntire's agents told him they had found American POWs just across the Mekong in Laos. The agents said they had already hired a group of Laotians to lead the prisoners into Thailand. All McIntire had to do was wait for delivery and then take credit for the rescue.

McIntire went to the 501st Military Intelligence Group in Seoul, Korea, to announce the imminent arrival of POWs. But officials at the MIG were not so easily convinced. They had heard the same type of scheme numerous times before and knew that it followed a predictable pattern. At some point, McIntire's agents would ask for money up front. Then there would be a series of glitches, each of which would be followed by a request for more money—for medicine, clothing, boots, or other items. If the tipsters were truly skilled, they could keep the process in motion for as long as a year. The MIG officials told McIntire to get more information.

McIntire returned to Thailand in March 1984. He met with his chief agent, who told him all was going well. As a matter of fact, he said, some prisoners were being led out of Laos that very day. They would arrive in Thailand in May. As proof of his sincerity, the agent offered to sell McIntire one of the POWs' dog tags. He also gave McIntire a copy of a sheet of notebook paper on which a POW had written autobiographical information.

McIntire promised to have the prisoners met by someone from the U.S. government. He returned to Seoul to arrange the welcoming committee. Again, officials at the MIG were unconvinced. They wanted to know the source of the information. If it were someone they had dealt with before, they would know how to gauge the information.

McIntire refused to give the name of his source; the agent had insisted on anonymity, saying he had been compromised before. If his name were known, the agent had argued, it would endanger his own life and that of the POWs.

The MIG officials told McIntire they had heard that line countless times, and it was the hallmark of a phony story. McIntire held fast. He did, however, pass on the POW autobiography and the name of the man whose dog tag was for sale. The man named on the dog tag was not even missing or unaccounted for. The autobiography had been written by Army Captain Walter H. Moon, who had disappeared in Laos in 1961.

Moon had been one of the Communists' "hard case" prisoners who had repeatedly tried to escape captivity. During one escape attempt, he had been shot in the head and recaptured. He had soon made another break for freedom and been shot in the side. Returned POWs who had seen the incident said Moon had died immediately.

During his imprisonment, Moon had been forced to write an autobiography in response to his interrogators' questions. Moon had signed the document and dated it 1961. In 1984 Bo Gritz somehow obtained the original. He gave a copy to Moon's widow, telling her Moon was still alive. But the document was now dated 1984. Gritz also gave a copy to Congressman Steve Solarz of New York, who passed it on to the DIA. Dozens of Laotian refugees at the Na Pho Camp in Thailand also had copies of the 1961 version, which they routinely offered for sale along with other MIA paraphernalia.

The MIG officials explained this saga to McIntire, who nonetheless insisted he would soon produce Walter Moon and the other prisoners. The officials then told McIntire he was welcome to wait for the POWs on his own time, but the U.S. government would not participate.

In the interim, Mark Smith had also set up a private network in Thailand. In 1983 Smith's informants told him rumors about POWs in Laos. Smith reported the rumors, which were so vague as to be useless.

In 1984 Smith's contacts gave him something more specific. They told him about an old C-130 crash site in Laos. They said American remains had been at the site for more than ten years. The contacts also told Smith about other crash sites containing such artifacts as parachutes, helmets, and dog tags. Again Smith reported the rumors. The MIG had heard the stories many times before. The sites in question had long been excavated and the artifacts duly recovered.

Still Smith could not be dissuaded. Like McIntire, he wanted to hear only one answer, that he had personally uncovered solid leads on live POWs. When the MIG failed to follow through on his worthless reports, Smith joined forces with McIntire. Together they took their information to their superior officer, Lieutenant Colonel Robert Howard.

The colonel had no way of knowing the leads were bogus. He accepted the reports and dutifully passed them on to Army Intelligence.

Smith and McIntire, meanwhile, were reassigned to the United States. There they awaited word of an impending POW rescue. When none came, McIntire approached intelligence authorities at Fort Bragg, resubmitting the entire batch of information that had been given to the MIG and Colonel Howard. Once again, the reports were sent up through channels, where they eventually reached the same DIA analysts who had already received two sets of the same reports. The analysts sent word back down to Fort Bragg to tell McIntire the information was still of no use.

McIntire was advised that in case he planned to go through yet a fourth channel, he should at least submit something new. The jab was wasted on McIntire. He and Smith had no sympathy for analysts forced to respond three times to urgent reports of the same old sightings that had been cleared up years before.

More determined than ever, McIntire and Smith concluded that the MIG and DIA were conspiring to debunk them. Their only alternative was to go outside the military. In Smith and McIntire's case, that alternative came in the form of Congressman Billy Hendon, who was delighted to hear from them. Hendon urged the two to seek more information in Thailand. In mid-1985 they set out for Bangkok.

Smith and McIntire had no trouble finding sources overseas (as one witness told the Kerry Committee, every taxicab driver and street vendor in Bangkok is running a sideline in POW scams). In one of the many bars along the Patpong Road, Smith and

McIntire met a Laotian who confided that he was on his way to Laos to pick up two American prisoners. He said he would sell the men for several million dollars.

Smith and McIntire returned to the United States, where they reported their find to Army Intelligence. The officials only rolled their eyes. The POWs who were about to be rescued had been the subject of live sighting reports for many years, mainly as a result of "wanted posters" circulating in Thailand. The entrepreneur who wanted to sell the prisoners had dabbled in false POW reports for years, often making announcements from his home base in Seattle, Washington.

Nevertheless, the DIA invited Smith and McIntire to the Pentagon to talk about POWs. The idea was to assuage the pair with a chance to meet with ranking officials and at the same time explain to them that their latest source was unreliable. While at the Pentagon, McIntire admitted he had "nothing tangible" on POWs.

The Pentagon visit, however, backfired. It only confirmed Smith and McIntire's notions of their own importance. They returned to Fayetteville convinced they could take on the government. They hired a local attorney, Mark Waple, who began piecing together the basis of a lawsuit. Central to the suit, which was filed in September 1985, was Smith and McIntire's claim that they had solid proof of live POWs.

The Special Forces community believed the story without question. It jumped in with moral support. Bob Brown contributed $5,000 to establish the Mark Smith Litigation Trust. He published the address in his magazine, so readers could contribute.

Activist Ted Sampley tried to generate excitement over the case. He called me to say that because of information provided by Smith and McIntire, the Army's Delta Force had been placed on alert. He said the elite team was at that very moment practicing jungle exfiltration.

The week of the Delta Force rumor, Sampley also called to tell me that Green Berets had infiltrated Laos; that they had conducted a rescue; and, finally, that POWs were being debriefed in Thailand. I started making travel arrangements to Bangkok. A contact at the Pentagon told me other journalists had done the same, but he advised that we all stand down. Sampley's stories were unfounded.

In December Smith and McIntire made an explosive announcement. They had an affidavit from an entrepreneur using the pseudonym John Obassy, who swore he had firsthand knowledge of U.S. captives in Laos. The Obassy contribution was pivotal. It would stir Congress to action and would persuade lawmakers and private citizens alike that the U.S. government might in fact have engaged in a cover-up.

The key to Obassy's success was his mastery of detail, which would unfold as the case progressed. As Obassy told it, he had been in Laos the previous October, when he had seen thirty-nine Americans working as slaves in a gold-mining operation.

"Each person had at least three armed guards on them," Obassy wrote. He also described Americans being held as free-roaming prisoners, allowed to move in a limited region. "I personally spoke with these people, who confirmed to me that they had been left behind. . . . They were afraid to leave their sanctuary areas in Laos."

Obassy wrote that he was using a false name because his life and the lives of the POWs would be endangered if his real name were revealed. "My true identity has been made known to the attorney who took this affidavit, Mr. Mark L. Waple, and to a United States congressman."

The congressman was Billy Hendon, who had brought Obassy over from Thailand to swear out the affidavit.

In January 1986 Smith and McIntire appeared before a Senate panel and testified that they had solid proof of POWs. They would deliver their proof to the Committee on Veterans Affairs within one week, they said.

Smith and McIntire did not disclose the nature of their proof, but Sampley made sure word got out that it was a recent videotape depicting live American prisoners. The tape was said to be in the custody of John Obassy, who was now in either Southeast Asia or the Middle East. Congress pressed for details of the video, and Smith admitted he had seen only portions of it when Obassy was in North Carolina for the affidavit. Significantly, Obassy had not let Smith view the parts containing POWs.

Congress had only one response: get the tape.

Smith set out for the Middle East.

With Smith out of the country and Congress already annoyed that the much-vaunted "POW proof" was still only hearsay, something was needed to bolster the case. Bo Gritz was brought in to add credibility.

Gritz swore out an affidavit that in April 1983 he had been taken to a secret Fort Bragg command center known as "the Cage," where a Green Beret general told him about an upcoming POW operation that was later described by Mark Smith.

Gritz's vague statement did little to help the lawsuit; aside from the comment about the general, Gritz devoted most of the affidavit to describing his own heroic efforts to save POWs. But Gritz's contribution did serve a useful purpose, diverting the skeptics long enough to buy time until Smith's triumphant return.

But he was hardly a triumphant hero. He still did not have the tape. But he said he had seen the entire 240 minutes and that it depicted live American prisoners. Breathless from the adventure, Smith composed a lengthy "Memorandum for the Record."

In the memo, Smith first described the serpentine process that had led to his viewing the tape. According to Smith, he had first attended a secret international summit at the Cactus Hotel in

Cyprus, then traveled by boat to East Beirut. He had finally seen the tape at secret Israeli Mossad headquarters in Beirut, in the company of Mossad's chief of intelligence for Syria and Lebanon.

Smith described opening scenes featuring Obassy in the company of senior officials from Vietnam and an unnamed third country. The Vietnamese were depicted leading troops into northern Laos, where they met with Pathet Lao forces.

"They came together and then I saw them put the prisoners on the road and start marching them down the road," Smith wrote.

Smith described a group of American and Korean POWs hooked to a medieval-sounding device. "They were handcuffed, had ankle shackles with bars between the ankles, had to march in step because each had a steel collar around their neck with rags wrapped on their necks to keep or prevent further injury. Between the necks of each prisoner was a wooden pole which was about four feet long—long enough to prevent the prisoners from reaching out to touch the prisoner in front or behind. Each was handcuffed."

Smith said the men were being forced to dig trenches for a gold-mining operation and were also being used to clear deadfall around huge trees being harvested for timber.

Despite this heavy outdoor work, the Americans as Smith described them had pale skin. They also had short stubble on their faces. Apparently the captors who would not allow them to touch one another did permit them to shave.

Smith wrote that while the Korean prisoners glowered in anger at the camera, the Americans showed no response to being filmed. "The Americans looked like whipped dogs."

They were guarded by another American, a mysterious trustee in a blue hat and sunglasses. "He does not have any stick or anything," Smith wrote. "He just supervises."

Obassy again appeared on screen, this time acting in a medical capacity. He peered down the men's throats and gave them injections.

Smith wrote that there were about a thousand other POWs spread out along the road, carrying sledgehammers, saws, wood-splitting tools, cooking utensils, and pans. The prisoners, he said, were from Vietnam, Laos, Thailand, and Korea. Smith did not say how he knew their nationalities.

The tape ended on a close-up of a pair of Smith and Wesson handcuffs being held by a white hand, presumably that of the mysterious blue-hatted trustee.

Smith gave the memo to Congressman Billy Hendon, who showed it to his House colleague Bob Smith. The memo should have prompted the congressmen to interrogate Mark Smith about the numerous questions it raised. The most obvious was about the involvement of Mossad. Why would Israeli Intelligence conceal its knowledge of U.S. POWs? Why would Mossad choose to break silence through a retired Army major who was now suing his own president? The memo also raised questions about the one thousand POWs. It would be impossible to hide that many prisoners for any length of time, particularly if they were placed along an open road, as Mark Smith claimed.

On January 27 the two congressional activists hand-carried the memo to the White House, where they presented it to Vice President George Bush. They also gave Bush a copy of a letter sent that same day to President Reagan, from attorney Mark Waple.

In his letter to Reagan, Waple said Obassy would allow the U.S. government to view the tape only after Obassy became "convinced of our sincerity." Waple begged for an urgent meeting among himself, Reagan, McIntire, Mark Smith, and Hendon.

Mindful that he was now asking the president to meet with men who had just filed suit against him, Waple assured Reagan that under the circumstances, he was willing to hold in abeyance "the unfortunate litigation which is pending in U.S. District Court."

Waple's letter to Reagan went unanswered, but George Bush did send a note to John Poindexter, asking him to "have someone look into this."

After a month had lapsed with still no action from the White House, Waple composed a second letter to Reagan. Hendon delivered it by hand the afternoon of Friday, February 28. This letter revealed how the U.S. government could convince John Obassy it was sincere: with $4.2 million cash, delivered under precise conditions.

The instructions had all the elements of an amateur blackmail plot, featuring an odd mix of useless would-be security measures. Obassy wanted Mark Smith, Bob Smith, Hendon, and Senator Dennis DeConcini to take the cash to Los Angeles International Airport, where they would be directed to a waiting commercial airliner. There would be no other passengers. One of the pilots was to be personally selected by Mark Smith; the remainder of the crew could be chosen by the U.S. government. Waple assumed the government would use its own agents, which was permissible "as long as they are under deep civilian cover."

The plane would have to be equipped to fly to Southeast Asia, but the exact destination would not be revealed until after the craft was airborne.

After landing at the designated site, the passengers would be taken by helicopter to another undisclosed location, to view the video. If the Americans were satisfied with what was on the tape, they would then be allowed to buy it, along with unspecified additional evidence.

Waple insisted on an immediate response. He gave Reagan the weekend to decide, insisting on an answer by the following Monday, March 3.

Bob Smith made a backup call to General Perroots, the DIA director. Perroots was out of town, so Smith wound up speaking to the deputy director, Brigadier General James Shufelt.

According to Shufelt, the call began with Smith saying, "I hope you are sitting down, because I have a bizarre story to relate." Shufelt could not have agreed more with that assessment.

Smith repeated the deal as outlined in the letter to Reagan and reiterated that a decision must be reached by the following Monday. Shufelt told Smith he would have to get back to him and hung up the phone. Shufelt immediately called ISA chief Jim Kelly and National Security Council member Richard Childress, both of whom expressed incredulity at the proposal.

There ensued a weekend of frenzied phone calls among members of an ever-widening circle of those with a "need to know." Key members of that group met the following Monday in Billy Hendon's office on Capitol Hill. Hendon and Congressman Bob Smith were there, along with Mark Smith, Waple, Generals Perroots and Shufelt, DIA General Counsel Bill Alard, and DIA Legislative Liaison Steve Lucas. Hendon acted as moderator and host, making it clear that he saw himself as the conduit between Mark Smith and the administration. Hendon underscored that he had great confidence in Mark Smith and believed he was telling the truth.

The DIA men asked Mark Smith what would happen if Obassy didn't get the money. They were amazed at his answer that the POWs would come out anyway, but in such a way as to embarrass the United States. The officials then asked if the money would therefore guarantee the safe release of the POWs. Smith said he did not know.

However, he added that he did know the names of the Americans shown in the video but would not reveal them. Hendon then enraged the DIA delegation by saying that he, too, knew the names but was also keeping them secret.

The generals expressed disgust that a U.S. congressman, especially one who professed great concern for POWs, would conceal the names of living prisoners (in the years since that meeting, Hendon has yet to reveal the names of the men he said he knew were in captivity).

Hendon closed the Monday meeting by reiterating the offer to sell the tape for $4.2 million, insisting to General Perroots that if the offer were refused, the answer had better be put in writing.

Despite the obvious signs that a scam was in the works, the government decided the tape should be bought and asked Ross Perot to put up the $4.2 million. The money was placed on deposit in the Bank of America in Singapore. Perot would not release the funds until he had proof that the tape existed and its contents were as advertised.

The Senate committee, meanwhile, had grown impatient with Smith and McIntire. The two litigants had ignored repeated requests to present what they had promised, irrefutable evidence of American POWs in Southeast Asia. An affidavit from their most credible witness, Lieutenant Colonel Robert Howard, had been a great disappointment; although he said he believed Smith and McIntire and had seen evidence on POWs, the colonel acknowledged that the evidence was all based on secondhand information. Fed up with the unfulfilled promises, the committee subpoenaed Smith and McIntire to appear before a hearing on March 15. The meeting was canceled when Smith and McIntire did not show up.

By now McIntire had taken a considerable backseat; his whereabouts on the date of the hearing remain unknown. Smith missed the hearing because he was out of the country, as were Hendon and Waple. All three were in Singapore, where Obassy was being held in jail for fraud: he had been convicted of conspiring to cheat a local businessman out of $40,000. Hendon bailed him out with $42,000 supplied for the purpose by Ross Perot, whose $4.2 million was still being held by the Bank of America.

It was now time for Obassy to prove to Perot that the tape was genuine. In the company of Mark Smith, Waple, and Hendon, Obassy took the tape to Fayetteville. He showed portions to Waple and Hendon but did not let them see the parts containing POWs. Obassy now agreed to appear before the Senate committee to answer questions about the tape.

Before he was scheduled to testify, I learned that John Obassy was really Robin Gregson, a British con man well known to Thai officials. His repertoire ran from smuggling to theft. His specialty was preying on people already in trouble, usually on the fringes of the drug and gem trade. In 1984 Gregson had been convicted of defrauding an Australian tourist out of $10,000 by promising to get the tourist's drug charges dropped. In 1985 Gregson was wanted on yet another warrant for fraud. His presence in the United States probably had less to do with the tape than with the fact that he was hiding from the Thai police.

I exposed Obassy as Gregson in *The Washington Times*. It was a small item but produced a tremendous response. Hendon called in a fury, saying I had just signed a death warrant for the thirty-odd POWs. "Their blood is on your hands!" he raged. In that same conversation, Hendon admitted he had known the truth about Gregson but believed him anyway and would support him "to the bitter end." Other activists, including Sampley and some of the more militant family members, made similar angry calls.

Gregson took advantage of the uproar. He supposedly was so upset at being unmasked that he burned the video, effectively extricating himself from a very awkward situation. Mark Smith, for his part, expressed no dismay that Obassy/Gregson would destroy the only existing evidence of live POWs. Instead, he faulted the newspaper for printing the story and demanded that Congress investigate where I had gotten my information on Gregson.

Smith later said he now had the tape. He promised he would

relinquish it to the Senate Veterans Affairs Committee. Delivery was set for 9 A.M. on June 25. The afternoon of June 24, Sampley called me to report that Smith had boarded a plane for Washington, POW tape in hand.

The next morning the hearing room was packed with eager witnesses to Smith's dramatic moment. Instinctively, the audience seated itself by ideology; Smith supporters on one side, detractors on the other. Jack Bailey, who has had a long career in the POW business, floated between the two factions, insisting the tape was genuine. "I've seen it," he said, "and it depicts live prisoners of war."

The excitement lasted until ten minutes past nine, when committee chairman Frank Murkowski delivered the bad news: Mark Smith was nowhere to be found.

The audience reaction was mixed. Some MIA wives shook their heads in disappointment. Bailey listened with a hurt expression. An Air Force officer snickered into his hand.

Clearly angry, Murkowski announced that he had instructed federal marshals to find Smith. Murkowski speculated that Smith had been depending on Gregson to supply the evidence and "Gregson has refused to provide anything. Whether Major Smith ever had anything at all is something my colleagues and I should consider."

Acting on advice from Waple, Smith did not ignore the second subpoena served by the U.S. marshals. He and McIntire appeared at a new hearing, where they were to produce—finally —their evidence of POWs.

The evidence consisted of maps of places where Smith and McIntire thought POWs might be held, plus three poor-quality photocopied pictures of unidentified men. One of the photocopies showed a smiling man holding a rifle. He was not under guard or restrained in any way. There was nothing in the picture to indicate what it was or where it had been taken; it could have been a safari memento or another recruiting ad for Private Delta Force. Still, Smith described the pictures with great solemnity. "These photographs were provided to me by a source in Thailand and depict, according to this source, who I consider to be reliable, Americans who were left in Southeast Asia at the conclusion of the Vietnam War." He said he did not know the names of the men.

The committee members were aghast. Senator Alan Simpson could not contain his wrath. "As we say in the West in a poker game, put up or shut up," Simpson said. "I've never seen such lightweight stuff in my life. I don't know what you're up to, but I can tell you it's not savory."

Smith said he could get the original pictures, along with classified POW files he announced he had stolen from the Army, although it would take some time. He never came up with the goods. In Fayetteville, the lawsuit was finally dismissed. McIntire has since distanced himself entirely from the POW issue.

As for Smith, he has moved to Bangkok, where his Army pension allows him to live well by Thai standards. He leads a low-key existence as a freelance POW guide, pointing American "Rambos" toward the Laotian border and running low-budget prisoner hunts. In 1993 he gave Mike Van Atta a "POW legbone" that turned out to be phony. Other than that, he hasn't produced any additional "evidence" of POWs.

But if the key figures in the Mark Smith Caper, as the DIA calls it, have faded into obscurity, other participants have not. Billy Hendon and Bob Smith, the congressmen, have catapulted off their Smith Caper contacts and have built successful careers around the POW issue.

11

The Grey Flannel Rambos

My first encounter with Billy Hendon was the closest I have come to making a command appearance in Washington. It was in the early days of the Mark Smith Caper, before I knew Smith and Hendon were connected. I had just started writing on POWs and was not yet familiar with all the players. I was startled to receive a call one Friday afternoon from a U.S. congressman, demanding to see me immediately. It was Hendon, saying he had vital POW information that could be delivered only in his office on Capitol Hill.

It was my introduction to the Grey Flannel Rambos, four men whose outward respectability conceals their spiritual debt to Bo Gritz.

They are by no means a formal organization, and their name is my own invention. They do not necessarily work together, and they move from friendship to enmity and back again, depending on their fluctuating agendas. But the Grey Flannel Rambos—Billy Hendon, Red McDaniel, Bob Smith, and John LeBoutillier—have several traits in common, including connections to politics, a love of the limelight, and an unremitting antagonism toward the DIA.

The group members are highly skilled at helping to further the conspiracy myth. Of the four, the greatest troublemaker is

Billy Hendon, whose imagination and stamina far outshine that of his fellows.

I first caught a glimpse of his abilities in 1985, when he made that surprising phone call in which he promised to deliver "the next Watergate."

As soon as I hung up the phone I proceeded to Hendon's office, where an aide ushered me into Billy's chamber. The six-foot, six-inch lawmaker was stretched out on a leather couch, arms clasped behind his head. He wore a pair of expensive cowboy boots, carefully propped on the armrest.

"Get out your notebook," he ordered. "This is important."

Hendon immediately launched into a presentation that drew on his considerable gift for drama.

"Three POWs," he drawled, holding up fingers to illustrate, "are right now on their way out of Laos."

The men were weak, Hendon said, but not so sapped they couldn't make the trek into Thailand. They were being led through the jungle by a small band of insurgents from the Lao resistance.

Hendon quivered with emotion as he spoke of the mission in progress. He was obviously deeply moved. At one point he bent as if he would drop to his knees. Pointing in the direction of the Vietnam Veterans Memorial, he thundered: "They are coming to sandblast their names off the Wall!"

And, he added cryptically, George Bush knew all about it.

Hendon told me the men would be out by Monday. The process was very delicate, he warned, and I could not write anything until the men were actually free. If I could keep the operation secret over the weekend, Hendon would arrange for me to meet the POWs. I would get an exclusive interview. I would get an update on Saturday or, at the very latest, Sunday afternoon.

By Tuesday there was still no word from Hendon. On Wednesday one of his aides called to say there had been a slight delay—one of the POWs was ill, and the group had had to move slowly. On Friday I heard that the rescue troop had run into hostile forces and was hiding in the jungle. The following Monday, the group was still having trouble.

The progress reports came farther and farther apart, until they finally stopped altogether. There was no follow-up from Hendon. He seemed completely unfazed that what he had described as my career-making scoop had fizzled out with no explanation. I was relieved I had listened to my husband, Michael, a senior editor at *The Washington Times,* when he advised me not to tell my editors they would soon have the next Watergate.

For Hendon, the fizzled story was business as usual. It was also an indicator that already he had grown complacent, accustomed as he was to having his caprices go unchecked.

Hendon stoked his POW career in 1983, when he was a Pentagon consultant while between terms in Congress. Hendon worked for the Office of the Secretary of Defense, International Security Affairs. He attached himself to a coworker who was the office liaison with the DIA's POW/MIA department. In the company of this coworker, Hendon made daily visits to the DIA, where he had free access to all the classified MIA files. He was reelected to the House of Representatives in 1984 and quickly moved to the forefront of the group of congressmen involved in the MIA issue.

While in office, Hendon cultivated favored reporters, who were amazed at what he could do for them. He could get documents, hidden reports, transcripts, and confidential letters. He was a benevolent dispenser of scoops, a source who not only gave out tips but also provided free research.

He was particularly helpful to ABC News. The quality of Hendon's help to the network was such that he once enabled ABC to virtually take over the DIA for about three weeks. The takeover began on a Friday afternoon, with an urgent Freedom of Information Act request for more than ninety specific documents, which were based on electronic transmissions sent to the DIA. Hendon had seen the documents during his tenure at the DIA and had made note of their individual date-time groups and coded identification numbers. He gave the numbers to ABC, enabling them to bolster their request with an unspoken threat: DIA could not say the materials didn't exist, because ABC had the identification numbers. As soon as the request came in, the Pentagon intelligence agency pulled in extra staff to work Saturdays and Sundays. The analytical branch was told to suspend all other projects until this one was complete. In the end, none of the documents was released because all were classified; but the episode still worked in Hendon's favor, because ABC now viewed him as an excellent source on MIAs.

This type of selective leaking may have angered the DIA, but it enabled Hendon to take advantage of the press. He knew that by doling out "hot tips" to favored journalists, he could influence them to report the stories from his point of view. It was an old Hendon method, dating back to his first term in office.

In 1982, for example, Hendon told certain of his press contacts a startling story of a recent failed POW rescue. Hendon portrayed himself as the central figure who had overcome great hurdles to secure the release of prisoners. He said the mission had progressed to the point where the prisoners were on standby, awaiting imminent rescue. He said the effort had failed at the last minute because someone in the U.S. government had leaked the story to the *Los Angeles Times* and the *San Francisco Chronicle*.

Hendon's contacts printed the story as presented, featuring the congressman as a heroic figure unseated by shady government foes. Had they approached Hendon's story with more skepticism, however, they might have uncovered at least part of a far more tortured sequence of events.

Hendon was indeed part of an official move to work with

Laos on the MIA question. But the effort was a vague, diplomatically couched maneuver to open a dialogue on recovering possible MIAs or their remains. Hendon was not the sole representative. His partner was another freshman congressman, John LeBoutillier from New York. Their boss on the project was Army Colonel Richard Childress, Ann Mills Griffiths's friend at the National Security Council.

The two congressmen made an interesting team. Hendon, a former faculty member at the University of Tennessee, likes to pass himself off as a simple backwoods-boy-made-good. He colors his speech with phrases such as "dadgummit" and can slip into an exaggerated southern accent at will. But he is just as savvy as the Harvard-educated LeBoutillier, a member of the blue-blooded Vanderbilt family. Acquaintances describe "LeBout" as belonging to a lesser branch of the clan and having lived for years with his mother in relative poverty at the family mansion on Long Island. Nevertheless, he moves with ease among the nation's social elite and can rope in connections when necessary. LeBoutillier and Hendon share similar social styles. They are talkative, aggressive, and highly personable and can establish a quick rapport with new acquaintances.

But for all their flashiness, Hendon and LeBoutillier were ill suited for diplomacy; before the "official dialogue" with Laos was over, LeBoutillier would narrowly escape prosecution and Childress would deride the two congressmen as little more than "hack politicians" in pursuit of "sad-sack dreams."

Childress knew he would have to tread carefully while setting up talks with Laos. The United States did not have diplomatic relations with the official Communist government and did in fact support some factions of the anti-Communist Lao resistance. The Laotian government was afraid the United States might be helping to organize a coup. The Communist leaders in Vientiane insisted that if the U.S. government wanted to talk about MIAs, it would have to go through official channels only. There was to be no contact of any kind with members of the Lao resistance.

Childress wrote to the Laotian government, affirming U.S. respect for official Laos. He promised that the United States would not work with the resistance and would not cultivate intelligence sources from within their ranks. He went so far as to rewrite White House guest lists so that resistance leaders would not be invited to any official functions.

But while Childress was striving to create the proper climate for dialogue, one of his emissaries, LeBoutillier, was working on a byzantine project that directly contradicted the White House guarantees to Laos.

Like other would-be Rambos before him, LeBoutillier thought he could find and rescue missing American servicemen. In June 1982 he approached the government's unofficial POW/MIA czar, Ann Mills Griffiths. LeBoutillier knew that with Griffiths's blessing, he could carry out any number of wild schemes, including the one he had in mind. He told Griffiths he was forming a secret intelligence operation to gather information on live POWs. LeBoutillier would pass on the intelligence to high-level government officials, who would then initiate a rescue.

LeBoutillier told Griffiths he needed a way to launder funds for the project, Skyhook II. Griffiths provided a solution, convincing a friend in California to reactivate a dormant charity, Save Our POW/MIAs, for the purpose of gathering funds. The friend, Betty Bartels, assumed that the project had White House approval. She allowed her charity to be used as a way station for funds destined for accounts in New York and Bangkok. The money was ultimately made available to an American expatriate living in Bangkok, retired Air Force Colonel Albert Shinkle.

Skyhook II worked well under these conditions, at least in

terms of the cash flow. Betty Bartels's charity would eventually launder about $200,000 for LeBoutillier.

But the project's secret network came to light soon after Skyhook II was formed. Acting more like an excited Boy Scout than a covert operative, LeBoutillier divulged his operation to trusted friends, who then told only their most trusted associates. It wasn't long before "Skyhook II" became the not-so-secret password among a certain clique of wealthy conservatives.

Shinkle was no less discreet. He went on a conspicuous spending spree, buying more than $150,000 worth of infantry gear for the Lao resistance. The U.S. embassy sent Childress an urgent cable, informing him that LeBoutillier was raising a private army against the Laotian government.

Childress was incensed that the carefully constructed groundwork with Laos had now been undercut. He suspected that Hendon was also involved and demanded to see the two congressmen. He told Hendon and LeBoutillier the White House would have nothing to do with them if they raised their own army.

Hendon maintained his innocence, and LeBoutillier emerged as being at fault. Childress asked LeBoutillier to write a letter promising to stop the mercenary activity. Childress sent the letter to relevant government agencies, then "fired" LeBoutillier.

Hendon was now the lone emissary to Laos. It was a heady position for Hendon, but one that would not last. After the business involving Skyhook II, Vientiane abruptly ended the talks in 1982. Hendon turned the entire episode to his advantage, telling the press that the failed initiative was in fact a POW rescue starring himself.

But Hendon was not the only one who succeeded in placing a unique spin on events in Laos. When the California papers reported Hendon's story of the failed rescue, LeBoutillier's first move was to tell the National League of Families board members that Hendon had violated national security laws. Later, LeBoutillier claimed it was he who had been on the verge of saving the POWs. He said the mission had been betrayed by Richard Childress, whom LeBoutillier described as leading an international drug-running and arms-smuggling operation.

Preposterous as they were, the accusations against Childress sparked an FBI investigation. The Bureau found nothing to substantiate the charges. The Senate, too, looked into the matter and concluded there was no basis for the claims.

LeBoutillier himself was investigated after the government learned he had arranged for a friend in Virginia to purchase handguns for Laotian mercenaries. The Bureau of Alcohol, Tobacco and Firearms tried to charge LeBoutillier with firearms violations. But LeBoutillier persuaded the U.S. Attorney that the government might have had something to do with the private army, and the court declined to prosecute.

From start to finish, the handgun affair dragged on for about four years. LeBoutillier lived under threat of prosecution until 1986. But that and other problems, such as breaking with Hendon and being voted out of office, did not deter him from embarking on a grandiose new project.

The new venture, if successful, would give LeBoutillier power over Hendon, Childress, Griffiths, and virtually any other official involved with MIAs. It would place him at the right hand of Ronald Reagan in a newly created post of Secretary for POW Affairs. Reagan had not created the position, nor does it exist now; LeBoutillier wanted it specially made, just for him.

LeBoutillier knew it was a long shot. To help expedite the scheme, he pulled in family and political connections, obtaining letters of support from Richard Nixon and other notables. He also copied Hendon's method of cultivating friendly journalists to further his cause. I was one of the potential "friendlies" on his list.

We had already talked several times when LeBoutillier called one morning to pass on a tantalizing career tip: according to LeBoutillier, *The Washington Times* was at that moment looking for the right reporter to send on a POW expedition to Southeast Asia. Using the activists' stock-in-trade tone of whispered urgency, LeBoutillier said that he knew from one of the newspaper's secretaries that managing editor Woody West was looking for a reporter to send to Southeast Asia.

"The timing couldn't be better," LeBoutillier told me. "Some men are getting ready to come out of Laos. Now go in there and tell him you have a strong lead on live prisoners."

As it turned out, West was not looking for someone to send overseas, though another reporter was already working a deal with Ross Perot to hunt for POWs in Laos. Nothing came of that effort, nor of LeBoutillier's live prisoners. Like Hendon before him, LeBoutillier let the tip fizzle without explanation or apparent concern. As near as I could determine, the tip was designed to establish LeBoutillier as my advocate so that I, in turn, would help him.

There soon arose many opportunities to help, by quoting LeBoutillier in stories he himself supplied. The stories were based on POW intelligence supposedly uncovered by the once-secretive Skyhook II.

LeBoutillier also took his case directly to the public, in the form of direct mail marketing. He produced his fund-raising appeals on elegant stock and adorned them with official-looking seals and other markings. They appeared to have come from Congress or the White House. Only after careful examination did it become clear they had come from a private source.

As the fund-raising effort gathered momentum, LeBoutillier did not lose sight of his main goal of becoming a cabinet secretary. He pressed his effort for the remainder of the Reagan years. The game was over, though, when George Bush was elected president. LeBoutillier had been among those accusing Bush of orchestrating a POW cover-up, and there was no way Richard Nixon or anyone else could convince Bush to make LeBoutillier part of his inner circle.

But all was not lost for LeBoutillier. His fund-raising apparatus was well in place, enabling him to concentrate fully on soliciting funds in the name of POWs. From July 1985 through August 1992, Skyhook II solicited nearly $1.9 million. In 1992 some of the cases featured in some unmailed Skyhook II letters were proved fraudulent, and LeBoutillier's professional fund-raisers consequently stopped working for him. LeBoutillier then hired a telemarketing company to solicit donations by phone. The company has continued to collect money for LeBoutillier, who appears to have found his niche in POW activism.

During the time LeBoutillier was feeling his way to a career as a telephone solicitor, Hendon, too, was pursuing his own equally unsavory course.

Like LeBoutillier, Hendon lost his 1982 bid for reelection. He had two years until his next campaign, which would revolve heavily around POWs. Before he could launch the campaign in full force, though, Hendon first had to rehabilitate himself after the indictment by LeBoutillier.

Hendon went straight to the site where LeBoutillier had denounced him. He acquired a spot on the platform of the National League of Families' 1984 general meeting, which would be held at Nellis Air Force Base in Nevada. The appearance was pivotal to Hendon's later success as a Grey Flannel Rambo.

Nellis was a curious choice for the conference. Located just outside Las Vegas, it is known as the home of the Thunderbirds precision flight team. But the base is also a test site for everything from experimental aircraft to nuclear weapons. Vast portions of the Nevada desert belong to Nellis; the tests conducted there are so sensitive that civilian aircraft are banned from flying over certain sections. In the mid-1980s the normally high security at Nellis was even tighter. The Air Force was working on a secret project known as Have Blue, which later became the F-19 Stealth fighter. An Air Force general died at Nellis while at the controls of a Stealth prototype. The Air Force closed ranks around the incident, concealing it in such a way as to imply a cover-up.

As a result, the atmosphere at Nellis reinforced the image of a secretive, uncooperative military. In retrospect, it is surprising the Air Force agreed to let Nellis be used by a group that was already deeply wary of government lies and cover-ups. From Hendon's perspective, the locale could not have been better.

Hendon played well to the cover-up angle, using it as part of his cleverly executed move to win back the League of Families. His opening lines, delivered with theatrical authority, elicited gasps and murmurs from the audience: "The cover-up continues to this day inside our government. I know. I've been there. Our men are being held right now, half a world away, against their will."

Hendon raised the question he knew was on everyone's mind: "Maybe I'm an outright liar, as some have said, and others, how shall we say it, have been induced, perhaps, to say." He added that he hoped the families would believe in him, but whether they did or didn't was really not important. What mattered was the POWs. In reassuring tones, Hendon promised he was there to "help you and your loved ones any way I can."

Throughout his speech, Hendon portrayed himself as constantly badgering a reluctant DIA to follow up on live sightings. He gave numerous specific examples of reports that had been discredited by the DIA. Hendon presented each story as having merit. With each new anecdote, he would look an audience member in the eye and say, "This could have been someone in your family."

He told of one incident that had taken place while he worked at the Pentagon. Hendon said the DIA had received a report that someone had seen a particular airman who was known to have died in a plane crash. The DIA had regarded the report as an obvious fabrication. Hendon had believed otherwise. While his supervisors weren't looking, he had copied details from the fake report. He had learned the name and address of the airman's unsuspecting widow. He had gone to her home.

"I told the former wife," Hendon informed his audience. "I felt I had an obligation to do it. She didn't know about [the report] until I walked into her house and told her."

Hendon defended his actions as noble. "That guy's name haunts me," he said. "It's with me on a daily basis." Much later, when I asked Hendon about the man whose name haunted him, he didn't know what I was talking about. Nevertheless, Hendon emerged restored from his weekend with the League. The group's leadership continued to hold him in disdain as a publicity-grabbing meddler, but the family members themselves, frequently shunted aside even by their own board of directors, looked on Hendon as a savior. If anyone could find POWs, they thought, it was Billy Hendon.

Fresh from his victory at the League convention, Hendon set about building his contacts. He deepened his relationship with then-Congressman Bob Smith; a wise investment, since Smith later went on to capture a secure seat in the Senate. When Hendon won back his own seat in 1984, he returned to Congress with an ally in place, New Hampshire's Bob Smith.

Hendon worked furiously during his second term in the House. But all his energy went into a single cause. However, back in North Carolina, the voters expected action on more than just the hunt for missing soldiers. In 1986 Hendon was again turned out of office. He moved across town from Capitol Hill to a tony POW think tank, the American Defense Institute (ADI), run by Eugene "Red" McDaniel.

A retired Navy captain, McDaniel has long been involved in the MIA issue. He is highly decorated, holding coveted awards that include the Navy Cross, two Silver Stars, and the Legion of Merit.

He spent six years as a POW in North Vietnam. Like John McCain, McDaniel was singled out by the Hanoi Hilton guards as a troublemaker and as a result suffered unspeakable torture. He nearly died after one three-week session during which his captors tried to extract information McDaniel did not have.

McDaniel's heroic background gives him much credibility among activists and even some skeptics. However, he has distributed several false POW pictures and has made greater gains in fund-raising than in learning the truth about MIAs.

McDaniel's alliance with Hendon was viewed as the melding of two powerful figures on the MIA scene. But their partnership only brought results similar to those created when Barnum met Bailey.

Hendon's first project for McDaniel was a high-profile scheme borrowed from Ross Perot, who was still telling people he was willing to ransom POWs at $25,000 apiece. Hendon's plan was to pay $2.4 million—not for the ninety-six men it would buy under Perot's approach, but for a single live POW. Twenty-one congressmen, including Bob Smith, pledged the funds.

Hendon devised a unique method of publicizing the reward. He would buy ten thousand copies of Vietnamese-language versions of popular videotapes, such as *Rocky* and the Indiana Jones movies. In the midst of these movies he would splice a plea for information on POWs, accompanied by an offer to pay $2.4 million for the information.

As Hendon described it to me, he envisioned hundreds of young Vietnamese lounging around on their living room mats, drinking beer and watching *Rocky,* only to have the film's action suddenly interrupted by the important announcement concerning POWs. Hendon thought this would launch the largest scavenger hunt in the history of Vietnam. He planned to publicize his gambit in Vietnamese-language newspapers in Southeast Asia and on radio stations in the Philippines. The effort stalled when the various sales managers approached by Hendon decided they did not want to be associated with the scheme; no one would sell him advertising space or airtime.

But the ADI was determined to go through with the ransom. In addition to the $2.4 million reward, McDaniel's group offered $1 million, payable in gold, for the release of a POW.

In 1988 McDaniel launched yet another pledge campaign, "HOME FREE!/The Committee of 40 Million." The plan was to have 40 million Americans pledge $25 each in an effort to raise $1 billion. McDaniel hoped to ransom more than four hundred POWs.

A year later, with no results from either program, Hendon came up with another scheme to publicize the $2.4 million reward. He would describe the offer on small leaflets sealed inside Ziploc bags, which would be attached to helium balloons that Hendon would launch from a boat in the South China Sea. He would also send balloons across the Mekong River from Thailand into Laos. The leaflets did not result in any POW leads, but the undertaking brought excellent publicity for Hendon.

He returned to Indochina later that year in the company of one of his Grey Flannel cohorts, Bob Smith. This trip was on behalf of Bobby Garwood and ushered in a strange alliance among Hendon, Smith, and the convicted collaborator.

Hendon was a latecomer among Garwood supporters but in 1989 interjected himself into an old dispute between Garwood and the DIA. The conflict centered around Garwood's claim that he had seen American POWs in Hanoi as late as 1978. They were supposedly inside a compound at No. 17 Ly Nam De Street. Garwood said he had seen the men on several occasions, while staying overnight at the compound.

Garwood's descriptions of the sightings contained enough detail to convince a willing listener. During one visit to the compound, Garwood said, he had seen a group of American

POWs milling about in a courtyard near a cistern. It soon became obvious Garwood had never been to No. 17 Ly Nam De Street, but he did provide a sketch of the cistern, most likely based on information given to him by someone who had actually seen it.

The cistern would come to figure prominently in 1989, when Hendon decided to champion Garwood. Hendon thought he could use the cistern to prove Garwood right—or, more accurately, prove the DIA wrong.

Hendon recruited Bob Smith and an ABC camera crew to join him in a raid on Ly Nam De Street. With cameras rolling, Hendon knocked on the gate at No. 17, which was now a military film studio. A befuddled film studio officer answered the knock. Hendon burst past him into the courtyard, where he circled in triumph at the discovery of a cistern.

The episode was aired on national television. The viewing public, unsure what all the fuss was about, heard Hendon's explanation that the cistern proved Garwood was telling the truth. It therefore followed, Hendon said, that Garwood had seen American POWs at the site in 1978.

The incident made a great impression on MIA family members and activists, many of whom reconsidered their positions on Garwood.

Hendon dabbled with more publicity stunts, at one point asking an MIA daughter to chain herself to a tree in Cambodia. Then he went to work picking the brain of the DIA's self-destructing POW/MIA director, Colonel Mike Peck. Hendon also had a new job, as an investigator for the Kerry Committee. He was hired by his friend Senator Bob Smith, the committee's vice chairman.

The committee was soon plagued by security leaks. Classified documents entrusted to the senators wound up in the hands of investigative journalists, notably syndicated columnist Jack Anderson. Angry committee members launched an internal investigation and ultimately fired Hendon.

Behind the scenes, Smith and Hendon maintained their alliance. Smith, who by now had embarked on a full-scale war against the DIA, enlisted Hendon to join him on yet another overseas trip pertaining to Bobby Garwood. This time Garwood would join the travel party.

It was Garwood's first return to his old adopted homeland. He hoped to use the trip to wipe away all lingering doubts about his credibility. He would accomplish this by leading Smith, Hendon, and a large press contingent to various places where, he claimed, he had seen POWs. As with the cistern episode, Garwood expected the public to believe that if he found certain landmarks he had described, he must have told the truth about POWs. The trip was timed to coincide with ABC's airing of the revisionist movie the Emr family made about Garwood.

A few days into the Vietnam trip, Garwood led the delegation to a spot on Thac Ba Lake in Yen Bai province, where he found two motellike structures where, he said, he had seen POWs in 1977.

To the uninitiated observer, the discovery made Garwood look good. He had described the buildings in a 1992 deposition. But Garwood couldn't have seen the buildings in 1977, because they were built after 1983.

The discovery at Thac Ba Lake was scheduled as part of a favorable story on Garwood to be aired on ABC's July 23, 1993, episode of 20/20. But on July 21, the day my third baby, Courtney, was due to be born, I learned that Hendon had made an advance trip to Thac Ba Lake, where he photographed the buildings Garwood would later find.

I described Hendon's photo trip in a story that appeared on the front page of the July 22 Washington Times. In that story, I quoted Senator Smith's aide Lisa Stocklan and Garwood's attorney, Vaughan Taylor, as saying Hendon did in fact take the photographs, but did not show them to Garwood. I also quoted Senator McCain as saying, "It should be thoroughly investigated, the role of Billy Hendon in this whole affair on Thac Ba Lake."

The Pentagon set out to do just that. I soon learned that investigators in Bangkok had obtained a sworn statement from a Vietnamese boatman, who said Hendon had paid him to find some buildings on Thac Ba Lake that Hendon could photograph. The statement was classified and would be sent to the Pentagon via cable from the Bangkok headquarters of the Joint Task Force–Full Accounting. A few weeks later, the document vanished. Without this crucial evidence, the investigation stalled.

Meanwhile, the *20/20* show canceled its piece on Garwood and scheduled new interviews to balance the story. But it seemed that Hendon once again had landed on his feet and was set to earn the accolade LeBoutillier had sought years earlier, as the acknowledged civilian expert on POWs. But in late July Hendon made a surprising move. He was known as a staunch opponent to any kind of normalization of relations between the United States and Vietnam; but now he wrote to President Clinton, asking him to lift the trade embargo on Vietnam "at the earliest possible moment."

In the eyes of most activists, Hendon had become a traitor. Family members considered the trade embargo to be an important lever in the search for MIAs. Hendon's proposal to lift the embargo sparked enormous dissent within the movement.

The Pentagon, too, was shocked by the proposal but had a completely different perspective. DIA analysts watched in amazement as the activists abandoned some of their government-bashing and instead focused on the Hendon crisis. The analysts also looked on as a disgusted Senator Smith slacked off on his war against the DIA to concentrate instead on distancing himself from Hendon. At the POW office, things grew relatively quiet. For a time the analysts were free to concentrate on solving genuine MIA cases without having their work interrupted by a constant stream of false reports.

Finally, something good had come from at least one of the Grey Flannel Rambos.

12

The Merry Prankster

Shortly after war broke out in the Persian Gulf, I received a call from longtime POW activist Ted Sampley. "Did you hear what happened to Wetzel?" he asked. "I mean, what *really* happened to Wetzel?"

Navy Lieutenant Robert Wetzel was an A-6 Intruder pilot shot down on the first day of the war. At the time of Sampley's call, the airman was listed as missing in action. According to Sampley, that designation was just a cover for the grisly truth: Wetzel had survived his shoot-down, only to parachute directly into a mob of angry Iraqis. Sampley said the anti-Semitic crowd had assumed from his nametag that Wetzel was Jewish. They had all happened to be carrying knives, so they had carved him up on the spot. Bits of Wetzel's body had been doled out as souvenirs.

"The Pentagon doesn't want anybody to know about this," Sampley confided. "But it's all right. I already told his family."

Wetzel eventually came home, alive and intact. Sampley later admitted he had never entirely believed the story but had told it anyway to publicize the plight of POWs.

Fortunately for Sampley, he did not wake up one morning to find himself surrounded by a crowd of angry Wetzels. In fact, over the course of his long career as an MIA rumormonger, Sampley has never received a thrashing either from the Wetzels or from any other family whose grief he has co-opted.

To Sampley's way of thinking, that is as it should be. He presents himself as somewhat culpable, but always forgivable; just a likable, bighearted oaf who sometimes gets carried away by the POW crusade.

A former Green Beret with multiple Bronze Star awards from Vietnam, Sampley has the outward appearance of the stereotypical downtrodden veteran outfitted by the local Army surplus store. But he is in fact a savvy businessman who is forthright about earning money off "the cause" and is a key figure in the MIA issue.

Unlike his colleagues who uncover POW "evidence" and solicit funds to embark on rescue missions, Sampley specializes in media manipulation and public relations. He has been invaluable to the activists, who rely on him to fan the flames of existing MIA stories, either through phone calls to legitimate journalists or on the pages of his own newspaper broadsheet, *U.S. Veteran News and Report*. In addition to his work in support of fellow activists, Sampley specializes in orchestrating stunts that are dramatic and at times dangerous.

In 1986, for example, when Sampley was in Washington, D.C., attending one of his many POW functions, he set up a publicity stunt that could have killed or seriously injured someone. Shortly before 2 A.M., bar closing time, Sampley and a few confederates erected a barrier at the top of a freeway on-ramp that handles traffic coming from Capitol Hill. They coated the ramp with oil, so that unsuspecting motorists would slither wildly before crashing into the barrier. The cars' headlights would illuminate a sign on the barrier that read "Free the POWs."

The next day I learned about the on-ramp trap from Sampley, who called to announce what he had done. He was proud of his effort but disappointed that the trick had not come off. While Sampley and friends had watched from a nearby hiding place, police officers had found and dismantled the arrangement before any cars ran into it.

When I told Sampley he had risked people's lives with the stunt, he accused me of being a spoilsport. He also said he was dismayed at missing the chance for newspaper coverage.

It was a rare lost opportunity. Over the next couple of years, Sampley would succeed in attracting considerable press coverage of antics designed for that specific purpose. His favorite trick was to chain himself and others—preferably attractive MIA daughters—to the gates of the White House and throw fake blood at police, onto the White House lawn, or at Secret Service agents.

On one occasion, Sampley placed bamboo cages containing live protestors on the front lawn of the house owned by Ronald Reagan's chief of staff Don Regan. The protestors were arrested. Another time, Sampley led a group to the home of former National Security Council head Frank Carlucci. In the midst of a major snowstorm, Sampley and his followers blocked Carlucci's driveway with 1,800 "care" packages addressed to POWs in Laos. On yet another occasion, Sampley orchestrated a "bounty hunt" for Ann Mills Griffiths and other leaders of the National League of Families. Hunters were challenged to hit their prey with cream pies, water balloons, and rotten tomatoes.

In 1988 Sampley—who at the time had no personal stake in the MIA issue—tried to turn one family's somber moment into a scandal that would help perpetuate the POW movement. Instead, Sampley's effort came across as a vulgar grab for center stage. The episode revolved around the case of a Navy pilot, Commander Edwin B. Tucker.

Tucker had been shot down over North Vietnam eleven years earlier. He was thought to have been captured and was listed as a

POW. He was later listed as killed in action. His remains were returned to the United States and were buried with full military honors in 1988 at Arlington National Cemetery.

Shortly after the funeral, Sampley called a press conference in Norfolk, Virginia, where Tucker's former aircraft carrier is based. Sampley announced that Tucker's body had been on display for fifteen years inside a glass case in Vietnam. Sampley said Tucker's family had been forced to pledge secrecy on the matter before being allowed to receive the remains.

In a scenario similar to the one he had created about Wetzel, Sampley said that Tucker had parachuted alive into a crowd of angry villagers, who had hacked at him with a hoe. "They carried him to a North Vietnamese hospital where he was put on an operating table and died," Sampley told reporters. The remains, along with Tucker's flight helmet, were then placed inside the glass case, Sampley said. "The Vietnamese public gawked at this display for fifteen years."

Sampley said that both the U.S. and Vietnamese governments had told Tucker's son he could have the remains only if he swore to keep the facts of the case secret.

It was an outrageous charge to make in a Navy town. Sampley had hoped to stir the anger of the tens of thousands of Navy families living in and around Norfolk. But the hoped-for public outcry did not take place, most likely because the dead pilot's son, Edwin B. Tucker, Jr., scoffed at Sampley's charge.

"There was no coercion, none of that whatsoever," the son said. He emphasized that there was "no agreement, secret or otherwise." He also questioned whether anyone would be foolish enough to place a body under glass and then allow it to decompose in public for fifteen years.

Over the next several years, Sampley continued to garner headlines with a variety of pranks and ill-founded press conferences.

In 1992 Sampley—now an official MIA family member through his marriage to the daughter of a man missing in Laos—finally organized a stunt that evolved into a national news story. He planned for a group of hecklers to disrupt President Bush's scheduled speech before the annual National League of Families assembly. League officials thought Sampley might try something at the convention and told the Secret Service not to let him gate-crash. As expected, Sampley tried to get in to see the president's speech. When he refused to leave, Sampley was arrested and charged with trespassing.

But the hecklers were already in place. Even with Sampley absent, they performed as scheduled. When Bush began his talk, Sampley's people drowned him out, yelling, "No more lies!" Bush asked the protestors to please let him finish. They yelled even louder. The exchange continued until Bush lost his cool and shouted, "Shut up and sit down!"

The quote made national headlines. It was a triumphant moment for the activists, who used the episode to trumpet their claim that Bush had nothing but disrespect for the families. Sampley jumped to claim credit, threatening more such outbursts if the president did not order the immediate release of all government documents pertaining to MIAs.

But if Sampley and his followers were pleased by the exchange, the National League of Families was highly embarrassed, and also very uneasy. The group's leaders were afraid that Bush would blame the entire organization for the disruption and that the episode might damage their relations with the government. The League took out newspaper ads apologizing to Bush.

While activists and family members were still abuzz over the confrontation, Sampley was already deep into his next project. It was his most scurrilous to date, a sustained campaign to label Senator John McCain an undercover agent of the KGB.

Sampley, who years earlier had defended Bobby Garwood's

actions as motivated by the need to survive, now accused McCain of being a weak-minded coward who had escaped death by collaborating with the enemy. Sampley claimed that McCain had first been compromised by the Vietnamese, then recruited by the Soviets.

To those who know McCain and are familiar with his behavior in captivity, the charge is ludicrous. McCain resisted his captors to such a degree that he was isolated in a special prison for troublemakers. He repeatedly refused special favors, including early release, and emerged as a spiritual and religious leader for other prisoners. Nonetheless, Sampley was persistent enough in his claims that the press in McCain's home state of Arizona picked up on the KGB story.

Sampley's antagonism toward McCain stems from the senator's failure to live up to Sampley's idea of how a former POW should embrace the MIA cause. In Sampley's estimation, McCain's personal experience should have caused him to champion the search for live POWs, the way it had Red McDaniel. Instead, McCain focused on the more neutral search for "truth," as well as on the prosecution of charlatans who took money from MIA families.

When McCain took the position that the United States should establish diplomatic relations with Vietnam in return for cooperation on the MIA issue, Sampley was outraged. He believed the United States should not have any dealings with its former enemy. Anyone who said otherwise—specifically, John McCain—was a traitor.

Sampley launched a private war on McCain. He searched into the senator's background, digging up old school records, military reports, and the like. Among his finds was an obscure clipping from a Cuban newspaper dated 1970. The article contained highlights of a Cuban psychiatrist's interview with POW McCain.

The interview itself contains nothing startling. The young

McCain boasts of his ability as a pilot, gives a message for his wife that he loves her and that she shouldn't worry about him, and talks about his father and grandfather, both Navy admirals. He says he had hoped to become both a test pilot and an astronaut.

Several times during the interview, the interpreter has trouble translating from English. McCain, who had been to the Spanish naval academy, supplies the words in Spanish.

Two decades after the fact, Sampley seized on McCain's use of Spanish as evidence that McCain had collaborated with the Cuban Communists. Sampley even called me at one point to promote his discovery as a news story. When I said there was no case, Sampley just laughed and changed the subject.

Sampley continued his research and eventually unearthed a 1973 interview in *U.S. News & World Report* in which McCain recounts his capture in Vietnam. In that article, McCain talks of landing in the middle of a lake and of being bludgeoned and bayoneted by an angry mob (the story was well known by the time Sampley found the article; perhaps it was the inspiration for his Wetzel and Tucker stories). McCain also talks about being beaten, tortured, and on the verge of death before finally agreeing to talk to his captors.

Amazingly, Sampley said that McCain's decision to talk to his guards meant McCain had Communist leanings.

Sampley thought he found further evidence of McCain's treason in the writings of Soviet defector Oleg Kalugin, a former KGB general. According to Sampley's interpretation of Kalugin's stories, a high-ranking Navy officer had agreed while imprisoned in Vietnam that he would work for the Soviets upon his return to the United States. Sampley said the Navy man was John McCain.

Sampley questioned everything about McCain, from childhood on, and began writing a lengthy article. Sampley framed the story in the context of McCain as undercover KGB agent furthering the cause of Communist Vietnam. Sampley likened McCain's case to that of the character portrayed by Laurence Harvey in *The Manchurian Candidate.* In that film, an American POW in the Korean War is brainwashed to do the bidding of his Communist captors. The prisoner is returned home, not knowing he is to be used as a political assassin. His actions will be triggered during a game of solitaire, when he turns up the queen of diamonds.

Sampley titled his article "Sen. John McCain: The Manchurian Candidate?" Sampley used the story as the lead piece for the December 18, 1992, issue of his broadsheet. He placed a photo of McCain on the cover, facing a large queen of diamonds.

To make sure his target saw the story, Sampley personally delivered several copies to McCain's Washington, D.C., office. Of course, the senator's staff had already seen the article.

Mark Salter, the senator's aide for POW/MIA affairs, was appalled that Sampley would come to the office. He ordered the activist to leave. Sampley said he had something he wanted to tell Salter, so the two went out into the hall. Salter followed as Sampley led him toward a stairwell. Salter asked what was going on.

Sampley wheeled and punched the aide. Salter fought back. The scuffle was broken up by Senate security guards.

When the dust had settled, Salter asked Sampley to sign a document agreeing to stay away from McCain and his staff. Sampley refused, so Salter took the activist to court for assault. Sampley was sentenced to two days in jail and was placed on probation for 180 days. He was also served with a restraining order prohibiting him from going near McCain or the people who worked for him.

After Sampley got out of jail, I asked him to explain what had happened. He said Salter had thrown the first punch, but he admitted to having gained the upper hand. He told me, blow for blow, what he had done to Salter.

"I worked him over pretty good," Sampley said. "I beat him up."

Even though he had spent time in jail, Sampley gave the distinct impression that he viewed the entire "Manchurian Senator" affair as a marvelous adventure.

He displayed a similar attitude toward a fight he instigated against Jan Scruggs of the Vietnam Veterans Memorial Fund. Scruggs is the man who came up with the idea to erect the Vietnam Veterans Memorial in Washington; he is now president of the fund that administers the memorial, a wall containing the names of service members killed in Vietnam. The wall has an accompanying statue, titled *The Three Servicemen*.

The trouble between Sampley and Scruggs began when Sampley acquired a public demonstration permit from the National Park Service that allowed vigils and other gatherings on federal land. Sampley set up what he said was a POW vigil booth along the walkway leading to the Vietnam Veterans Memorial. Its outward purpose was to hold an ongoing vigil for missing servicemen, but its location made it ideal for reaching a tailor-made market of service families, veterans, and other citizens paying respect to fallen warriors. Sampley stocked his vigil booth with POW paraphernalia, such as bumper stickers, badges, and flags, plus pamphlets, copies of his newspaper, and a bevy of T-shirts and other souvenirs bearing the likeness of *The Three Servicemen*.

Scruggs was offended that Sampley would turn the memorial into a self-serving commercial opportunity. Scruggs was even more disturbed that Sampley would market images of *The Three Servicemen*. The copyright to the statue is owned jointly by the Vietnam Veterans Memorial Fund and the sculptor, Frederick Hart. All income deriving from the statue's likeness belongs to the fund and the sculptor. The fund uses its portion of profits to help maintain the memorial. Hart donates his share to a nonprofit group that provides name rubbings and other services to Vietnam veterans and their families.

Hart contacted Sampley and asked that he stop selling the

T-shirts. Sampley refused. Hart and Scruggs then asked Sampley to do what other vendors had done: enter into a licensing agreement that would permit him to sell images of the statue. Again, Sampley said no.

Hart and Scruggs threatened litigation, saying they would not file suit if Sampley would enter into an agreement.

Sampley responded in the pages of *U.S. Veteran News and Report,* using the same tactics he had employed against McCain. He cast aspersions on both Hart and Scruggs, portraying them as greedy scam artists profiteering off the pain of the American people. Sampley targeted Hart in particular as a former antiwar protestor "who had been gassed in ugly confrontations with the police." Sampley did not mention that Hart kept no royalties for himself, instead printing that the sculptor had made a fortune off the statue. Sampley also recounted the original controversy surrounding the wall designed by Maya Lin (Sampley had been against the design and in 1982 wrote then–Interior Secretary James Watt protesting its funereal nature).

As for his own profiteering, Sampley took the high ground. He claimed that Homecoming II, which ran the vigil booth, was using the T-shirt proceeds to underwrite various POW-related projects.

Tom Burch, an attorney who is active in POW/MIA issues, told Hart and Scruggs he was willing to mediate with Sampley. Burch was a natural choice for dealing with Sampley. As chairman of the National Vietnam Veterans Coalition, Burch uses methods similar to Sampley's. In July 1993, for example, Burch called on activists to mail a brick or, preferably, a cinder block to the White House, in protest against President Clinton's "stonewalling" on POWs.

Notwithstanding his love for theatrics, Burch did not want to see his fellow veterans embroiled in public controversy. As one rabble-rouser to another, Burch did his best to convince Sampley to pay the licensing fee.

When Sampley again declined to cooperate, Hart and Scruggs filed suit. The court sided with the copyright holders.

Documents filed with the court revealed the extent to which Sampley had made use of the statue and, indeed, of the entire POW issue.

The material showed that he had created a self-contained financial network that revolved around POWs and MIAs. One of Sampley's companies, Red Hawk, manufactured the POW T-shirts and sold them to his nonprofit Homecoming II, which in turn sold them at the vigil booth. Although Sampley could say he was destitute, with only one personal bank account containing $100, the organizations were quite healthy. His reported earnings from the cash-only T-shirt concession amounted to nearly $2 million over three years.

The cash flow was abundant. In August 1991 alone, Homecoming II wrote ten checks to Red Hawk, totaling more than $18,000. Some of the checks were written on the same day or only a few days apart.

Despite the constant influx of money, Sampley did not pay the people who worked at the vigil booth. They were considered volunteers. Sampley also used them to compile data for his POW/MIA biography project and to fold copies of *U.S. Veteran News and Report*.

In return for their work, which continued in shifts around the clock, the volunteers got a place to sleep at the Homecoming II House in Annandale, Virginia.

I visited the house shortly before Christmas of 1992 and found a stark arrangement that worked entirely to Sampley's benefit. Residents explained that they had to buy their own food and personal goods, even though they worked full time for no pay.

Among the volunteers was Cheyenne Borton, an eighteen-year-old girl who was the only female in a houseful of middle-aged men. Cheyenne explained how Sampley had arranged the volunteers' sleeping quarters: "When the house is full, you just pick a place on the floor."

Despite its similarities to a nineteenth-century workhouse, the Homecoming II facility did not come under scrutiny in the course of the Hart/Scruggs lawsuit. The judge did not look into the financial dealings of the house, nor did he examine its relationship to Sampley's Red Hawk corporation. He merely looked at the concession stand sales figures and ordered Sampley to pay royalties in the amount of $359,442.92.

It was only a symbolic victory for Hart and Scruggs. Sampley said he wasn't going to pay and successfully resisted all attempts to collect on the judgment.

I asked Sampley how he had managed to avoid doing what the court had ordered. "I immediately put Red Hawk out of business," he said. "I sold everything they owned, and paid bills. I closed down Homecoming II. I heard that Scruggs was planning to levy the vigil site, so I gave it away. I put everything into another nonprofit group."

When sheriffs arrived to foreclose on Sampley, there was nothing to seize.

Sampley, who says he has spent more than a half-million dollars defending himself on the T-shirt charge, emerged energized by the conflict. When it seemed as if the fight with Scruggs had progressed as far as it would go, Sampley turned to new attention-grabbing projects and reverted to one of his stock-in-trade publicity stunts, the bamboo cage. In the fall of 1993 he erected a cage outside the Camp Lejeune Marine Corps base and arranged for three MIA wives to starve themselves inside. While in the cage, the women ingested varying combinations of water, juice, and vitamins, but none took any food. The fast was a protest against President Clinton's plan to lift the trade embargo against Vietnam.

When Sampley called to tell me about the cage, I asked how long the women could hold up. He responded with what sounded like concern. "I'm kind of worried about them," he said. "They're all over forty."

Still, Sampley fairly bubbled with excitement as he told me the cage had drawn many distinguished visitors, including U.S. marines and Ross Perot.

As insurance against the media missing a chance to speak to the starving women, Sampley had a phone line installed inside the cage. On the twelfth day of their fast, the women were taken to the hospital. Their ordeal had no impact on Clinton, who, on September 14, 1993, went ahead with his plan for a modified lifting of the trade embargo. He lifted it entirely in early 1994.

Despite Sampley's many ill-conceived escapades, he is not without his charm. Like Hendon and LeBoutillier, he has a special knack for establishing quick rapport. He is also well informed on the POW issue. Unlike the two ex-congressmen, however, he is funny and self-deprecating.

Sampley has used these attractive qualities to gain the attention he seems to crave from high-powered persons. He earned the good graces of Tracy Usry, for instance, who served for many years as an aide to Senator Jesse Helms. Through his contact with Usry, Sampley enjoyed a lengthy career as an expert witness to various legislative committees and panels. He was even invited to the White House to brief President Clinton on the topic of MIAs. Sampley told the new president that prisoners were still being held in Southeast Asia but did not discuss the one subject of his true expertise: chicanery in the guise of POW activism.

13

The Lao Resistance

It is obvious why John LeBoutillier, Billy Hendon, Bo Gritz, and others have focused their attentions on Laos. A large number of the men who remain missing disappeared in Laos, and only a handful of American POWs ever returned from there. It would seem logical for Laos to be the most fruitful area for POW leads—at least, that is how Hendon and the others have presented matters.

The truth is, Laos contains few possibilities as far as the hunt for MIAs is concerned, even for those who vanished there. The vast majority of men lost in Laos were pilots who disappeared along the North Vietnamese–controlled Ho Chi Minh Trail; they were either caught by the Vietnamese themselves or were handed over to them for transfer to North Vietnam.

Most prisoners not sent to Vietnam were killed outright. Others were tortured to death, starved, or were deliberately allowed to die of dysentery. In recent years, Laotian officials have acknowledged killing the Americans, saying they didn't realize at the time that it was important to keep them alive.

The few POWs actually held in Laos had a slim chance of surviving. Even their captors, rural natives accustomed to the sparse diet and cyclical outbreaks of disease, had to struggle; their life expectancy was only forty years.

Remote areas of Laos remain inhospitable, as American crash site investigators have learned. William Gadoury, who has regularly camped out at the excavations, found the conditions daunting, even with a medical doctor on hand to treat the first sign of illness.

"Sometimes, lying in my cot there at night," he told the Kerry Committee, "I wonder, if I didn't have the cot, if I didn't have the mosquito net, and the military rations and all the things that we have out there, how long could I last?"

At the end of the war, U.S. negotiators thought perhaps forty of the approximately three hundred men missing in Laos could have survived under such conditions. When the Vietnamese announced that only ten men would come back from Laos, the Americans set about finding ways to account for the others.

It was a slow and difficult process. The peace terms had been negotiated with Vietnam, not Laos; there was no binding agreement for Vientiane to reveal the fate of American MIAs. The Pentagon tried to solve what cases it could, by whatever means available.

The DIA thought it could make some progress with the help of Emmet Kay, a civilian pilot shot down over Laos in May 1973, after Operation Homecoming. He was held by the Pathet Lao, then released in September 1974. But Kay had little to offer toward resolving MIA cases. He said that he had not seen any other Americans in captivity and that the Pathet Lao had told him that all his countrymen had been released in 1973.

The DIA also thought there might be an opportunity to obtain more information in 1975, when the anti-Communist resistance grew in opposition to the new Pathet Lao government. Perhaps informants could be among the underground. But the resistance was not at all unified to the degree of its famed French namesake. The "Lao resistance" was an umbrella term describing roughly seven thousand Laotians affiliated with one of many fragmented groups that in truth posed no threat to the Lao People's Democratic Republic. It would be difficult, if not impossible, to establish, much less maintain, reliable contacts in the Lao underground.

Every now and then refugees came out of Thailand with information on MIAs in Laos, but the DIA had no way to follow up on the reports.

Thus the Pentagon remained woefully uninformed on the fate of most of the men missing in Laos until 1981, when the DIA hired a knowledgeable analyst named Soutchay Vongsavahn, a former Laotian general living in the United States.

Soutchay organized the hunt for MIAs in Laos as only an insider could do. He provided the DIA with maps depicting every known prison, detention site, and reeducation camp in the country. He also pored over the refugees' live sighting reports and produced answers for some of the outstanding cases.

With Soutchay's help, DIA learned that "American POWs" reportedly forced to work at the Ban Phon Tiou tin mines were actually legitimate French and Soviet employees. "Americans" in Savannakhet province were really Soviet mining engineers. A "POW" in Vientiane was an Australian journalist. "Prisoners" in Houa Phan province were Soviet medical workers. "Captives" on the Plain of Jars were American Mennonite missionaries working with Hmong tribesmen.

Finally, genuine progress was being made. But while Soutchay's unique knowledge was resolving many cases, the activists were promoting their sketchy suppositions about MIAs in Laos. Unaware that the term "Lao resistance" was something of a misnomer, the activists took it upon themselves to set up private-agent networks. The activists created the impression that they were the only ones aggressively trying to discover the truth in Laos, since they were the only ones clever enough to work with the Lao resistance.

MIA family members in particular have been vulnerable to the boast that the activists have gone in where the U.S. government could not or would not. But in virtually every case, the activists' "Lao resistance" has turned out to be one of two notoriously shady sources: former soldier Kambang Sibounheuang or members of the Nosavon family. Each is as unreliable and unscrupulous as the other.

The first to turn MIA charlatan was General Phoumi Nosavon, who served as deputy premier of Laos for a brief period in the 1960s, after he took part in a CIA-financed coup. The CIA eventually split with Phoumi, and the old general wound up in Bangkok, where he surrounded himself with the trappings of a commander in exile. He called his group the United Front of Lao People for the Liberation of Laos (UFLPLL).

Phoumi milked every American who came his way, holding out the promise of POWs in exchange for cash or matériel. He gave phony information to Mark Smith, Melvyn McIntire, and Jack Bailey, among others. He once took $10,000 from an Australian television network in exchange for a "Pathet Lao chemical round" that turned out to be conventional ordnance painted black. Phoumi even tricked Bo Gritz into paying twice for the rental of troops to be used during Gritz's failed Operation Lazarus.

When Phoumi died, his son Phoumano took over the UFLPLL. The younger Nosavon did little in the way of liberating Laos, but he continued the POW hijinks. Phoumano's best-known operation was one of the most celebrated and convoluted MIA scams ever perpetrated, and it involved Army Captain Donald Gene "Butch" Carr.

Carr and his pilot, Air Force Lieutenant Daniel Thomas, were on a secret mission on board a small OV-10A Bronco plane in July 1971. In the course of writing this book, I learned previously undisclosed details of that mission and the fate of Donald Carr. "Butch" Carr and Thomas were not looking for a North

Vietnamese presence in Laos, as previously thought, but had been assigned to extract troops who were on a secret mission for U.S. forces. Carr and Thomas were not flying alone, as was believed, but were accompanied by two helicopters from Nakhon Phanom Royal Thai Air Base in Thailand. When the flight arrived at the recon site, a heavy cloud cover prevented the Americans from seeing into the jungle below. Carr and his pilot found a hole in the clouds, dove through it, and were never heard from again. One of the men from the helicopter support flight, retired Lieutenant Colonel Jerry Gilbert, told me Carr's OV-10A had never activated the automatic beeper that would have been triggered by the air crew ejecting.

Gilbert also told me the accompanying helicopters had circled for about two hours, hoping the cloud cover would break up so they could see what had become of the Bronco. The helicopters had finally been forced to return to base before running out of fuel. Gilbert said the helicopter crews had believed the Bronco had been shot down and that Carr and Thomas were dead. Both men were later listed as missing in action and, much later, as Killed in Action/Body Not Recovered.

The Carr case took on elements of mystery as early as 1973, when a corporal from North Vietnam's 473rd Division defected at Quang Tri. The defecting corporal told U.S. officials that in July 1971 he had seen an Air Force lieutenant colonel who had been shot down while piloting an OV-10. The defector described the prisoner as having a thick mustache and beard. The DIA showed the defector photographs from the classified "Blue Book" depicting missing American servicemen. The defector selected two photos of Donald Carr.

The DIA was intrigued, even though in his Blue Book picture, Carr was clean-shaven. Other details, such as coloring and body size, were also wrong; yet the time and place of Carr's disappearance corresponded roughly to the information given by the defector.

Some analysts thought the sighting was genuine. Others believed the defector might have seen or heard about two POWs: a man in a lieutenant colonel's uniform, as well as Donald Carr. The question was, whom had the defector seen or heard about, and when? The sighting was already two years old when DIA took the report.

The debate was renewed in 1993, after DIA acquired an old photograph depicting two unidentified Americans being captured by enemy troops in Laos. The picture had been taken from the air, most likely by the crew of a helicopter sent to rescue the Americans. One of the men in the photo is wearing a pilot's jumpsuit and is standing; the other, in Army camouflage fatigues, is lying down with his head raised and appears to have a broken leg. The photograph was part of an album sold by a former U.S. serviceman, who said the picture had been circulating in his unit in Vietnam around July 1971, when Carr disappeared. Before Jerry Gilbert came forward with his revelations about Carr's last mission, some at the DIA thought the circumstantial evidence was strong enough to conclude that the man with the broken leg was Carr and that he must have been captured alive. Others did not think it was Carr. The matter was still being debated in 1994.

Whatever the fate of Donald Carr, his name and likeness somehow began circulating among the scam artists of Southeast Asia. Phoumano Nosavon learned all the relevant details and called Boston businessman Jay Sullivan. Since 1986 Sullivan and a partner had spent more than $700,000 looking for POWs; Phoumano was hoping to entice them to spend even more.

Phoumano gave Sullivan the most tantalizing news a POW hunter could hear, that he had a roll of pictures of a live American held captive in Laos. Phoumano said he had acquired the pictures while working with retired Air Force Lieutenant Colonel Jack Bailey as part of a Drug Enforcement Agency sting against a mysterious Laotian known only as "Mr. X." Sullivan asked to see the pictures.

Phoumano sent two photos, Sullivan told me. One was recent, depicting Carr with a banana leaf behind him. The other was much older, showing Carr at his wedding. Phoumano asked Sullivan to compare the two pictures, to determine whether the man with the banana leaf was Donald Carr.

Sullivan gave the pictures to a secret contact he knew from when he had worked at Electronic Data Systems, Ross Perot's old outfit. The contact agreed it was Carr.

Sullivan wanted to see what was on the rest of the banana leaf roll. The other pictures would lend a clue as to where the POW was being held, and by whom. In August 1991 Sullivan went to Thailand to get the rest of the pictures. Phoumano greeted him in Bangkok with the news that he was no longer working with Jack Bailey, who had only just obtained the negatives from the entire roll and was keeping them for himself. Sullivan was disappointed, but Phoumano perked him up with a fresh report on Donald Carr. Phoumano said he now knew Carr was being held by Laotian and Vietnamese military officers in a camp in northern Laos. Phoumano promised to put Sullivan into touch with the captors.

Phoumano directed Sullivan and an American partner to a hotel in Chiang Khong, an old smugglers' crossroads in northern Thailand. At Chiang Khong, Sullivan met several times with a group of Laotians who claimed to be holding Donald Carr at a remote camp in Phong Saly province, along the Vietnamese border. Sullivan gave the Laotians a small down payment for the release of Carr. Sullivan never heard from them again.

Sullivan spent the next several months flying back and forth between Boston and Bangkok, chasing further leads from Phoumano. Then the Pentagon learned that the Carr "banana leaf" photo was actually of Gunther Dietrich, a German bird smuggler. The picture had been taken at a Bangkok bird farm.

Phoumano now insisted that Dietrich was really a brainwashed Donald Carr. Sullivan continued trying to follow up on additional leads on other POWs held in secret border camps. Then, in March 1992, Sullivan came upon the Bangkok bird farm that was the site of the Dietrich/Carr photograph. Only then did he realize the whole thing was a scam.

"I almost cried," Sullivan told me. "It killed me, because I knew this was where the banana leaf picture was taken. That was a real heartbreak."

Phoumano has continued to peddle false information from his "resistance" headquarters in Thailand. The other self-styled resistance leader who also claims knowledge of POWs is based in the United States.

Kambang Sibounheuang first came to my attention in October 1989, when he called me at work to announce a "very big story." Kambang said he was a high-ranking leader of the Lao resistance and had information on American POWs. He wanted to meet right away, "to arrange for the information." A few years earlier, I might have dropped everything and gone to an appointed rendezvous spot, hoping for a scoop, as I had with Billy Hendon. But by now I had heard scores of similar offerings.

"Tell me more," I said.

"Live POWs. American. A very big story," Kambang answered.

"Who are they?"

"I cannot give you ID."

"Where are they being held?"

"I cannot say."

And so it went. I told Kambang it sounded like a very small nonstory and asked him to call again if he had anything of substance.

I fully expected to hear from Kambang again within a day or two, so I used that time to find out who he was. I learned he had played a key role in a case that had foreshadowed the popular photo cons that flourished around 1991.

Kambang had been an enlisted soldier in the Royal Lao Army; when he reached the United States in 1975, he gave himself a retroactive promotion to the rank of captain. He did indeed belong to a resistance group called the Neutralists, run by the exiled Laotian General Kong Le, the man Bo Gritz boasted of having ferried to Paris. Kambang's job in the United States was to help secure U.S. government support for the Neutralists.

Kambang waited ten years to approach the government for funds; even then, he did so in a roundabout way, and his pitch had little to do with the Neutralists.

In April 1985 Kambang called the DIA, saying he wanted to talk about POWs. At a meeting with the Laos/Cambodia desk officer, Warren Grey, Kambang outlined his upcoming plans to visit his family in Thailand. Kambang said that if the DIA gave him $4,000, he would spend part of his trip looking for POWs.

The DIA declined the offer but told Kambang the agency would welcome any POW evidence he happened to find. Kambang made careful note of what would constitute proper evidence: names, signatures, fingerprints, authenticator codes, and so on. He promised to call long distance from Thailand to report anything he found.

Since the agency was under intense scrutiny from all quarters, Grey realized that the encounter with Kambang, if not handled properly, could come back to haunt the DIA in some future investigation. In July 1985 the DIA sent Kambang a follow-up letter, saying the agency assumed that since it hadn't heard from him, he had not found any leads while visiting his family.

Kambang responded as if he had just been shaken from a daze. He wrote back, thanking the DIA for reminding him about the prisoners. He said that as a matter of fact he had learned about thirty-seven Americans held captive in Laos.

Kambang had few details on the POWs and rambled on about various Soviet advisers who had been killed by the resistance during recent months. Then he got to the bottom line: the Neutralists needed money, which Kambang would be pleased to accept on their behalf. The money would be used for bribes, guards, medicine, and other items. Kambang cautioned that he could not guarantee results: "American prisoners of war is not too many now, and very difficult to get the information and location because they moved them around 2 times a month, because they know we are looking for them now."

The DIA understandably did not respond to this second request for money, and Kambang did not write again either. He did not want to waste his time when he had other, more lucrative avenues to pursue.

Kambang was working in Tennessee at the time, as a security guard in Nashville. There he met Frank Lockhart, an electronics salesman who told Kambang he had a Ph.D. in psychology. The two became friends. Kambang regaled Lockhart with tales of his adventures with the Lao resistance, and Lockhart soon agreed to collaborate on a book about Kambang's exploits.

Meanwhile, Kambang was feeding other stories to two Bo Gritz cronies, Lance Trimmer and Gordon Wilson. Kambang told them of Americans being held captive in the center of Hanoi. He also said that prisoners were being kept in remote mountain caves in Laos and forced to work on American military equipment abandoned after the war. One of the POWs was named "Mr. Morgan." Kambang said Kong Le had more information in Paris.

Trimmer and Wilson wanted to mount a rescue. Not realizing that their own leader, Gritz, supposedly had an in with Kong Le, they pressed Kambang to ask the exiled general if they could visit him. Kong Le, who thought the men were U.S. government envoys empowered to work with the Neutralists, agreed to see them. Kambang demanded to accompany Trimmer and Wilson on the trip, so they bought him a plane ticket to Paris.

While in France, Kambang arranged to obtain a POW photograph to give to Trimmer and Wilson. Kambang did not actually receive the picture until he was back in the United States. By that time, Kong Le had concluded that Wilson and Trimmer were not U.S. agents and had severed contact with them. Kambang then decided he would give the picture to his friend Lockhart, who was still working on the book.

The photo depicts a Caucasian man wearing a pair of low-slung black pants, with no shirt. The man is looking down and is standing in what appears to be a shallow stream surrounded by thick vegetation. Kambang identified him as "Mr. Roly," an American in custody of the Pathet Lao. An excited Lockhart took the picture to Red McDaniel in Washington. McDaniel in turn showed it to the DIA, whose analysts instantly recognized it as a picture given to its Stony Beach team in Thailand by a source who said it was "Harold D. Stephenson."

The DIA had already determined that the photo was probably taken from a propaganda film and did not depict Stephenson or any other American MIA. But Lockhart, using an MIA list supplied by McDaniel, insisted the photo was of Air Force Lieutenant Colonel Charles S. Rowley, who had been shot down over Laos in 1970. Lockhart's identification was based solely on the fact that "Rowley" sounded like "Roly."

The DIA dutifully contacted Rowley's mother, who said the picture was not of her son. Rowley's brother, Walter, was also unequivocal: "No. No. By no stretch of the imagination could it be him." Expert photo analysts at the DIA, CIA, and FBI concurred that the man in the picture was not Charles Rowley.

Lockhart and Kambang, however, were not satisfied with the consensus of the DIA, CIA, FBI, and members of the Rowley family. They insisted "Roly" must be Rowley, because the two names sounded so much alike. Kambang tried to raise money to rescue Mr. Roly and even persuaded *Life* magazine to print the picture as part of a special issue on POWs. Kambang's efforts succeeded only in angering Kong Le, who expelled him from the Neutralists for exploiting the MIA issue. Kambang kept the firing to himself and instead claimed to be the successor to his "uncle," Kong Le. Kambang pressed on with the Mr. Roly picture. In 1993 he gave it to Dr. Charney to analyze as part of a renewed attempt to prove it was really Charles S. Rowley.

The Rowley business was on temporary hold, though, when Kambang first called me in 1989 with his "very big story" and told me he was a leader of the Lao resistance. By that time he was working for the Arlington, Virginia, police. He told his contacts he was a patrol officer, but he was really a clerk who sometimes performed meter maid duties. (Eventually he would lose his job after giving phony dog-tag information to his police superiors, but during my fleeting acquaintance with him, Kambang was still employed there.)

As I had expected, he followed up on the first phone call to say he had new information on POWs, from his "Uncle" Kong Le in Paris.

"How do I know I can trust your information?" I asked.

"I am very trustworthy!" he answered. "I am policeman for Arlington!"

I told Kambang I knew an Arlington police officer.

"Who's that?" he challenged.

"Jim Page." Jim and his wife, Dawn, were good friends.

Kambang hung up the phone. I never heard from him again.

I might have forgotten all about Kambang, if not for an odd coincidence a few days later. A *Washington Times* photographer, Brig Cabe, stopped me in the hallway to relate an interesting tale. Brig had just returned from an assignment at an American Legion

post in northern Virginia. One of the legionnaires, a World War
II veteran, had confided to Brig that he and others from the post
were preparing a secret mission into Laos. They were going to
rescue a number of POWs, including Morgan Donahue, a genuine
MIA whose name has been used in many POW schemes (including
one by Red McDaniel to raise $10,000). The veterans were work-
ing with a colonel in the Lao resistance. The colonel had approached the men after noticing POW bumper stickers on their
cars.

The resistance colonel had instructed the legionnaires to go
to Thailand posing as businessmen. Each was to supply $10,000
and take it to Thailand. They were to make their way to Nakhon
Ratchasima, where they would be met by local resistance agents.
The group would proceed to a cave at Boualapha and rescue two
heavily guarded Americans.

Brig was concerned about the legionnaires' health, if not
their lives; these were men in their sixties who were planning to
hack through the mountains and fend off active-duty troops a third
their age.

I told Brig about my recent encounter with the Lao resistance. Was there some connection?

Brig asked his new friends at the Legion to set him up with
the colonel from the Lao resistance. Brig told the legionnaires not
to say he was a journalist but to describe him only as "an interested
man of means."

The "colonel" turned out to be Kambang Sibounheuang. At
his first meeting with Brig, Kambang said the resistance desperately needed money. Brig gave him the clear impression he was
willing to help, as long as Kambang could produce POWs.

Kambang worked hard to establish himself as a friend in
Brig's eyes. He brought other Laotians to meet Brig and even
happily joined Brig's wife and children for a pizza feast. Still Brig
insisted on seeing proof of the POWs.

With Brig hovering over him, tape recorder in hand, Kambang called a contact in Thailand. The entire conversation was in Thai. I had the tape translated. The dialogue did not inspire trust.

"I need something on the Americans," Kambang began.

"Huh?"

"The prisoners. I need something on the American prisoners."

"Who?"

"Send me right away."

"What?"

The friend eventually realized what Kambang was talking about. The resulting conversation gave a glimpse of things to come. "I have received the cassette recording," Kambang said, still in Thai, "but the voice is that of a Lao, not an American. The Americans over here will know that the voice is not that of an American when they listen to the tape."

About a week later, Kambang passed on the tape anyway. It was from a man calling himself Morgan Donahue. As Kambang had realized, the "Donahue" on the tape is clearly not a native English speaker. His voice, inflection, and tone are those of a Lao who cannot even imitate English. He intones his sentences as if reciting a chant. Much of the message is nonsense. He is supposedly speaking from a remote cave in Laos, but in the background children are laughing and playing, and a helicopter is heard flying low overhead.

When Brig went to Bangkok on an assignment that had nothing to do with POWs, he arranged to meet Kambang's Laotian contacts, who supposedly had some glass slides imprinted with Morgan Donahue's fingerprints. The Laotians showed up as promised, with only a photocopied dog tag that did not even belong to Donahue, plus a piece of paper on which were written random English words.

"I told them this was not acceptable evidence," Brig recalls.

"I told them to go back to the cave and cut off Donahue's finger. I told them it was a small price to pay for the man's freedom, after all these years. It would prove beyond a doubt that it was Donahue."

The Laotians made a number of excuses why they couldn't get back to the cave right away to cut off the finger. They told Brig they needed money. He gave them about $160, took their pictures, and sent them on their way.

Back in the United States, Kambang's only explanation was that something funny was going on with his friends.

After that encounter, Kambang—perhaps unnerved by the request for a finger—abandoned his efforts to recruit Brig for a POW rescue. He returned to Tennessee, where he went to work as a bailiff for Nashville Judge Hamilton Gayden. Kambang made the most of his powerful new contact, enchanting him with stories of secret prison compounds and brave resistance agents. Within months, Gayden was hot on the trail of POWs. Kambang's best work was yet to come.

14

Akuna Jack and the Panic of '91

In the summer of 1991, my husband, Michael, and I took our daughter Erin to Hawaii to view the solar eclipse. We stopped over in Los Angeles on the trip back home to Virginia. I was dozing in the airport lounge, awaiting our next flight, when Michael handed me the front page of the *Los Angeles Times*. I woke up fast when I saw a picture of three portly middle-aged men standing near some trees. They were holding a strangely coded sign that appeared to be dated May 25, 1990. The men were described as American POWs.

Each man had been identified by one of three different families. The families swore the POWs were Air Force Colonel John Leighton Robertson, shot down over Vietnam in 1966; Air Force Major Albro Lynn Lundy, Jr., shot down over Laos in 1970; and Navy Lieutenant Larry James Stevens, shot down over Laos in 1969.

"My God," I thought. "After all this time, are these men still being held?"

Virtually overnight, the United States became mesmerized by that very question. Senator John Kerry, a Vietnam veteran, served as an informal national spokesman when he addressed the question on the *Nightline* show and proclaimed, "We have got to get answers."

The Robertson, Lundy, and Stevens families said they already had answers: all three men were alive in captivity. Albro L. Lundy III, who identified his father as the man in the middle of the three-POWs picture, appeared on network television, saying, "There's no doubt in anyone's mind that they are who they are." Deborah Robertson Bardsley, who said her father was the man on the left, told Cable News Network, "I'm convinced, because when this photo was first placed in my hands my [recognition] was so immediate and total and absolute." Deborah's sister Barbara, appearing on *Good Morning, America,* was equally certain: "I looked at that picture—I said, 'That's Daddy.' I did not have one moment of doubt."

They were thoroughly convincing. Even POW czar Ann Mills Griffiths, who is often disdainful of families' claims, was moved to announce that these families were credible.

The government mobilized. The Pentagon launched an urgent investigation of the photo and dispatched a fourteen-member fact-finding team to Hanoi. The FBI began to analyze the photo to determine where it had been taken and whether it was genuine. The State Department embarked on its own inquiry, asking the governments of Vietnam, Laos, and Cambodia for help. The State Department's Kenneth Quinn, who was on an official tour of Southeast Asia when the photo was first publicized, was ordered to make it a high priority when dealing with Indochinese officials.

Various self-styled experts came forward to decode the picture's sign, which bore the strange symbols "PHOTO LD.25.5.1990 NNTK! .K.B.C.19." A former Army infantry sergeant told *The Washington Times* that the "LD" portion signified a type of military map and that "NNTK" were coordinates that would reveal where Robertson, Lundy, and Stevens were being held. Another former infantryman said that "NNTK" corresponded to Morse code for "attention anyone" and that "PHOTO" was a clue that the men were imprisoned in the village of Phu To, west of Hanoi. A former cryptographer said the letters meant the POWs were about to be killed; and an anonymous Pentagon official said the symbols stood for the South Vietnamese version of the Navy's Sea Air Land (SEAL) commandos, and that the picture had been taken on the Cambodian border in 1970.

Excitement continued to mount. Massive enlargements of the "Three Amigos" picture appeared on roadside billboards throughout the United States. Morning talk shows were dominated by discussions about POWs. Newspapers began printing special reports on the MIA issue.

Then, just a few days after the Robertson/Lundy/Stevens photo first appeared in print, the *Today* show broadcast a snapshot of a balding, tan-complexioned man relaxing in a wooded setting. Two MIA parents, Dan and Betty Borah, declared that the man was their son, Navy Lieutenant Daniel Vernor [sic] Borah, who had been shot down over Vietnam in 1972.

The nation, still in a state of shock over the "Three Amigos" picture, was stunned. Here was another live prisoner. The media demanded a statement from the Pentagon. The DIA gave a meager, unsatisfying response, saying only that it had not been able to get a copy of this latest picture.

The press turned up the heat. *Newsweek* devoted its July 29, 1991, issue to examining "The MIA Mystery," with an emphasis on the Robertson, Lundy, Stevens, and Borah cases. Major Lundy's wife, Johanna, appeared on the cover, holding the by-now-famous "Three Amigos" photo.

Journalists scrambled to outdo one another on what had rapidly become the biggest ongoing story of the day. Privately, some believed they were on their way toward earning a Pulitzer Prize.

During the final week in July, with POWs a topic of nightly

newscasts and daily newspaper reports, there came a revelation so shocking as to eclipse the attention focused on Robertson, Lundy, Stevens, and Borah. Retired Air Force Lieutenant Colonel Jack Bailey, a professional POW hunter, announced that he had found a live prisoner currently held in Laos. Bailey said he had dispatched a Laotian agent into the jungle to photograph the prisoner. The resulting picture had been declared genuine by the man's family and by the noted anthropologist Dr. Michael Charney. Bailey displayed the recent POW photo alongside a 1965 snapshot of the missing man. The two pictures bore a striking resemblance to each other.

Bailey said he had supplied the blue polo shirt, watch, and sandals worn by the man in this new POW picture. Bailey said he had given the items to the Laotian agent. "I told him that if he found any POWs [to] have them put that stuff on so I'd know it was taken on the trip," Bailey said. Bailey also said he had given the agent a camera and specially marked film.

The announcement was nothing less than explosive. Whereas the "Three Amigos" and Borah pictures had come through mysterious channels and with little explanation of their origins, Bailey's photo had a clear history. This was the first time since Operation Homecoming that a POW had been proven to be alive at a certain time and in a specific place. The impact was so great that Bailey's picture lent additional authenticity to the other POW photos.

In response to Bailey's remarkable news, *The Wall Street Journal* commissioned a poll, which found that 70 percent of the American public believed that POWs were being held against their will in Southeast Asia. Of that number, 75 percent believed the U.S. government was not doing what was required to gain the prisoners' release.

Additional unidentified POW pictures continued to surface. Less than a week after Bailey's revelation, Senator Bob Smith declared that the Senate must take action. Smith introduced a resolution to create a Select Committee on POW/MIA Affairs. He said the committee should investigate matters pertaining to the government's handling of the MIA issue over the previous twenty years. The Senate approved Smith's resolution. By October 1991 the Senate had selected ten members for the committee. John Kerry would be chairman, and Smith would be vice chairman. The "Kerry Committee" went to work.

Meanwhile, the truth emerged about the "Three Amigos" photo. It turned out that the picture was the work of Cambodian con artists—low-level government officials who routinely devised POW scams. The hoaxsters had access to an old copy of the U.S. government's "Blue Book," a once tightly guarded publication containing pictures of American MIAs. The con artists had used the Blue Book as a reference while scouring foreign magazines for pictures they could pass off as POWs.

The "Three Amigos" picture had originally come from a 1923 edition of *Soviet Life* magazine. The men in the photo were actually three farmers showing off after a harvest. The Cambodian con artists had copied the photo from the magazine and tampered with one portion so that a large banner became a coded sign.

The con had been perpetrated via two channels, both of which involved members of the Grey Flannel Rambos. First, the Cambodians had told the U.S. government they had information on Robertson, Lundy, and Stevens. The DIA, which had received many fake letters and tapes allegedly from the three airmen, had determined that the Cambodians' information could not be verified and filed it away as a dubious "live sighting" report. But the DIA's self-destructing POW/MIA boss, Colonel Mike Peck, had given a copy of the report to Colonel Robertson's daughter Shelby Robertson Quast. Peck had told Mrs. Quast how to get in touch with the Cambodians who had made the report. With the help of

Billy Hendon, Mrs. Quast had obtained a copy of the "Three Amigos" photo and embarked on a trip to Cambodia in a futile attempt to purchase her father's freedom.

Meanwhile, the Cambodian hoaxsters had got word to another Grey Flannel Rambo, Red McDaniel, that they would trade Robertson, Lundy, and Stevens for the $2.4 million advertised on Hendon's reward balloons. McDaniel had tried to drum up interest in the photo on Capitol Hill, telling lawmakers they could view the POWs, with no obligation to buy, for only $500.

When no one in Congress had shown interest in the "Three Amigos" picture, McDaniel, acting with the permission of the Robertson, Lundy, and Stevens families, had released it to the press.

The truth also came out about the "Borah" photo. The man in the picture was a seventy-seven-year-old hill tribesman named Ahroe, who lived in the village of Muang Nong, Laos. He was half French, half Laotian. The picture was part of a roll photographed by a Laotian refugee who had given copies to another refugee, who had sent them to his cousin in America, Kambang Sibounheuang.

Kambang had shown the pictures to his new boss in Nashville, Judge Hamilton Gayden. Kambang and Gayden say they had tried for months to learn the identity of the man in their new pictures. Finally, Gayden had found a likely match in the same issue of *Life* magazine that contained the "Mr. Roly" photo. Gayden had thought the new POW photos depicted Daniel V. Borah, who was known to have been captured after being shot down over Vietnam in 1972.

As Gayden later told me, he and Kambang had deliberately withheld the photos from the DIA, so the agency wouldn't "slam-dunk" the identification. Instead, Gayden had contacted the Borah family, who had verified that the pictures were of their son. The family had then called in Senator Smith for guidance. The DIA had learned about the photos and asked Smith for copies. Smith had inexplicably refused and had then appeared with Mr. Borah and one of the pictures on the *Today* show. While on the show, Smith had accused the DIA of trying to suppress the photo.

Despite the revelations that the POW pictures were fake, the Robertson, Lundy, Stevens, and Borah families continued to believe that the photos depicted their missing men. The families believed that the U.S. government was lying about the pictures' origins. Members of the Borah family even went to Laos to meet with Ahroe, who confirmed that he was the man in the picture. Ahroe allowed himself to be fingerprinted and photographed to prove he was not a brainwashed Daniel Borah. The family still believed their man was in the POW snapshot.

The families' claims notwithstanding, the press and public reluctantly accepted that the "Three Amigos" and "Borah" pictures were hoaxes. Other pictures that had also surfaced as portraying unnamed POWs were also proved false. Of all the POW pictures that came out in the summer of 1991, only one—the photo released by Jack Bailey—was now known to be genuine.

Or so the public thought. To the DIA, it was a different story. The agency knew there was something seriously wrong with this "surefire" POW picture—and that something was the involvement of Bailey.

Over the years, the DIA had dealt with Bailey numerous times, and those dealings had been both frustrating and fruitless. There was a regular pattern with Bailey: dramatic MIA-related claims that fizzled out when the DIA tried to follow up on them.

The analysts believed Bailey was a fraud. They called him "Akuna Jack" after his old smuggling boat, the *Akuna,* and viewed him as a man who had earned more than $3.2 million hoodwinking the public about himself, his work, and POWs.

Bailey's most basic lies have been about himself. In publicity leaflets, he claims to be an American legend on a par with "Lucky" Lindbergh and the *Mercury 7* astronauts. He says he is "one of the highest-decorated American fighting men of any war," whose medals include the Silver Star, one of the nation's highest awards for gallantry in action. He says he was a test pilot with Chuck Yeager; a combat pilot in the Korean War; and a fighter pilot in Vietnam flying 256 missions during two tours. Bailey also says he retired as the commander of Langley Air Force Base in Virginia, the headquarters of the U.S. Tactical Air Command. He portrays himself as a dedicated humanitarian who, when not engaged in combat, has found time to establish orphanages in Korea, Vietnam, Nicaragua, and Honduras.

None of the claims is true. Bailey's service record is good, but not in the sense he claims. He was never a test pilot, nor was he even stationed in Korea during the war. He was a safety officer during his one tour in Vietnam, with neither the mandate nor the time to fly 256 combat missions. He has a perfectly respectable but unremarkable collection of military decorations. There is no Silver Star. He was not the commander at Langley. He didn't establish any orphanages, although he helped out at a few, at his commander's request.

Amid the distortions, it is possible to trace with some degree of accuracy Bailey's involvement with POWs. After retiring from the Air Force in 1969, Bailey worked at a series of jobs that eventually led him back to Southeast Asia. He acquired a rusted old smuggling ship, the *Akuna III*. The boat was to be used for Bailey's nonprofit organization, Operation Rescue.

In fund-raising letters, Bailey said his unarmed *Akuna III* would deter pirate attacks on boat people fleeing communism in a 700,000-square-mile area of the South China Sea. Although maritime law mandates that Bailey would have had to physically rescue any refugees he found floating on the open sea, he said he could not legally take them on and could only give them food and medicine. For this, he said, he needed a minimum of $18,000 per month.

The fund-raising letters told horrifying stories of young girls being passed from pirate to pirate, continuously raped, sometimes in front of their own families. The girls were either sold into slavery or murdered. Other fund-raising appeals told of refugees starving to death or being trapped alive inside sinking ships. One letter had a photograph of one of these sinking death ships; Bailey's crew apparently did not rescue the victims but instead took pictures of the disaster in progress.

Bailey began telling U.S. authorities about live POW sightings passed on to him by the boat people. The DIA was immediately suspicious. Most of the boat people came from the old IV Corps area of Vietnam, which had the lowest concentration of U.S. personnel during the war. Bailey's live sighting reports were vastly out of proportion to anything that had been received previously.

In 1982 Bailey took some observers along on a rescue mission so they could publicize his work. The guests included Bob Brown, Jim Coyne, and Tom Reisinger, all from *Soldier of Fortune;* plus Richard Woodley, on assignment from *People* magazine. The trip was a disaster. The ship broke down at sea, and a flustered Bailey threatened to throw one of the guests overboard. The resulting story in *People* portrayed Bailey as a well-intentioned, yet bumbling, Don Quixote. It would have embarrassed most men in Bailey's position into going out of business, or at least toning down their claims. Instead, Bailey stepped up his POW activity. He switched from reporting secondhand live sightings to turning in what he said were genuine POW bones. He produced several sets of remains, all of which were fake. One of his dramatic presentations, to the U.S. embassy in Bangkok, turned out to be a combination of pig bones and human remains from persons no taller than five feet. He had identified them as belonging to specific servicemen who were not even missing.

Another of his finds turned out to be the remains of an Asian woman. After learning that he hadn't solved an MIA case with these bones, Bailey kept them anyway, wrapped in an American flag, and used them to dramatize fund-raising speeches.

Bailey told the press about each new set of bones he produced, always saying the remains had come from Laos. From Bailey's standpoint, the claims merely reflected popular activist sentiment, that the key to the MIA mystery lay in Laos. To the Laotians, who read of Bailey's exploits in the press, the claims were outrageous. Laotian officials held the U.S. government responsible for Bailey's actions. Vientiane warned that if Bailey persisted, Laos would cancel the carefully negotiated joint excavation of the crash site at Pakse and future joint excavations would be jeopardized.

Washington tried to rein Bailey in. An official from the Pentagon's office of International Security Affairs, where Billy Hendon briefly worked, wrote Bailey a letter of reprimand. The official, James Kelly, explained that Bailey was interfering with international relations, contaminating crash sites, and upsetting MIA families by falsely identifying remains. Kelly asked him to stop looking for bones in Laos.

Bailey ignored the request. He then sent out new handwritten letters describing his adventures in Laos. One such letter told of his trudging through the jungle in search of POWs, stopping only to deliver babies in remote villages.

The Laotian government did not seem to notice these new letters, and the Pakse project went on as scheduled. The U.S. government made no further complaints about Bailey interfering in international relations. In 1985 alone, the year of the Pakse crash site excavation, Bailey reaped nearly half a million dollars in donations.

Bailey became one of the most visible figures on the MIA scene. He increased his involvement with MIA families and friends. None of the hunts produced a POW or remains, and one former prisoner, Dieter Dengler, wrote to the National League of Families, complaining that Bailey had improperly used his name and likeness for a fund-raising drive.

But neither Dengler nor the League could prevent Bailey from going about his business. He sent POW reports to MIA families, in care of Senators Bob Dole and Nancy Kassebaum. He gave twelve worthless pictures to one of the DIA's Stony Beach officers at a meeting in Bangkok. He courted his favorite journalists and fattened his album of glowing press reports.

In 1989 Bailey's local newspaper, *The Orange County* (California) *Register,* ran a story on Bailey, portraying him in heroic terms. Among those impressed by the article was a Los Angeles–based private investigator, Nicholas Cain. Cain is also an action/adventure novelist and Oriental-goods retailer, and his wholesale supplier had only recently claimed to have information on POWs. Cain was unsure how to proceed and called Bailey for help. The supplier's story turned out to be a hoax, but Bailey seemed unconcerned. He shrugged off the incident and then took Cain into his confidence.

Bailey showed Cain a mysterious photo of an American POW crouching in front of a banana leaf. Bailey said the man was Army Captain Donald Gene Carr, a Special Forces officer missing in Laos.

Bailey said he was not yet ready to pursue the photo and asked Cain to join him in Thailand to make a documentary about Asian gangs.

Once in Thailand, Bailey took Cain to a country estate owned by his Thai girlfriend, Candy. The estate contained some wilderness area, and Cain remarked that the property reminded him of Vietnam.

"Jack kind of looked at me and said, 'Yeah, it's almost like a POW camp,' " Cain told me. "And then he sort of snickered. It took me aback, but then I thought, 'Naw, he wouldn't do a scam.' "

Cain soon changed his mind.

"Jack got out this old camera and said we could work on a POW video. He had me do a stand-up saying we were on the border between Vietnam and Laos." Bailey asked Cain to say they were near a secret POW camp. Cain refused. The two had an argument, with Cain accusing Bailey of fraud. The next morning, Cain returned to Los Angeles.

Back in the United States, Cain said nothing about the POW film. He assumed that Bailey had given up on it and had chosen to stay in Thailand with Candy. Over the next two years, Cain gradually forgot about "Akuna Jack."

Bailey remained active, though, and eventually got out his old banana leaf "POW" picture and decided to look up the Carr family. It was almost an act of whimsy on Bailey's part, but it had an impact on the Carr family like nothing had since Don Carr disappeared. Matthew Carr, Don's half brother, struggled to maintain composure when he recounted receiving a faxed photocopy of the banana leaf shot: "The moment I saw it, I knew it was Butch." Don Carr's son, Don Jr., was desperate to know if this was really the father he hadn't seen since he was five. Don Jr. begged his mother, Carol Collins, to help with the investigation. Carol found an old picture from her 1965 marriage to Don and relinquished it to Dr. Charney so he could compare it against the banana leaf picture.

Bailey was still working on the Carr case when Red McDaniel released the Robertson/Lundy/Stevens "Three Amigos" photo. Bailey knew that McDaniel also had a copy of the banana leaf picture and was afraid McDaniel would release that as well. Bailey did not want to be upstaged by McDaniel and decided to beat his rival into print.

That was when Bailey went public with his explosive POW story, saying he had found Donald Carr.

Among those startled to read about Donald Carr was Jay Sullivan, the Boston businessman who had obtained a copy of the banana leaf picture from Phoumano Nosavon. More startled still was Nick Cain, who recognized the photo as the one he had seen in 1989, long before Bailey was now saying the Carr pictures had been taken.

Cain tried to stop Bailey from going any further with the story. He wrote to the National League of Families, the DIA, and Senator John Kerry, informing them that the Carr story was a fraud. Cain realized that Bailey had already gained much ground with his claim about providing the watch and shirt in the banana leaf picture, so he proposed a sting to catch Bailey committing a new POW-related fraud. Cain offered to reestablish contact with Bailey and help set a trap. The project never got under way. Someone, most likely an employee at the National League of Families, sent Bailey a copy of the sting proposal. Bailey cut off all contact with Cain.

Bailey surely knew that Cain's revelations would eventually catch up with him, but he continued the Carr scam anyway, unwittingly abetted by a new ally, Judge Norman Turner of Riverside, California. Turner was among those who joined the families before the press in the summer of 1991, insisting the MIAs were still alive. Turner vouched for Bailey's character, harking back to the days when the two had been fighter pilots together in Vietnam.

But Turner had been fooled by Bailey. The two had met at a southern California cocktail party, and Bailey had talked Turner into thinking they had served together in the war. They had not. Bailey had used a number of tricks to deepen Turner's trust in him. The most influential was the phony Silver Star; Turner had a genuine Silver Star from Vietnam, and he knew what it meant to earn one.

During the course of the 1991 POW outcry, Turner grew increasingly disturbed by Bailey's behavior. At one point, Bailey told Turner that he wanted to announce that a live POW would be coming home within thirty days.

I asked Turner why he, an intelligent and moral person, had stayed with Bailey after that. "I was bothered by that and other things," Turner told me. "Jack had given me four different versions of how he got the Carr photo. But every time I decided I couldn't believe Bailey, I went back to those pictures. I really believed we were onto something. I believed it was Donald Carr."

Inevitably, Turner came into contact with Carr's former wife, Carol Collins, who had been unable to function since hearing that Don might still be alive. Carol had divorced Don Carr during one of his tours in Vietnam. She had remarried, been widowed, and wound up as Don's legal next of kin when that right was assigned to her by Don Jr. Ever since Don Sr.'s disappearance, Carol had been wracked with guilt over the divorce. She still loved him deeply.

Carol accompanied Bailey and Turner to Bangkok, where they met with Phoumano Nosavon, who said he was raising an army to rescue POWs. Phoumano and Bailey rattled off wild plans to save the prisoners but were unable to accomplish the most preliminary steps.

Meanwhile, after analyzing a stream of letters from Cain, the DIA was certain Bailey had lied about the Carr photo. When the DIA found the photo's model, Gunther Dietrich, ABC News sent two investigators to Bangkok to do a story on the Carr case.

One of the ABC investigators, reporter Jimmy Walker, told me that Bailey had at first been cooperative and full of "tips." In the course of one of many network-supplied meals, Bailey had told the news team that POWs were being held in Burma. He had confided that he knew this because he was actually a general in the Burmese rebel forces. He had spun other tales, as well: that staggering numbers of Americans were being held in a camp in Laos and that the Pathet Lao had just killed one sixty-year-old POW. He had also said he hoped to rescue Donald Carr within two or three weeks.

Bailey had eventually ran out of "tips" and had gone on camera for an interview on the Carr case. Walker confronted him with the truth about Gunther Dietrich. Bailey punched him.

When the episode was aired in the United States, Senator John McCain asked the Justice Department to investigate POW fraud, particularly as perpetrated by Jack Bailey. Both the FBI and a federal grand jury began to pursue indictments (they would eventually spend two years on their investigations, without making any arrests).

Bailey responded that McCain was part of a government conspiracy to hide the truth about POWs. Bailey suggested that Gunther was part of the plot and that he was in fact a brainwashed Donald Carr.

Bailey's speculation outraged Carol Collins, but it also made her wonder if the charge might be true. "I had been jerked around so much by Jack Bailey, I decided to go see Gunther for myself," she told me.

Carol teamed up with Judge Turner, flew to Germany, and found Dietrich awaiting trial on a bird-smuggling charge.

"I knew the minute he opened the door it wasn't Don," Carol told me. "I also knew it was the man in the pictures. My heart just went into my shoes. I knew we'd all been had."

Turner photographed Dietrich from many angles and even had Dietrich pull up a pants leg to expose his knee. Donald Carr's scar from an old football injury was conspicuously absent. The eye color was also wrong. So were Dietrich's height, weight, and bone size.

Dietrich told the Americans that he was the man in the photos. He remembered when they had been taken, several years previously. The shirt, watch, and sandals were his own. No one had given them to him.

Back in the United States, Carol told the Carr family what she had found. She encountered a curious reaction. Some in the family thought Gunther really was a brainwashed Donald. Marie Barzen, Donald's former stepmother, told me that Carol had been fooled by Gunther. "She was going by things that could have been altered—eye color, scars, body size," Marie said.

Dr. Charney examined Turner's pictures of Dietrich and concurred with Carol. The man in the banana leaf photo was really Gunther Dietrich. Still, some in the family continued to believe the brainwashing story.

Bailey's associate Larry Stark, a former civilian POW who is vice president of Operation Rescue, gave the amazing explanation that it didn't actually matter if Carr were in the picture. "Even if it is Gunther, why discredit the picture?" Stark asked me. Completely ignoring Bailey's involvement in the Carr fraud, Stark said the photo had been staged by the DIA as part of a conspiracy to debunk the POW issue. "The government knows Carr is alive," Stark told me. "The DIA built a story around Carr so they could discredit the story, and Bailey, and write off Carr."

As for Bailey, he reacted to being exposed and investigated in much the same way he responded to the story in *People*. He remained completely unchastened. Even with FBI agents working full-time to put him in jail for fraud, Bailey latched onto another phony POW photo and organized one more overseas adventure. He summoned Norm Turner to meet him in Thailand, swearing he had stumbled upon a genuine photo of Navy Lieutenant Larry James Stevens (one of the "Three Amigos"), this time alone in captivity.*

---

*Kambang told the DIA that he, too, had knowledge of Stevens. The Pentagon flew Kambang to Thailand and polygraphed his source, who showed deception in all his responses.

Turner, who reminded himself that the boy who cried wolf had once really seen a wolf, was taken in by Bailey's pleading. Turner boarded a jet for Bangkok, anxious to see the Stevens picture. "It turned out to be crap," Turner told me. "We had a shouting match and I left." After his long association with Bailey, during which he had spent about $10,000 looking for Donald Carr, Turner had finally seen enough. "I'm disgusted with him," Turner told me. "I don't want anything more to do with him."

Carol Collins and Don Carr, Jr., agree. Neither will ever allow Jack Bailey into their lives again.

Sadly, their lessons came too late. Even if Carol, Don Jr., Norm Turner, Nick Cain, and the FBI are all wise to Bailey and the other POW frauds, the American public is not. Even with the "Three Amigos" and "Borah" photos discredited and Bailey exposed as a charlatan, the public will forget the various details and will remember only that there came a time, in the summer of 1991, when it became abundantly clear that POWs were alive in captivity in Southeast Asia.

Epilogue

The Kerry Committee spent more than a year examining every conceivable aspect of the MIA issue. The senators delved into matters surrounding MIA accounting; methods of gathering intelligence; the Paris Peace Accords; Operation Homecoming; the DIA's POW/MIA office; the actions and policies of Presidents Nixon, Ford, Carter, and Reagan; and much more. In the process, committee members conducted more than one thousand interviews and took more than two hundred sworn depositions from witnesses ranging from Kambang Sibounheuang and Bo Gritz to Richard Nixon and Henry Kissinger. The senators held more than two hundred hours of public hearings, which were telecast on C-SPAN and frequently reported on by the press. Committee investigators pored over tens of thousands of documents and even gained access to highly secret intelligence reports. The panel sent one investigator to work full-time seeking information in Moscow and dispatched several delegations to Russia, North Korea, and Southeast Asia.

In the end, the Kerry Committee concluded that men had not been knowingly abandoned in Southeast Asia; that there was no U.S. government conspiracy to cover up evidence of live prisoners; and that the answers to the MIA mystery could be provided only by Hanoi.

And yet the Kerry Committee did not so much lay questions to rest as provide a springboard for continued chicanery.

One of the most prolific activists has been the committee's own vice chairman, Senator Bob Smith. Nearly a year after the panel completed its work, Smith was still deeply embroiled in the POW affair. Among other things, he tried to prosecute his enemies, whom he made the targets of what he dubbed "Operation Clean Sweep." The operation was designed to prompt a government investigation of officials responsible for the "mind-set to debunk." Those targeted by "Operation Clean Sweep" included DIA Director James Clapper and Soutchay Vongsavahn, who had done so much to solve MIA cases from Laos. Smith wanted Defense Secretary Les Aspin to launch the investigation, but Aspin sensibly declined.

Smith has continued the manipulative tradition established years earlier by Billy Hendon. In October 1993 Smith told the DIA an unlikely story about a Pathet Lao defector who somehow had intimate knowledge of POWs on a remote island off South Vietnam. Smith gave differing versions of the Laotian defector's story, saying there had been one hundred, and then six hundred, POWs lined up for execution on the island in either 1981 or 1982. Smith insisted that the American embassy in Australia had known about the executions soon after they took place. Smith demanded that the DIA release the embassy's report on the incident. No such report existed, but the bureaucrats at the DIA scrambled to satisfy Smith's request.

Smith has also persisted with stories about pilot distress symbols trampled in the grasses of Southeast Asia. Smith says he has satellite photographs of the symbols, which were part of the escape-and-evasion training given to pilots. Smith's claims are in part based on fact. In the event of shoot-down, a pilot was supposed to trample certain symbols, such as a modified letter K, into the grass to indicate he was alive, in captivity, or injured. But dozens of former fighter pilots, including my father-in-law, have told me they only vaguely remember having been taught a brief class on locator codes and doubt they would have been able to use them properly, if at all. It is significant that during the course of the war, not a single pilot was ever rescued as a result of a locator symbol. Expert analysts have repeatedly said that Smith's distress signal photos show only naturally occurring topographical features. One genuine symbol turned out to have been carved by a Laotian farmboy, who said he had done it for aesthetic reasons.

A newcomer to the POW issue, Fred Kirkpatrick, has continued in the tradition of Jack Bailey. An American citizen who lives in Ho Chi Minh City, Kirkpatrick presents himself overseas as a United States senator. He has tried to secure work from Vietnam as an emissary to the United States in various fields, including POW/MIA affairs. In 1993 Kirkpatrick told MIA daughter Deborah Robertson Bardsley he could lead her to her father, who was supposedly one of the men in the "Three Amigos" photo. Deborah went to Vietnam, accompanied by a camera crew from the Discovery Channel. The ensuing documentary clearly shows Kirkpatrick repeatedly promising to produce the missing Robertson, then telling a deflated Deborah the plans have fallen through. After the program aired, Kirkpatrick insisted he hadn't given Deborah any false information.

Other longtime activists have also been hard at work. Mike Van Atta organized a spirited rally outside the New Jersey home of former President Nixon. Ted Sampley reprised the old Smith and McIntire tactic and filed a lawsuit against President Clinton, Commerce Secretary Ron Brown, and Senator John Kerry. Sampley charged that the men had deceived the American public about

POWs. He also accused Kerry of covering up evidence of live POWs so that the senator's cousin could set up a business deal in Vietnam.

In the spring of 1993, a dramatic discovery seemed poised to revive the excitement of two years earlier. Harvard researcher Stephen J. Morris announced that he had unearthed an old Soviet document proving that about seven hundred American POWs had been left behind in Vietnam. Morris had found the document in Moscow, in Soviet Communist Party archives. It was purportedly the transcript of a 1972 speech by Vietnamese Army Lieutenant General Tran Van Quang before the North Vietnamese Politburo. In the speech, Quang said that Hanoi had held 1,205 POWs at a time when it admitted holding only 368.

When Morris announced his discovery, he did not use the cautious language favored by academicians; instead, he spoke unequivocally, declaring his find authentic. Yet there was much to suspect about the Quang document.

It said that after the United States failed in the attempt to rescue its prisoners at Son Tay, North Vietnam increased the number of its prisons from four to eleven. In truth, though, North Vietnam was so shaken after Son Tay that it in fact decreased—not increased—the number of its prison camps.

The document also said that there was a secret secondary camp system in which prisoners were held according to rank. One such camp supposedly held a hundred colonels. But nowhere near that number of colonels was ever held captive, let alone in a special prison.

The document had other inconsistencies, as well, including numbers and ranks for POWs that did not correspond with Pentagon figures.

I addressed those problems in an article for *The Washington Times* and wrote that the document was most likely Soviet-generated propaganda. The Quang report was eventually determined to be a forgery.

In June 1994 I learned that the forgery was actually the work of the CIA. The agency created the document as part of an effort to force Vietnam to release additional information on MIAs. The CIA specifically wanted a copy of the Vietnamese "Blue Book," a handwritten record of the wartime whereabouts and eventual fate of American POWs. The phony and inflammatory Quang document was deliberately placed where an unwitting Morris would find it. The spy agency gambled that Morris would publicize the document and that the Vietnamese would go to great lengths to prove it false. The ploy worked. Soon after the Quang document was made public, Vietnamese officials gave the CIA a copy of the coveted "Blue Book."

Meanwhile, the Quang document became a celebrated cause among the activists, including some new and disturbing participants.

The most worrisome of these is Joe Jordan, a former enlisted Navy communications technician. Jordan calls himself the Strike Force Commander of the National Vietnam POW Strike Force, located in Houston, Texas. Jordan has a fondness for weapons and likes to pose for pictures while brandishing high-powered firearms, often in the company of young women. During the 1992 Republican National Convention, Jordan was on the Secret Service watch list of people considered to be a potential danger to the president.

Jordan has turned his wrath against General Clapper of the DIA and has sent him numerous unsettling letters. In September 1993 Jordan sent Clapper a fax that began "Dear Slippery Jim: I just wanted to write to you today and tell you today and tell you what a real loser, liar, coward, incompetent, ignorant, arrogant, slimeball, traitor, faggot, turncoat, communist, queer-lover, slacker and generally worthless piece of human garbage you are

(Sorry Jim, no more Mr. Nice guy!).'' The letter went on to deride Clapper about the Quang document and other matters pertaining to a POW cover-up. Jordan concluded by saying he planned to stage a mock court-martial of Private Clinton outside the White House. "We might expand the festivities to include you or do something appropriate in front of your family residence," Jordan wrote, "so I suggest you plan accordingly."

Apart from his campaign against Clapper, Jordan also contacted an MIA daughter to say that her father had recently been returned to the United States. Jordan said the woman's father was part of a secret government program that would be ruined if she told anyone what she had just learned. Even other close family members could not be told. The daughter, in tears, called her Air Force casualty assistance officer to say that Jordan had predicted that when she finally met her father, he would literally spit in her face for not trying to rescue him since his disappearance in 1966. The casualty officer assured the woman that in the event her father ever returned, he would do no such thing.

In June 1994 Jordan purchased some 4,500 Vietnamese photographs showing dead American servicemen. The pictures are duplicates of those that the DIA acquired in 1992 and 1993. They are gruesome, depicting such horrors as insects crawling on the dead men's eyes. Jordan wrote to Ann Mills Griffiths of the National League of Families to announce that many of the pictures would be published in a special edition of Ted Sampley's newspaper. In his letter to Griffiths, Jordan wrote, "It is our intent to inflame the families like a swarm of hornets and turn them loose on the government of the United States." When Sampley did in fact publish the photos in the June 17, 1994, edition of *The U.S. Veteran Dispatch,* the families were not so much inflamed as sickened.

"I cannot begin to tell you how shocked I was to find those pictures in my mailbox," said one MIA wife, who asked me not to use her name in order to avoid angering other activists. "I have not been able to get them out of my mind."

The activists are not entirely to blame for the issue's continued longevity. Old problems stemming from government insensitivity have also kept matters volatile. Mary Lou Hall, whose actions delayed a presumptive finding of death being applied to her husband, Harley, was given three of Harley's teeth in 1993. Mary Lou told me the teeth had been given to U.S. delegates by a Vietnamese villager, who had kept them as souvenirs for twenty years. The Pentagon returned the teeth to Mary Lou and insisted she accept them as Harley.

Mary Lou correctly argues that the teeth prove nothing. "I'm going to take these teeth, because they are Harley's, but I'm not going to bury them," she told me. "They're not his remains." As late as 1994, Mary Lou was still fighting to prevent the government from forcing her to accept the teeth as her husband.

The POW issue has had some positive side effects. Karen Kirkpatrick, a cousin of Donald Carr, has made the most of her encounter with Jack Bailey. Karen told me that the Carr scam had resulted in her learning considerable new information about Don's disappearance. For the most part, though, the myth of live POWs has been an unhappy burden on the American people. It has fostered mistrust and falsified the national history. More important, it has destroyed the lives of MIA families. It has turned the tragedy of MIAs into a subculture with near-religious overtones, made up of believers, nonbelievers, and heretics. In late 1993, when the Shelton children asked the government to end Charles Shelton's designation as the last symbolic POW, many activists were angry and accused the Shelton children of betraying the POW/MIA issue.

The Shelton episode helps illustrate that there is only one reasonable course of action on the issue. It is time to dismantle the POW myth. There are several ways in which this should be done.

First of all, it is important to recognize that the constant rounds of official inquiries only lend credibility to the myth of live POWs. The government must put an end to these endless investigations and not cave in to pressures from self-serving lobbyists. Senator Smith has asked for yet another presidential commission. His request should be refused. It should be sufficient to accept the findings of previous panels, dating from the 1975 Montgomery Committee, that none of our men are alive in captivity.

Second, Congress must enact legislation to punish those who knowingly disseminate false information. This single act of law would make life difficult for the charlatans, including those who operate from the halls of Congress. Concurrent with such legislation, the government must adopt a new approach, as outlined by Senator John McCain. "The burden of proof should be on those who have evidence, instead of the other way around," McCain said.

The DIA should also acknowledge the existence of deserters in Vietnam. There is no harm in telling the truth about deserters but much harm in continuing the lie. The Pentagon should simply state that there are a number of known cases of men who did not want to come home.

The MIA list must be revised to give an accurate reflection of who is truly missing. Otherwise, the inflated figure will continue to give the false impression that scores of Americans have vanished as a result of the conflict in Southeast Asia.

The government would be wise to sever connections with Ann Mills Griffiths of the National League of Families and to remove her as its unofficial POW/MIA czar. The continued presence of Griffiths at the DIA only hinders the process of resolution and fosters suspicion that the country can ill afford.

The nation should also put a halt to all government-sponsored POW Day designations. Official observations should be made only in honor of the missing. It is an important distinction, in that the term "POW" implies that a man is alive; "MIA" means only that he is gone.

The United States should not abandon its admirable concern for the fate of MIAs. But it must make clear that the responsibility for a full accounting rests with Hanoi. The Vietnamese kept extensive, meticulous records during the war. Some of the archival material has already been released. The United States needs to maintain continued pressure on Hanoi to relinquish the rest of its pertinent files.

The government also needs to take a firm stance that the MIAs are dead. It needs to explain that there may be some cases in which the truth may never be learned. That is a sad but inescapable fact of warfare. President Clinton would do the nation a service if he were to take such a stance in the course of the next Veteran's Day or Memorial Day observance.

If these recommendations are not acted on, the myth of live POWs will go unabated. People such as Jack Bailey, Bob Smith, Kambang Sibounheuang, and the others will be free to carry on as before. They will continue to gain status and make money at the expense of America's MIA families. They will perpetuate the legacy of shattered lives, of women like MIA wife Carol Collins.

Carol lives each day with the aftermath of Jack Bailey's Carr scam. In describing the effects of her ordeal, Carol's words are heartrending. They seem to carry some long-ago echo from a sister in spirit, the heroically dedicated suicide victim, Marian Shelton: "The marrow has been sucked out of my bones. I can't laugh anymore. I don't know how to feel."

Notes

Note: Full publication data on all books mentioned are included in the Bibliography following.

Prologue

xvi The figure on how much the government pays for MIA-related efforts comes from the *Report of the Select Committee on POW/MIA Affairs, p. 9.*

xviii–xix Intelligence sources confirm the existence of "Duck Soup," whose true nature remains classified.

xxi Hrdlicka and Collins made these statements in their testimony before the Senate Select Committee on POW/MIA Affairs (Kerry Committee).

xxii Pentagon policy was to promote known POWs at regular intervals.

Part One: The Setup

1. Perspective

8 Details on the Communist treatment of French POWs were first published by Bernard Fall in *Military Review,* U.S. Army Command and General Staff College, Fort Leavenworth, Kans., December 1958.

9 Kushner told his story to a number of news organizations, including the Associated Press and *Army Times,* in 1973.

13 Results of these studies were published in *Injuries and Illnesses of Vietnam War POWs,* Volumes I–III.

14 "Follow-up studies conducted by the Navy": Results of these studies were published in *Five-Year Medical Follow-up of Vietnam POWs: Preliminary Results.*

2. The List

19 "There are now 2,231 names": This number continues to decrease as Vietnam returns remains to U.S. control.

22 "John Walsh's squadron commander": Walsh's commander, Lieutenant Colonel Walter Stueck of Georgetown, Texas, told the Minneapolis *Star Tribune* that Walsh had once stated that in the event he disappeared in action, he wanted to be listed as MIA rather than KIA. Stueck told the paper that after Walsh was shot down, "I flat-out lied" about Walsh's fate. Stueck's quote was picked up by the Associated Press and was included in an article dated February 13, 1991.

23 Coker made this speech on October 27, 1973. The speech is excerpted in the Kerry Committee final report, pp. 356–7.

24 Anderson's comments were carried by the UPI on March 10, 1981. Anderson returned to the United States in 1970 and was arrested by the FBI in 1972 on an outstanding warrant for desertion. He was convicted of the charge, served eight months in jail, and was sentenced to three years probation.

25 "A top secret report": Refers to Report No. 2874-A, Special Folder/Top Secret, Politburo Minutes No. 73, Point 47.

26 "The KGB and Beheiren continued": Refers to Report No. 438-A, Special Folder/Top Secret, Politburo Minutes No. 73, Point 47.

27 Accounts of Dienst's arrest and conviction for desertion were carried by United Press International and the Associated Press on July 12, 1982, and August 3, 1982, respectively. The status of Kiel and Clark was mentioned in a letter dated October 22, 1992, from the commandant of the Marine Corps to the director of the Pentagon's POW/MIA Central Documentation Office. A copy of the letter is in the author's files.

28 For a full list of the "Vessey Discrepancy Cases," see the appendix of the Kerry Committee final report.

30–31 A copy of the memo describing Stanton's offer to sell MIA records is in the author's files.

34 "In 1992 Senator Smith scoured": A complete list of Smith's "Compelling Cases" is contained in the appendix to the Kerry Committee final report.

3. The DIA Office

38 Peck told me about the rumpled clothes, etc., during a 1991 interview for a story I was writing for *Soldier of Fortune.*

44 Information on Smith's involvement with the unreliable teenager comes from confidential Pentagon sources, who say Smith admitted knowing the boy was unreliable.

47 In a January 4, 1994, memo to me from the Pentagon, my source wrote: "It was a proven fact that Hendon had copied and taken from DIA classified documents; several of the employees of POW-MIA/DIA at the time were aware that Hendon had copied the classified files, and at least one of those individuals was suspected of having helped Hendon to copy them. When Hendon copied the files he removed the classification markings and made many of the documents into unmounted vu-graphs or transparencies. In 1986 in a meeting that Hendon called with DIA to discuss three case files, Senator DeConcini, Congressman Bilirakis and Congressman McEwen also attended. During the course of that meeting, Hendon displayed a number of the transparencies from his files . . . at least one of the

documents/transparencies still contained the classified control number. A check of DIA files determined that the document was still classified.''

48 "McCain wrote to then–Defense Secretary Caspar Weinberger'': Copies of the letters are in the author's files.

51–52 A discussion of Griffiths's power and how she wields it is contained in the Kerry Committee's final report.

53 Peck told me about his plans for the time capsule during interviews for the *Soldier of Fortune* article.

53 "Peck takes pains to cultivate an image of himself as lady-killer'': This is true of my own personal experience with Peck and is part of his reputation among his colleagues. See "Mike Peck's Mythic Battle,'' by Cathryn Donohoe, *The Washington Times,* June 7, 1991.

56 "living in a cell'': There are no cells beneath the Navy Annex.

57 The report, allegedly from Albro Lundy, Jr., and others like it, are in the author's files.

4. The Turncoats

60–62 Documentation on the Mehrer case, including copies of personal correspondence from his girlfriend and brother, is in the author's files.

62 Documentation on Nolan is in the author's files.

64 Investigators are still trying to determine the identity of Chaigar.

66 "In 1986 Cambodian guerrillas'': A copy of this report is in the author's files.

66–68 Documentation on Laporte is in the author's files. For an in-depth examination of the Laporte case, see "The Legend of Doc Laporte'' by Karen Tumulty, *Los Angeles Times Magazine,* April 14, 1991.

70–81 Extensive documentation on the Garwood case, including transcripts of POW testimony and the results of a lengthy DIA investigation, is in the author's files.

74 "Eight men from the Dublin City team'': This account is primarily based on the recollections of Paul Olenski, supported by newspaper articles published in 1968.

75 Men from the patrol were so distraught by Brown's death that survivors continue to hold annual memorial services.

77 "If he had stayed a prisoner'': This statement was made in a deposition to prosecutors in connection with Garwood's trial. A copy of this and depositions from seventeen other former POWs are in the author's files.

78 A transcript of McCain's statement is contained in the *Congressional Record* of June 29, 1993.

5. The Government Cabal

82 A detailed examination of negotiations regarding POWs is contained in the Kerry Committee's final report.

85 "In one of the first lists of negotiating points": Habib made this statement in his testimony before the Kerry Committee.

89 Nixon caused a sensation at *The Washington Times* during a 1985 visit. The normally cacophonous newsroom went completely silent as, one by one, reporters realized that Nixon was gazing down at them from the second-floor mezzanine. The former president was accompanied by the paper's editor in chief, Arnaud de Borchgrave, who seemed thoroughly amused that his reporters were rendered universally speechless.

6. Presumptive Findings

97 "During a campaign debate": The debate was carried on national television on October 6, 1976. The latter statement was made in Buffalo, New York, on September 30, 1976.

99 "The reclassification process had no impact": Oksenberg made this statement in testimony before the Kerry Committee.

104 "It is of course misleading": In some cases, POWs came home to find their wives had divorced them and remarried.

107 Information on the mortician is based on confidential interviews with intelligence sources. Material on the mortician is also contained in the final report of the Kerry Committee, pp. 288–9.

7. Scandal in Paradise

114 The Navy gave this response to McCollum in a letter dated July 8, 1983. A copy is in the author's files.

114 "The letter closed with a threat": A copy of the letter, dated October 9, 1985, is in the author's files.

119 "Dr. Dunlap pleaded with Marsh to reconsider": A copy of this letter, dated July 10, 1986, is in the author's files.

120 "Both the Senate and the GAO feel that": Summaries of the GAO and Senate findings are contained in the final report of the Kerry Committee.

Part Two: The True Conspiracy

8. Enter the Hero

125 The claim about Caristo's part in rescue missions is in *Soldier of Fortune,* February 1992.

128 Gritz's résumé and information on his childhood are contained in his self-published book *Called to Serve.*

131 Information on Shipman's role comes from a confidential intelligence source. Also, see 1988 National Security Council report on Gritz, excerpted in the Kerry Committee final report, pp. 314–15. For Gritz's version of events, see his two privately published books, *Called to Serve* and *A Nation Betrayed.*

131 Information on Fort Apache comes from a confidential intelligence source.

132 Extensive reports on Operation Velvet Hammer are contained in *Soldier of Fortune,* "POW/ MIA Special," and *The Heroes Who Fell from Grace* by Charles J. Patterson and G. Lee Tippen.

9. Rescue Fever

145 The comment regarding Carlos Norman Hathcock II was printed in *The Insider,* Vol. III, No. 11, November 1993. A copy is in the author's files.

145 Information on the activities of Joyce Cook comes from a confidential intelligence source.

148 Gritz's descriptions of his dealings with Kong Le and Operation Brokenwing are contained in *A Nation Betrayed.*

150 "POW insiders": The story on "My Favorite Flake" appears in *Soldier of Fortune,* "POW/MIA Special."

151 Barnes made his assorted claims during interviews with the author; also, see *BOHICA* by Scott Barnes with Melba Libb.

154 Van Atta has continued to list these credits in issues of his newsletter, *The Insider.*

155 A copy of the letter to Vessey is in the author's files.

155 Copies of the exchange of letters between Van Atta and the DIA are in the author's files.

156 A summary of the activities of Team Falcon is contained in the Kerry Committee final report, pp. 310–12.

157 A copy of Barnes's suit against Perot is in the author's files.

10. For a Small Price . . .

159 A copy of the suit is in the author's files.

160–164 Information on Smith and McIntire's activities comes from confidential intelligence sources and is also detailed in affidavits filed in connection with the lawsuit against the president et al.

165–166 Copies of the Obassy and Gritz affidavits are in the author's files.

166 A copy of the Smith memo is in the author's files.

168 "Mindful that he was now asking": A copy of the letter is in the author's files.

169 A copy of Bush's note is in the author's files.

170 "According to Shufelt": Shufelt wrote the ensuing account in a detailed memo, a copy of which is in the author's files.

171 "An affidavit from their most credible witness": A copy of the Howard affidavit is in the author's files.

11. The Grey Flannel Rambos

177 Information on Hendon's activities while working at the Pentagon comes from confidential intelligence sources. The name of his coworker has been withheld to protect him.

179–182 Detailed information on the failed "Laotian initiative" and the roles therein of Bartels, Childress, Griffiths, Hendon, and LeBoutillier is contained in the Kerry Committee's final report, pp. 305–10 and 317–18.

183 "LeBoutillier also took his case": Copies of this and other Skyhook II solicitations are in the author's files.

184 A discussion of Skyhook II fund-raising techniques is contained in the Kerry Committee final report, pp. 331–2 and 334–5.

185 Information on the Have Blue program and the general's death comes from a confidential intelligence source.

185 A tape recording of Hendon's speech to the families is in the author's files.

187 "McDaniel's heroic background": For a discussion of McDaniel's involvement in distributing POW photos and other information, see the Kerry Committee final report, p. 323.

189 "The committee was soon plagued": An account of Hendon's firing was carried by Reuter on July 1, 1992.

190 "To the uninitiated observer": A copy of Garwood's 1992 deposition is in the author's files. Also, line drawings of the annual satellite photos of Thac Ba Lake clearly show that the buildings did not exist in 1977; copies of the drawings are in the author's files.

191 A copy of Hendon's letter asking Clinton to lift the trade embargo is in the author's files.

12. The Merry Prankster

195–197 "On one occasion": Sampley has received extensive press coverage of his many stunts; copies of news articles documenting the activities are in the author's files. Many of the clippings were mailed to the author by Sampley.

197 "It was his most scurrilous": Sampley did much to publicize his own article about McCain as KGB agent and repeatedly tried to persuade the author to pursue the story for *The Washington Times*.

198 "Sampley launched a private war": The article appeared in the January 24, 1970, edition of *Granma*. Sampley obtained it after it had been translated into English and transcribed in a weekly bulletin issued by the CIA's Foreign Broadcast Information Service.

199 "Sampley continued his research": The interview was published in the issue dated May 14, 1973.

200 Accounts of the scuffle were given to me by both Sampley and Salter. Sampley himself told me what his sentence was.

203 "When Sampley again declined": On June 24, 1992, Judge Charles R. Richey of the U.S. District Court for the District of Columbia ruled that the copyright to *The Three Servicemen* was properly held by the Vietnam Veterans Memorial Fund and sculptor Frederick Hart. Judge Richey entered a permanent injunction against Sampley and his companies, ordering them to stop selling likenesses of the statue. On December 10, 1992, Judge Richey entered a judgment of $359,442.92 against Sampley and his companies for copyright infringement.

203 "The cash flow was abundant": Copies of Sampley's financial records are in the author's files.

204 "When sheriffs arrived": Sampley told me this himself.

13. The Lao Resistance

206 "Most prisoners": Admissions by the Laotian officials are discussed in the Kerry Committee's final report.

209 A discussion of Kambang is contained in the Kerry Committee final report under the heading "Dissemination of Unreliable Information." At one point, the report describes him thus: "To date, no information provided by Kambang has resulted in a serious lead about the identification, location or repatriation of a live American POW/MIA, and most of it has been determined to be fraudulent."

214 "Kambang had been an enlisted soldier": The DIA conducted an extensive check into Kambang's background and wrote its findings in a report that was given to the Kerry Committee. At one point, the report read, "He states he was a Captain in the Royal Lao Army. Our best information is that he was an enlisted man in the Royal Lao Army."

214 "Since the agency": A copy of DIA's letter to Kambang is in the author's files.

215 "Kambang had few details": A copy of Kambang's letter to DIA is in the author's files.

216 The quotes from Rowley's family were published in the November 1987 issue of *Life* magazine.

217 "Kambang's efforts succeeded only in angering": A summary of Kambang's falling-out with Kong Le is contained in the DIA's report on Kambang, published in the Kerry Committee final report: "Kambang was removed from his position with the Neutralist faction after the leader of the Neutralists, former Lao General Kong Le, learned that Kambang had fabricated POW-related information and had attempted to use the POW issue for personal gain." In his brief conversations with me, Kambang claimed to be Kong Le's nephew; the DIA assured me he was not related to the former general.

217 The DIA report states: "In 1990, Kambang passed bogus dog-tag information to his superiors in the Arlington (Virginia) Police Department where he worked as a clerk. The information was determined to be fabricated and DIA traced the information back through the Arlington Police Department to Kambang. The Department was informed that Kambang was an established POW/MIA source of questionable reliability."

219 "With Brig hovering over him": A copy of this tape is in the author's files.

219 "About a week later": A copy of the tape allegedly from Morgan Donahue is in the author's files.

14. Akuna Jack and the Panic of '91

227 These claims are contained in the publicity material Bailey distributes. His service record contradicts the claims; a copy is in the author's files. Additional information on Bailey is contained in the Kerry Committee final report, under the heading "Dissemination of Unreliable Information."

229 "The fund-raising letters": Bailey specifically told me his crew did not rescue the drowning refugees.

229 The threat to throw a guest overboard was reported in *People* magazine and was also confirmed to me by Brown, Coyne, and Woodley.

229 "turned out to be a combination of pig bones": The remains Bailey turned in to the embassy were sent to the Army's Central Identification Laboratory at Fort Shafter, Hawaii. The lab described its analysis of the bones in an unclassified cable to the Defense Department, dated November 27, 1984. A copy of the cable is in the author's files.

230 "Washington tried to rein Bailey in": A copy of the letter from Kelly is in the author's files.

231 ~~Dieter Dengler told me Bailey had recruited him to help rescue his old cellmate, MIA~~ Eugene DeBruin, who, Bailey said, was alive in Laos. Before embarking on the mission, Bailey had Dengler write a publicity letter in support of Bailey and his efforts. Dengler told me that while on the mission, it became obvious Bailey had no information whatsoever on DeBruin. An angry Dengler withdrew permission to use the letter and returned home. Bailey later used the letter anyway in a fund-raising drive; he continued to use it despite repeated protests from Dengler. In Dengler's correspondence with the National League of Families, he wrote of Bailey, "I can see now how he fooled also me, he told me . . . the money needed to be raised right away, if not, everything is lost. I am so glad that I went over to Asia which made me realize that he is a dishonest parasite." A copy of the letter to the League, dated August 15, 1989, is in the author's files.

231 "He gave twelve worthless pictures": This is based on information from confidential intelligence sources.

232 "Jack got out this old camera": Cain made this same charge in letters to the DIA and the National League of Families. Copies of the letters are in the author's files.

232 "Bailey was still working": Bailey's associate Larry Stark confirmed to me that Bailey released the banana leaf photo after reading a newspaper article that quoted McDaniel as saying he was planning to release additional POW pictures.

233 "Cain tried to stop Bailey": A copy of the letter containing the sting proposal is in the author's files.

234 "Carol accompanied Bailey": Carol told me the trip had been a "wild-goose chase" and that she had returned from it greatly disillusioned.

235 "Bailey had eventually ran out of 'tips' ": Bailey punched Walker while the cameras were rolling; the episode was later aired on national television.

Epilogue

240 "One of the most prolific": Smith has kept up a stream of memos pertaining to Operation Clean Sweep and other matters regarding the POW/MIA issue. Copies of many of these memos are in the author's files.

241 "A newcomer to the POW issue": A business card signed by Kirkpatrick, identifying himself as a U.S. senator, is in the author's files.

241 "Other longtime activists": A copy of Sampley's suit against Clinton et al. is in the author's files.

243 "Jordan has a fondness for weapons": Information on Jordan being placed on the Secret Service watch list comes from confidential intelligence sources.

243 "Jordan has turned his wrath": A copy of this and other similar letters from Jordan to various officials and business leaders are in the author's files.

244 "Apart from his campaign": The MIA daughter told her casualty assistance officer about her conversations with Jordan. The officer described the daughter's complaints in an official memo for the record. A copy of the memo is in the author's files.

245 "The POW issue": Karen Kirkpatrick is no relation to Fred Kirkpatrick.

Bibliography

Barnes, Scott, with Melba Libb. *BOHICA*. Canton, Ohio: Bohica Corporation, 1987.*

Blakey, Scott. *Prisoner at War: The Survival of Commander Richard A. Stratton*. Garden City, N.Y.: Anchor Press/Doubleday, 1978.

Clarke, Douglas L. *The Missing Man: Politics and the MIA*. Washington, D.C.: National Defense University Press, 1979.

Dengler, Dieter. *Escape from Laos*. San Rafael, Calif.: Presidio Press, 1979.

Dimas, David D. *A Family Waits!* La Mirada, Calif.: Orion Publications, 1987.

Doyon, Jacques. *Les Soldats Blancs de Ho Chi Minh* (The White Soldiers of Ho Chi Minh). Paris: Fayard, 1973.

Dudman, Richard. *40 Days with the Enemy: The Story of a Journalist Held Captive by Guerrillas in Cambodia*. N.Y.: Liveright, 1971.

Esper, George, and the Associated Press. *The Eyewitness History of the Vietnam War, 1961–1975*. New York: Ballantine Books, 1983.

Fall, Bernard B. *Street Without Joy*. Harrisburg, Pa.: Stackpole Co., 1964.

Follett, Ken. *On Wings of Eagles*. New York: William Morrow and Company, 1983.

Grant, Zalin. *Survivors: Told in the Words of Nine American Prisoners of War*. New York: W. W. Norton, 1975.

Gritz, James "Bo." *Called to Serve*. Sandy Valley, Nev.: Lazarus Publishing Company, 1991.†

————. *A Nation Betrayed*. Self-published.

*Presents an activist's point of view.
†Presents an activist's point of view.

Groom, Winston, and Duncan Spencer. *Conversations with the Enemy: The Story of PFC Robert Garwood.* New York: Putnam's, 1983.

Hinkle, Lawrence F. *Notes on the Physical State of the Prisoner of War as It May Affect Brain Function.* Washington, D.C.: Bureau of Social Science Research, 1963.

Hubbell, John G. *P.O.W.: A Definitive History of the American Prisoner of War Experience in Vietnam, 1964–1973.* New York: Reader's Digest Press, 1973.

Hunter, Edna J. *Prolonged Separation: The Prisoner of War and His Family.* San Diego, Calif.: Center for POW Studies, Naval Health Research Center, 1977.

Jensen-Stevenson, Monika, and William Stevenson. *Kiss the Boys Goodbye: How the United States Betrayed Its Own POWs in Vietnam.* New York: Dutton, 1990.*

McConnell, Malcolm. *Into the Mouth of the Cat: The Story of Lance Sijan, Hero of Vietnam.* New York: W. W. Norton & Co., 1985.

Naval Health Research Center. *Five-Year Medical Follow-up of Vietnam POWs: Preliminary Results.* San Diego, Calif.: 1979.

————. *Injuries and Illnesses of Vietnam War POWs. I. Navy POWs.* San Diego, Calif.: 1977.

————. *Injuries and Illnesses of Vietnam War POWs. II. Army POWs.* San Diego, Calif.: 1975.

————. *Injuries and Illnesses of Vietnam War POWs. III. Marine Corps POWs.* San Diego, Calif.: 1977.

————. *Injuries and Illnesses of Vietnam War POWs. IV. Comparison and Captivity Effects in North and South Vietnam.* San Diego, Calif.: 1977.

————. *The Prisoner of War: Coping with the Stress of Isolation.* San Diego, Calif.: 1974.

O'Daniel, Larry J. *Missing in Action: Trail of Deceit.* New Rochelle, N.Y.: Arlington House, 1979.

Patterson, Charles J., and G. Lee Tippin. *The Heroes Who Fell from Grace.* Canton, Ohio: Daring Books, 1985.†

Richelson, Jeffrey T. *The U.S. Intelligence Community* (2nd ed.). Cambridge, Mass.: Ballinger, 1989.

Rowe, James. *Five Years to Freedom.* Boston: Little, Brown, 1971.

Sanders, James D., Mark A. Sauter, and R. Cort Kirkwood. *Soldiers of Misfortune.* Washington, D.C.: National Press Books, 1992.‡

Santoli, Al. *Everything We Had: An Oral History of the Vietnam War by Thirty-Three American Soldiers Who Fought It.* New York: Random House, 1981.

————. *To Bear Any Burden: The Vietnam War and Its Aftermath in the Words of Americans and South East Asians.* New York: Dutton, 1985 (has several chapters pertaining to MIAs and POWs).

*Presents an activist's point of view.
†Presents an activist's point of view.
‡Presents an activist's point of view.

Sauter, Mark, and Jim Sanders. *The Men We Left Behind.* Washington, D.C.: National Press Books, 1993.*

Schemmer, Benjamin. *The Raid.* New York: Harper & Row, 1976.

Schwinn, Monika, and Bernard Diehl. *We Came to Help.* New York: Harcourt Brace Jovanovich, 1976.

Simons, Lt. Frank D. *You Don't Cry for Heroes: A Vietnam Journal and the POW Dilemma.* Rochester, Ind.: Civil Fact Finding Commission for POW/MIA in Southeast Asia, 1988.†

Soldier of Fortune magazine. Jim Graves, ed. "POW/MIA" Special. Boulder, Colo.: Omega Group, Ltd., 1983.

Stanton, Shelby L. *Green Berets at War: U.S. Army Special Forces in Southeast Asia, 1956–1975.* Novato, Calif.: Presidio Press, 1986 (noteworthy for the MIA appendix, which contains material from purloined Army files; other portions of book may not be reliable).

Stockdale, Jim and Sybil. *In Love and War.* New York: Harper & Row, 1984.

U.S. Congress, House of Representatives. *Final Report, House Select Committee on Missing Persons in Southeast Asia.* 94th Congress, 2nd Session. Washington, D.C., 1976.

————. Subcommittee on Asian and Pacific Affairs. *New Information on U.S. MIA-POWs in Indochina.* 97th Congress, 1st Session. Washington, D.C., 1983.

————. Subcommittee on Asian and Pacific Affairs. *MIA/POWs in Southeast Asia: A Continuing National Priority.* 98th Congress, 1st Session. Washington, D.C., 1983.

U.S. Congress, Senate. *Report of the Select Committee on POW/MIA Affairs.* 103rd Congress, 1st Session. Washington, D.C., 1993.

U.S. Department of Defense. Defense Intelligence Agency. *Pathet Lao Knowledgeability Regarding U.S. Unaccounted-for Personnel.* Washington, D.C., 1977.

————. Defense Intelligence Agency. *Recent Reports of U.S. PWs and Collaborators in Southeast Asia.* Washington, D.C., 1977.

Webb, Kate. *On the Other Side: 23 Days with the Viet Cong.* New York: Quadrangle Books, 1972.

Westmoreland, William C. *A Soldier Reports.* New York: Doubleday, 1976.

*Presents an activist's point of view.
†Presents an activist's point of view.

Index

SUSAN KATZ KEATING was raised in Riverside, California, and Dublin, Ireland. She attended the University of California at Davis, and served briefly in the U.S. Army. She became interested in POWs while working as editor of the weekly *Dixon Tribune,* then researched and wrote about the POW/MIA issue during eight years at *The Washington Times.* Her work has appeared in a number of publications, including *Reader's Digest, American Legion,* and *Soldier of Fortune.* She lives in northern Virginia with her husband and three children.

About the Type

This book was set in Perpetua, a typeface designed by the English artist Eric Gill and cut by The Monotype Corporation between 1928 and 1930. Perpetua is a contemporary face of original design, without any direct historical antecedents. The shapes of the roman letters are derived from the techniques of stonecutting. The larger display sizes are extremely elegant and form a most distinguished series of inscriptional letters.